A TRUE STUDY ON PERSIAN LITERATURE

A TRUE STUDY ON PERSIAN LITERATURE

J. Symonds

CYBER TECH PUBLICATIONS
4264/3, Ansari Road, Daryaganj, New Delhi-110002 (India)
Ph.: 011-23244078, 011-43559448 Fax: 011-23280028
E-Mail: cyberpublicationsdelhi@yahoo.com
Website: www.cybertechpublications.com

A TRUE STUDY ON PERSIAN LITERATURE

J. Symonds

First Edition 2010

Published by : Asian Offset Printers

G.S. Rawat for **Cyber Tech Publications**
4264/3, Ansari Road, Daryaganj, New Delhi-110002 (India)
Ph.: 011-23244078, 011-43559448 Fax: 011-23280028
E-Mail: cyberpublicationsdelhi@yahoo.com
Website: www.cybertechpublications.com

Preface

Pre-Islamic Persian literature consists of religious texts, the most notable of which is the Avesta, a collection of liturgic fragments, and the later Pahlavi writing of the Sassanid period. The Islamic conquest of Iran in the 7th cent. was accompanied by a linguistic infusion: one century later, approximately 50% of the Persian literary lexicon consisted of Arabic terms. As Islam became the dominant theme, Arabic became the literary language, until the emergence of local dynasties in the 10th cent.. The first extant Islamic Persian poetry dates to the Samanid state (874–999); the first famous representative of this literature was the poet Rudaki (d. 940 or 944). To Rudaki are attributed a lost mathnawi (epic poem with rhyming couplets) version of the fables of the kalila wa dimna as well as a few qasidahs (panegyrics). Other major figures of this period are Abu Shukur of Balkh, who is credited with the introduction of rubaiyyat, Persian poetic quatrains; Daqiqi, a Samanid court poet and a precursor of Firdawsi; and Baba Tahir Uryan, author of rubaiyyat expressive of pain.

Persian language and literature originated and developed in Iran. Basically, the first major civilization in what is now Iran was that of the Elamites, who may have settled in southeastern Iran as early as 3000 BC. At present about two-thirds of the people of Iran are descended from Aryans who are believed to have begun migrating to Iran from the plains of central Asia during the middle of the second millenium BC. A new language and culture merged as a result of this contact between the new settlers and the original inhabitants. The development of the Persian language may be divided into four phases: (1) Avesta (2) Old Persian (3) Middle Persian (4) Modern Persian.

— *Author*

CONTENTS

1

INTRODUCTION

Persian literature spans two and a half millennia, though much of the pre-Islamic material has been lost. Its sources often come from far-flung regions beyond the borders of present-day Iran, as the Persian language flourished and survives across wide swaths of Central Asia. For instance, Rumi, one of Persia's best-loved poets, wrote in Persian but lived in Konya, now in Turkey and then the capital of the Seljuks. The Ghaznavids conquered large territories in Central and South Asia and adopted Persian as their court language.

There is thus Persian literature from areas that are now part of Afghanistan, Pakistan, India and Central Asia. Not all this literature is written in Persian, as some consider works written by ethnic Persians in other languages, such as Greek and Arabic, to be included.

Surviving works in Persian languages (such as Old Persian or Middle Persian) date back as far as 650 BCE, the date of the earliest surviving Achaemenid inscriptions. The bulk of the surviving Persian literature, however, comes from the times following the Islamic conquest of Persia circa 650 CE. After the Abbasids came to power (750 CE), the Persians became the scribes and bureaucrats of the Islamic empire and, increasingly, also its writers and poets.

Persians wrote both in Arabic and Persian; Persian predominated in later literary circles. Persian poets such as Sa'di, Hafiz, Rumi and Omar Khayyam are well known in the world and have influenced the literature of many countries.

CLASSICAL PERSIAN LITERATURE

Pre-Islamic Persian Literature

Template:Also see Very few literary works remain from ancient Persia. Most of these consist of the royal inscriptions of Achaemenid kings, particularly Darius I (522-486 BC) and his son Xerxes. Zoroastrian writings mainly were destroyed in the Islamic conquest of Persia. The Parsis who fled to India, however, took with them some of the books of the Zoroastrian canon, including some of the Avesta and ancient commentaries (Zend) thereof. Some works of Sassanid geography and travel also survived albeit in Arabic translations.

No single text devoted to literary criticism has survived from pre-Islamic Persia. However, some essays in Pahlavi such as "Ayin-e name nebeshtan" and "Bab-e edteda'I-ye" (Kalile va Demne) have been considered as literary criticism (Zarrinkoub, 1959). Some researchers have quoted the Sho'ubiyye as asserting that the pre-Islamic Persians had books on eloquence, such as'Karvand'. No trace remains of such books. There are some indications that some among the Persian elite were familiar with Greek rhetoric and literary criticism (Zarrinkoub, 1947).

Persian Literature of the Medieval and Pre-modern Periods

While initially overshadowed by Arabic during the Umayyad and early Abbasid caliphates, modern Persian soon became a literary language again of the Central Asian lands. The rebirth of the language in its new form is often accredited to Ferdowsi, Unsuri, Daqiqi, Rudaki, and their generation, as they used pre-Islamic nationalism as a conduit to revive the language and customs of ancient Persia.

In particular, says Ferdowsi himself in his Shahnama: "For thirty years, I endured much pain and strife, with Persian I gave the Ajam verve and life".

Poetry

So strong is the Persian aptitude for versifying everyday expressions that one can encounter poetry in almost every classical work, whether from Persian literature, science, or metaphysics. In short, the ability to write in verse form was a pre-requisite for any scholar. For example, almost half of Avicenna's medical writings are in verse.

Works of the early era of Persian poetry are characterized by strong court patronage, an extravagance of panegyrics, and what is known as "exalted in style". The tradition of royal patronage began perhaps under the Sassanid era and carried over through the Abbasid and Samanid courts into every major Persian dynasty. The Qasida was perhaps the most famous form of panegyric used, though quatrains such as those in Omar Khayyam's Ruba'iyyat are also widely popular.

"Khorasani style", whose followers mostly were associated with Greater Khorasan, is characterized by its supercilious diction, dignified tone, and relatively literate language. The chief representatives of this lyricism are Asjadi, Farrukhi Sistani, Unsuri, and Manuchehri. Panegyric masters such as Rudaki were known for their love of nature, their verse abounding with evocative descriptions.

Through these courts and system of patronage emerged the epic style of poetry, with Ferdowsi's Shahnama at the apex. By glorifying the Iranian historical past in heroic and elevated verses, he and other notables such as Daqiqi and Asadi Tusi presented the "Ajam" with a source of pride and inspiration that has helped preserve a sense of identity for the Iranian peoples over the ages. Ferdowsi set a model to be followed by a host of other poets later on.

The thirteenth century marks the ascendancy of lyric poetry with the consequent development of the ghazal into a major verse form, as well as the rise of mystical and Sufi poetry. This style is often called "the Eraqi style", and is known by its emotional lyric qualities, rich meters, and the relative simplicity of its language. Emotional romantic poetry was not something new however, as works such as Vis o Ramin by Asad Gorgani, and Yusof o Zoleikha by Am'aq exemplify. Poets such as Sana'i and Attar (who ostensibly have inspired Rumi), Khaqani Shirvani, Anvari, and Nezami, were highly respected ghazal writers. However, the elite of this school are Rumi, Sadi, and

Hafez. Regarding the tradition of Persian love poetry during the Safavid era, Persian historian Ehsan Yarshater notes, "As a rule, the beloved is not a woman, but a young man. In the early centuries of Islam, the raids into Central Asia produced many young slaves. Slaves were also bought or received as gifts. They were made to serve as pages at court or in the households of the affluent, or as soldiers and bodyguards. Young men, slaves or not, also, served wine at banquets and receptions, and the more gifted among them could play music and maintain a cultivated conversation. It was love toward young pages, soldiers, or novices in trades and professions which was the subject of lyrical introductions to panegyrics from the beginning of Persian poetry, and of the ghazal."

In the didactic genre one can mention Sanai's Hadiqatul Haqiqah as well as Nezami's Makhzan-ul-Asr?r. Some of Attar's works also belong to this genre as do the major works of Rumi, although some tend to classify these in the lyrical type due to their mystical and emotional qualities. In addition, some tend to group Naser Khosrow's works in this style as well; however the true gem of this genre is Sadi's Bustan, a heavyweight of Persian literature.

After the fifteenth -century, the Indian style of Persian poetry (sometimes also called Isfahani or Safavi styles) took over. This style has its roots in the Timurid era and produced the likes of Amir Khosrow Dehlavi, and Bhai Nand Lal Goya.

Essays

The most significant essays of this era are Nizami Arudhi Samarqandi's "Chah?r Maq?leh" as well as Zahiriddin Nasr Muhammad Aufi's anecdote compendium Jawami ul-Hikayat. Shams al-Mo'ali Abol-hasan Ghaboos ibn Wushmgir's famous work, the Qabus nama (A Mirror for Princes), is a highly esteemed Belles-lettres work of Persian literature. Also highly regarded is Siyasatnama, by Nizam al-Mulk, a famous Persian vizier. Kelileh va Demneh, translated from Indian folk tales, can also be mentioned in this category. It is seen as a collection of adages in Persian literary studies and thus does not convey folkloric notions.

Biographies, Hagiographies, and Historical Works

Among the major historical and biographical works in classical Persian, one can mention Abolfazl Beyhaghi's famous Tarikh-i Beyhaqi, Lubab ul-Albab of Zahiriddin Nasr Muhammad Aufi (which has been regarded as a reliable chronological source by many experts), as well as Ata al-Mulk Juvayni's famous Tarikh-i Jahangushay-i Juvaini (which spans the Mongolid and Ilkhanid era of Iran). Attar's Tadkhirat al-Awliya ("Biographies of the Saints") is also a detailed account of Sufi mystics, which is referenced by many subsequent authors and considered a significant work in mystical hagiography.

Literary Criticism

The oldest surviving work of Persian literary criticism after the Islamic conquest of Persia is Muqaddame-ye Shahname-ye Abu Mansuri, which was written in the Samanid period. The work deals with the myths and legends of Shahname and is considered the oldest surviving example of Persian prose. It also shows an attempt by the authors to evaluate literary works critically.

Persian Story Writing

One Thousand and One Nights is a medieval Persian literary epic which tells the story of Scheherazade (Šarzad in Persian), a Sassanid queen who must relate a series of stories to her malevolent husband, King Shahryar (Šahryar), to delay her execution. The stories are told over a period of one thousand and one nights, and every night she ends the story with a suspenseful situation, forcing the King to keep her alive for another day. The individual stories were created over many centuries, by many people and in many styles, and many have become famous in their own right. Notable examples include Aladdin, Ali Baba and the Forty Thieves, and The Seven Voyages of Sinbad the Sailor.

The nucleus of the stories is formed by a Pahlavi Sassanid Persian book called Hazar Afsanah, a collection of ancient Indian and Persian folk tales. During the reign of the Abbasid Caliph Harun al-Rashid in the eighth century, Baghdad had become an important cosmopolitan city. Merchants from Persia, China, India, Africa, and Europe were all found in Baghdad. During this time, many of the stories that were originally folk stories were thought to have been collected orally over many years and later compiled into a single book. The compiler and ninth-century translator into Arabic is reputedly the storyteller Abu abd-Allah Muhammad el-Gahshigar. The frame story of Shahrzad seems to have been added in the fourteenth century.

Dictionaries

Dehkhoda names 200 Persian lexicographical works in his monumental Dehkhoda Dictionary, the earliest, Farhang-i Avim and Farhang-i Menakhtay, from the late Sassanid era. The most widely used Persian lexicons in the Middle Ages were those of Abu Hafs Soghdi and Asadi Tusi, written in 1092. Also highly regarded in the Persian literature lexical corpus are the works of Mohammad Moin.

In 1645, Ravius and Lugduni completed a Persian-Latin dictionary. This was followed by J. Richardson's two-volume Oxford edition (1777) and Gladwin-Malda's (1770) Persian-English Dictionaries, Scharif and S. Peters' Persian-Russian Dictionary (1869), and 30 other Persian lexicographical translations through the 1950s. In 2002, Professor Hassan Anvari published his Persian-to-Persian dictionary, Farhang-e Bozorg-e Sokhan, in eight volumes by Sokhan Publications.

Currently English-Persian dictionaries of Manouchehr Aryanpour and Soleiman Haim are widely used in Iran.

PERSIAN PHRASES

* Thousands of friends are far too few, an enemy is too much.
* Hezaaraan dust kam and, yek doshman ziaad ast.
* The wise enemy is better than the ignorant friend.
* Doshman daanaa behtar az dust e naadaan ast.
* The wise enemy lifts you up, the ignorant friend casts you down.

* Doshman e daanaaa bolandat mikonad. Bar zaminat mizanad naadaan e dust.

The influence of Persian literature on World literature

Sufi Literature

William Shakespeare referred to Iran as the "land of the Sophy". Some of Persia's best-beloved medieval poets were Sufis, and their poetry was, and is, widely read by Sufis from Morocco to Indonesia. Rumi (Maulana) in particular is renowned both as a poet and as the founder of a widespread Sufi order. The themes and styles of this devotional poetry have been widely imitated by many Sufi poets. See also the article on Sufi poetry. Many notable texts in Persian mystic literature are not poems, yet highly read and regarded. Among those are Kimiya-yi sa'adat and Asrar al-Tawhid.

AREAS ONCE UNDER GHAZNAVID OR MUGHAL RULE

Afghanistan and Central Asia

Afghanistan and the Transoxiana can claim to be the birthplace of Modern Persian. Most of the great patrons of Persian literature such as Sultan Sanjar and the courts of the Samanids and Ghaznavids were situated in this region, as were writers such as Rudaki, Unsuri, and Ferdowsi. As such, this rich literary heritage continues to survive well into the present in countries like Tajikistan, Uzbekistan and Afghanistan.

Indian Subcontinent

With the emergence of the Japanese Ghaznavids and their successors such as the Ghurids, Timurids and Mughal Empire, Persian culture and its literature gradually moved into the vast Indian subcontinent. Persian was the language of the nobility, literary circles, and the royal Mughal courts for hundreds of years. (In modern times, Persian has been generally supplanted by Urdu, a heavily Persian-influenced dialect of Hindustani.)

Under the Moghul Empire of India during the sixteenth century, the official language of India became Persian. Only in 1832 did the British army force the Indian subcontinent to begin conducting business in English. (Clawson, p.6) Persian poetry in fact flourished in these regions while post-Safavid Iranian literature stagnated. Dehkhoda and other scholars of the 20th century, for example, largely based their works on the detailed lexicography produced in India, using compilations such as Ghazi khan Badr Muhammad Dehlavi's Adat al-Fudhala, Ibrahim Ghavamuddin Farughi's Farhang-i Ibrahimi, and particularly Muhammad Padshah's Farhang-i Anandraj. Famous South Asian poets and scholars such as Amir Khosrow Dehlavi and Muhammad Iqbal of Lahore found many admirers in Iran itself.

Western Literature

Persian literature was little known in the West before the nineteenth century. It became much better known following the publication of several translations from the works of late medieval Persian poets, and it inspired works by various Western poets and writers.

German Literature

- In 1819, Goethe published his West-östlicher Divan, a collection of lyric poems inspired by a German translation of Hafiz (1326-1390).
- The German essayist and philosopher Nietzsche was the author of the book Thus Spoke Zarathustra (1883-1885),[5] referring to the ancient Persian prophet Zoroaster (circa 1700 BCE).

English Literature

- A selection from Ferdowsi's Shahnameh (935-1020) was published in 1832 by James Atkinson, a physician employed by the British East India Company.
- A portion of this abridgment was later versified by the British poet Matthew Arnold in his 1853 Rustam and Sohrab.
- The American poet Ralph Waldo Emerson was another admirer of Persian poetry. He published several essays in 1876 that discuss Persian poetry: Letters and Social Aims, From the Persian of Hafiz, and Ghaselle.

Perhaps the most popular Persian poet of the nineteenth and early twentieth centuries was Omar Khayyam (1048-1123), whose Rubaiyat was freely translated by Edward Fitzgerald in 1859. Khayyam is esteemed more as a scientist than a poet in his native Persia, but in Fitzgerald's rendering, he became one of the most quoted poets in English. Khayyam's line, "A loaf of bread, a jug of wine, and thou", is known to many who could not say who wrote it, or where.

The Persian poet and mystic Rumi (1207-1273) (known as Molana in Iran) has attracted a large following in the late twentieth and early twenty-first centuries. Popularizing translations by Coleman Barks have presented Rumi as a New Age sage. There are also a number of more literary translations by scholars such as A.J. Arberry.

The classical poets (Hafiz, Sa'di, Khayyam, Rumi, Nezami and Ferdowsi) are now widely known in English and can be read in various translations. Other works of Persian literature are untranslated and little known.

Swedish Literature

During the last century, numerous works of classical Persian literature have been translated into Swedish by baron Eric Hermelin. He translated works by, among others, Farid al-Din Attar, Rumi, Ferdowsi, Omar Khayyam, Sa'adi and Sana'i. Influenced by the writings of the Swedish mystic Emanuel Swedenborg, he was especially attracted to the religious or Sufi aspects of classical Persian poetry.

More recently Rumi, Hafiz and Fakhruddin 'Iraqi are available in translation by Ashk Dahlén, scholar in Iranian Studies, who has made Persian literature known to a wider audience in Sweden.

CONTEMPORARY PERSIAN LITERATURE

History

In the nineteenth century, Persian literature experienced dramatic change and entered a new era. The beginning of this change was exemplified by an incident in the mid-nineteenth century at the court of Nasereddin Shah, when the reform-minded prime minister, Amir Kabir, chastised the poet Habibollah Qa'ani for "lying" in a panegyric qasida written in Kabir's honor. Kabir saw poetry in general and the type of poetry that had developed during the Qajar period as detrimental to "progress" and "modernization" in Iranian society, which he believed was in dire need of change. Such concerns were also expressed by others such as Fath-'Ali Akhundzadeh, Mirza Aqa Khan Kermani, and Mirza Malkom Khan. Khan also addressed a need for a change in Persian poetry in literary terms as well, always linking it to social concerns.

The new Persian literary movement cannot be understood without an understanding of the intellectual movements among Iranian philosophical circles. Given the social and political climate of Persia (Iran) in the late nineteenth and early twentieth centuries, which led to the Persian Constitutional Revolution of 1906-1911, the idea that change in poetry was necessary became widespread. Many argued that Persian poetry should reflect the realities of a country in transition. This idea was propagated by notable literary figures such as Ali-Akbar Dehkhoda and Abolqasem Aref, who challenged the traditional system of Persian poetry in terms of introducing new content and experimentation with rhetoric, lexico-semantics, and structure. Dehkhoda, for instance, used a lesser-known traditional form, the mosammat, to elegize the execution of a revolutionary journalist. 'Aref employed the ghazal, "the most central genre within the lyrical tradition" (p. 88), to write his "Payam-e Azadi" (Message of Freedom).

Some researchers argue that the notion of "sociopolitical ramifications of esthetic changes" led to the idea of poets "as social leaders trying the limits and possibilities of social change."

An important movement in modern Persian literature centered on the question of modernization and Westernization and whether these terms are synonymous when describing the evolution of Iranian society. It can be argued that almost all advocates of modernism in Persian literature, from Akhundzadeh, Kermani, and Malkom Khan to Dehkhoda, 'Aref, Bahar, and Rafat, were inspired by developments and changes that had occurred in Western, particularly European, literatures. Such inspirations did not mean blindly copying Western models but, rather, adapting aspects of Western literature and changing them to fit the needs of Iranian culture.

Following the pioneering works of Ahmad Kasravi, Sadeq Hedayat and many others, the Iranian wave of comparative literature and literary criticism reached a symbolic crest with the emergence of Abdolhossein Zarrinkoub, Shahrokh Meskoob, Houshang Golshiri and Ebrahim Golestan.

Persian Literature in Afghanistan

Persian literature in Afghanistan has also experienced a dramatic change during last century. At the beginning of the twentieth century, Afghanistan was confronted with economic and social change, which sparked a new approach to literature. In 1911, Mahmud Tarzi, who came back to Afghanistan after years of exile in Turkey and was influential in government circles, started a fortnightly publication named Saraj'ul Akhbar. Saraj was not the first such publication in the country, but in the field of journalism and literature it launched a new period of change and modernization. Saraj not only played an important role in journalism, it also gave new life to literature as a whole and opened the way for poetry to explore new avenues of expression through which personal thoughts took on a more social colour.

In 1930 (1309 AH), after months of cultural stagnation, a group of writers founded the Herat Literary Circle. A year later, another group calling itself the Kabul Literary Circle was founded in the capital. Both groups published regular magazines dedicated to culture and Persian literature. Both, especially the Kabul publication, had little success in becoming venues for modern Persian poetry and writing. In time, the Kabul publication turned into a stronghold for traditional writers and poets, and modernism in Dari literature was pushed to the fringes of social and cultural life.

Three of the most prominent classical poets in Afghanistan at the time were Qari Abdullah, Abdul Haq Betab and Khalil Ullah Khalili. The first two received the honorary title Malek ul Shoara (King of Poets). Khalili, the third and youngest, was drawn toward the Khorasan style of poetry instead of the usual Hendi style. He was also interested in modern poetry and wrote a few poems in a more modern style with new aspects of thought and meaning. In 1318 (AH), after two poems by Nima Youshij titled "Gharab" and "Ghaghnus" were published, Khalili wrote a poem under the name "Sorude Kuhestan" or "The Song of the Mountain" in the same rhyming pattern as Nima and sent it to the Kabul Literary Circle. The traditionalists in Kabul refused to publish it because it was not written in the traditional rhyme. They criticized Khalili for modernizing his style.

Very gradually new styles found their way into literature and literary circles despite the efforts of traditionalists. The first book of new poems was published in the year 1957 (1336 AG), and in 1962 (1341 AH), a collection of modern Persian poetry was published in Kabul. The first group to write poems in the new style consisted of Mahmud Farani, Baregh Shafi'i, Solayman Layeq, Sohail, Ayeneh and a few others. Later, Vasef Bakhtari, Asadullah Habib and Latif Nazemi, and others joined the group. Each had his own share in modernizing Persian poetry in Afghanistan. Other notable figures include Leila Sarahat Roshani, Sayed Elan Bahar and Parwin Pazwak. Poets like Mayakovsky, Yase Nien and Lahouti (an Iranian poet living in exile in Russia) exerted a special influence on the Persian poets in Afghanistan. The influence of Iranians (e.g. Farrokhi Yazdi and Ahmad Shamlou) on modern Afghan prose and poetry, especially in the second half of the twentieth century, must also be taken into consideration.

Prominent Afghanistani writers like Asef Soltanzadeh, Reza Ebrahimi, Ameneh Mohammadi, and Abbas Jafari grew up in Iran and were influenced by Iranian writers and teachers.

Persian Literature in Tajikistan

The new poetry in Tajikistan is mostly concerned with the way of life of people and is revolutionary. From the 1950s until the advent of new poetry in France, Asia and Latin America, the impact of the modernization drive was strong. In the 1960s, modern Iranian poetry and that of Mohammad Iqbal Lahouri made a profound impression in Tajik poetry. This period is probably the richest and most prolific period for the development of themes and forms in Persian poetry in Tajikistan. Some Tajik poets were mere imitators, and one can easily see the traits of foreign poets in their work.

Only two or three poets were able to digest the foreign poetry and compose original poetry. In Tajikistan, the format and pictorial aspects of short stories and novels were taken from Russian and European literature. Some of Tajikistan's prominent names in Persian literature are Golrokhsar Safi Eva, Mo'men Ghena'at, Farzaneh Khojandi and Layeq Shir-Ali.

Novels

Well-known novelists include:

- Simin Daneshvar
- Bozorg Alavi
- Ebrahim Golestan
- Zoya Pirzad

Satire

- Iraj Mirza
- Ebrahim Nabavi
- Kioumars Saberi Foumani
- Hadi Khorsandi
- Obeid Zakani
- Dehkhoda
- Bibi Khatoon Astarabadi
- Emran Salahi

Literary Criticism

Pioneers of Persian literary criticism in nineteenth century include Mirza Fath `Ali Akhundzade, Mirza Malkom Khan, Mirza `Abd al-Rahim Talebof and Zeyn al-`Abedin Maraghe`i.

Prominent twentieth century critics include:

- Allameh Dehkhoda
- Badiozzaman Forouzanfar
- Mohammad-Taqi Bahar
- Jalal Homaei
- Mohammad Moin
- Saeed Nafisi
- Parviz Natel-Khanlari
- Sadeq Hedayat
- Ahmad Kasravi.
- Abdolhossein Zarrinkoub
- Shahrokh Meskoob

Saeed Nafisi analyzed and edited several critical works. He is well known for his works on Rudaki and Sufi literature. Parviz Natel-Khanlari and Gholamhossein Yousefi, who belong to Nafisi's generation, were also involved in modern literature and critical writings. Natel-Khanlari is distinguished by the simplicity of his style. He did not follow the traditionalists, nor did he advocate the new. Instead, his approach accommodated the entire spectrum of creativity and expression in Persian literature. Another critic, Ahmad Kasravi, an experienced authority on literature, attacked the writers and poets whose works served despotism.

Contemporary Persian literary criticism reached its maturity after Sadeq Hedayat, Ebrahim Golestan, Houshang Golshiri, Abdolhossein Zarrinkoub and Shahrokh Meskoob. Among these figures, Zarrinkoub held academic positions and had a reputation not only among the intelligentsia but also in academia. Besides his significant contribution to the maturity of Persian language and literature, Zarrinkoub boosted comparative literature and Persian literary criticism. Zarrinkoub's Serr e Ney is a critical and comparative analysis of Rumi's Masnavi. In turn, Shahrokh Meskoob worked on Ferdowsi's Shahnameh, using the principles of modern literary criticism. Mohammad Taghi Bahar's main contribution to this field is his book called Sabk Shenasi (Stylistics). It is a pioneering work on the practice of Persian literary historiography and the emergence and development of Persian literature as a distinct institution in the early part of the twentieth century. It contends that the exemplary status of Sabk-shinasi rests on the recognition of its disciplinary or institutional achievements. It further contends that, rather than a text on Persian 'stylistics', Sabk-shinasi is a vast history of Persian literary prose, and, as such, is a significant intervention in Persian literary historiography.

Jalal Homaei, Badiozzaman Forouzanfar and his student, Mohammad Reza Shafiei-Kadkani, are other notable figures who have edited a number of prominent literary works.

Critical analysis of Jami's works has been carried out by Ala Khan Afsahzad. His classic book won the prestigious award of Iran's Year Best book in the year 2000.

Persian Short Stories

Historically, the modern Persian short story has undergone three stages of development: a formative period, a period of consolidation and growth, and a period of diversity.

The Formative Period

The formative period was ushered in by Mohammad Ali Jamalzadeh's collection Yak-i Bud Yak-i Nabud (1921; tr. H. Moayyad and P. Sprachman as Once Upon a Time, New York, 1985), and gained momentum with the early short stories of Sadeq Hedayat (1903-51). Jamalzadeh (1895-1997) is usually considered as the first writer of modern short stories in Persian. His stories focus on plot and action rather than on mood or character development and in that respect are reminiscent of the works of Guy de Maupassant and O. Henry. In contrast, Sadeq Hedayat, the writer who introduced modernism to Persian literature, brought about a fundamental change in Persian fiction. In addition to his longer stories, "Bgf-e kur" (his masterpiece; see above ii.) and "Haji Aqa" (1945), he wrote collections of short stories including Seh Ghatra Khun (Three

Drops of Blood, 1932; tr. into French by G. Lazard as Trois gouuttes de sang, Paris 1996) and Zenda be Gur (Buried Alive, 1930). His stories were written in a simple and lucid language, but he employed a variety of approaches, from realism and naturalism to surrealistic fantasy, breaking new ground and introducing a whole range of literary models and presenting new possibilities for the further development of the genre. He experimented with disrupted chronology and non-linear or circular plots, applying these techniques to both his realistic and surrealist writings. Unlike Hedayat, who focused on the psychological complexity and latent vulnerabilities of the individual, Bozorg Alavi depicts ideologically motivated personages defying oppression and social injustice. Such characters, seldom portrayed before in Persian fiction, are Alavi's main contribution to the thematic range of the modem Persian short story. This commitment to social issues is emulated by Fereydun Tonokaboni (b. 1937), Mahmud Dawlatabadi (b. 1940), Samad Behrangi (q.v.; 1939-68), and other writers of the left in the next generation.

Sadeq Chubak was one of the first authors to break the taboo. Following the example of William Faulkner, John Steinbeck, Erskine Caldwell, and Ernest Hemingway, his blunt approach appears in the early short story collections Khayma Shab-bazi (The Puppet Show, 1945) and Antar-i ke Luti-ash Morda Bud (1949; tr. P. Avery as "The Baboon Whose Buffoon was Dead", New World Writing 11, 1957, pp. 14-24), Later stories like "Zir-e Cheragh-e Ghermez", "Pirahan-e Zereski", and "Chera Darya Tufani Shoda Bud" describe the naked bestiality and moral degradation of the personages with no trace of squeamishness. His short stories mirror rotting society, populated by the crushed and the defeated. Chubak picks marginal characters-vagrants, pigeon-racers, corpse-washers, prostitutes, and opium addicts-who rarely appear in the fiction of his predecessors, and whom he portrays with vividness and force. His readers come face to face with grim realities and incidents that they have often witnessed for themselves in everyday life but have shunned out of their mind through complacency.

A distinctive trait of post-war Persian fiction in all the three stages of development is the attention devoted to narrative styles and techniques. In matters of style two main trends prevail. Some authors, like Chubak and Al-e Ahmad, follow colloquial speech patterns; others, such as Ebrahim Golestan (b. 1922) and Mohammad Etemadzadeh "Behazin" (b. 1915), have adopted a more literary and lyrical tone.

Although the work of all four writers stretch into later periods, some brief remarks about their differing techniques, which delineated future paths, need mentioning at the outset. Golestan experimented with different narrative styles, and it was only in two late collections of stories, Juy o Divar o Teshna (The Stream and the Wall and the Parched, 1967) and Madd o Meh (The Tide and the Mist, 1969) that he managed to find a style and voice of his own. His poetic language draws inspiration both from syntactical forms of classical Persian prose and the experiments of modernist writers, most notably Gertrude Stein.

The influence of modernism is evident also in the structure of Golestan's short stories, in which the traditional linear plot line is abandoned in favor of disrupted chronology and free association of ideas. Contrary to most other modern Persian authors, Golestan pays little heed to the state of the poor and the dispossessed. Instead, his short stories are devoted to the world of Persian intellectuals, their concerns, anxieties and private obsessions. His short stories resemble well-made decorative objects d'art, pleasing perhaps to the cognoscenti but leaving the majority of readers unmoved.

Golestan's brand of modernism has influenced the later generation of writers like Bahman Forsi (b. 1933) and Hooshang Golshiri (b. 1937). Although the stories of Behazin show similar indebtedness to classical Persian models, he does not follow Golestan's modernist experiments with syntax. Behazin is an author whose stories, delivered in a lucid literary style, express his leftist social beliefs. In some of his later works like the short story collection Mohra-ye Mar (The Snake Charm, 1955), he turns to literary allegory, imbuing ancient tales with a new message, a technique, which allows him to express his critical views obliquely. Behazin's predecessors in the sub-genre of the allegorical tale were Hedayat (in Ab-e Zendegi, 1931) and Chubak ("Esa'a-ye Adab" in the collection Khayma-Shab-Bazi).

Period of Growth and Development

This second period in the development of the modern Persian short story began with the coup of 19 August 1953, and ended with the revolution of 1979.

Jalal Al-e Ahmad is among the proponents of new political and cultural ideas whose influence and impact straddle the first and the second periods in the history of modern Persian fiction. His writings show an awareness of the works of Franz Fanon and the new generation of third-world writers concerned with the problems of cultural domination by colonial powers.

Al-e Ahmad, Behazin, Tonekaboni, and Behrangi can all be described as engaged writers because most of their stories are built around a central ideological tenet or thesis and illustrate the authors' political views and leanings. Among poets of this period, Forough Farrokhzad (1935-1967) has a special place as the first female poet of the Persian language acclaimed by her contemporaries and who left a lasting legacy despite her short life. Her legacy and influence is not primarily (or uniquely) political; however, she was among the first women able to set a personal and original mark. In this sense she is elevated to iconic status.

Another notable author from this period is Simin Daneshvar (b. 1921), the first woman writer of note in contemporary Persian literature. Her reputation rests largely on her popular novel Savusun ("The Mourners of Siy?vosh," 1969). Simin Daneshvar's short stories deserve mention because they focus on the plight and social exclusion of women in Persian society and address topical issues from a woman's point of view.

Gholam Hossein Saedi's (1935-85) short stories, which he called ghessa, often transcend the boundaries of realism and attain a symbolic significance. His allegorical stories, which occasionally resemble folkloric tales and fables, are inhabited by displaced persons, trapped in dead ends (Sepanlu, p. 117).

They emphasize the anxieties and the psychological perturbations of his deeply troubled characters. Sadeghi (1936-84) was yet another author who focused on the anxieties and secret mental agonies of his characters.

Hooshang Golshiri (b. 1937) and Asghar Elahi (b. 1944) created memorable psychological portraits through interim monologue and stream of consciousness techniques. Golshiri, the author of the long story "Shazda Ehtejab" (Prince Ehtejab, 1968), is particularly noted for his successful experiments with extended interior monologues. A bold, innovative writer eager to explore modern methods and styles, Golshiri uses stream of consciousness narrative to reassess familiar theories and events.

PERIOD OF DIVERSITY

Poetry

Of the hundreds of contemporary Persian poets (classical and modern), notable figures include Mehdi Akhavan-Sales, Simin Behbahani, Forough Farrokhzad, Bijan Jalali, Siavash Kasraie, Fereydoon Moshiri, Nader Naderpour, Sohrab Sepehri, Mohammad-Reza Shafiei-Kadkani, Ahmad Shamlou, Nima Yushij, Manouchehr Atashi, Houshang Ebtehaj, Mirzadeh Eshghi (classical), Mohammad Taghi Bahar (classical), Aref (classical), Parvin Etesami (classical), and Shahriar (classical).

Classical Persian Poetry in Modern Times

A few notable classical poets have arisen since the nineteenth century, among whom Mohammad Taghi Bahar and Parvin Etesami have been most celebrated. Mohammad Taghi Bahar had the title "king of poets" and had a significant role in the emergence and development of Persian literature as a distinct institution in the early part of the twentieth century. The theme of his poems was the social and political situation of Iran.

Parvin Etesami may be called the greatest Persian poetess writing in the classical style. One of her remarkable series, called Mast va Hoshyar (The Drunk and the Sober), won admiration from many of those involved in romantic poetry.

Modern Persian Poetry

Nima Yushij is considered the father of modern Persian poetry, introducing many techniques and forms to differentiate the modern from the old. Nevertheless, the credit for popularizing this new literary form within a country and culture solidly based on a thousand years of classical poetry goes to his few disciples such as Ahmad Shamlou, who adopted Nima's methods and tried new techniques of modern poetry.

The transformation brought about by Nima Youshij, who freed Persian poetry from the fetters of prosodic measures, was a turning point in a long literary tradition. It broadened the perception and thinking of the poets that came after him. Nima offered a different understanding of the principles of classical poetry. His artistry was not confined to removing the need for a fixed-length hemistich and dispensing with the tradition of rhyming but focused on a broader structure and function based on a contemporary understanding of human and social existence. His aim in renovating poetry was to commit it to a "natural identity" and to achieve a modern discipline in the mind and linguistic performance of the poet.

Nima held that the formal technique dominating classical poetry interfered with its vitality, vigor and progress. Although he accepted some of its aesthetic properties and extended them in his poetry, he never ceased to widen his poetic experience by emphasizing the "natural order" of this art. What Nima Youshij founded in contemporary poetry, his successor Ahmad Shamlou continued.

The Sepid poem (which translates to white poem), which draws its sources from this poet, avoided the compulsory rules which had entered the Nimai' school of poetry and adopted a freer structure. This allowed a more direct relationship between the poet and his or her emotional roots. In previous poetry, the qualities of the poet's vision as well as the span of the subject could only be expressed in general terms and were subsumed by the formal limitations imposed on poetic expression.

Nima's poetry transgressed these limitations. It relied on the natural function inherent within poetry itself to portray the poet's solidarity with life and the wide world surrounding him or her in specific and unambiguous details and scenes. Sepid poetry continues the poetic vision as Nima expressed it and avoids the contrived rules imposed on its creation. However, its most distinct difference with Nimai' poetry is to move away from the rhythms it employed. Nima Yioushij paid attention to an overall harmonious rhyming and created many experimental examples to achieve this end.

Ahmad Shamlu discovered the inner characteristics of poetry and its manifestation in the literary creations of classical masters as well as the Nimai' experience. He offered an individual approach. By distancing himself from the obligations imposed by older poetry and some of the limitations that had entered the Nimai' poem, he recognized the role of prose and music hidden in the language. In the structure of Sepid poetry, in contrast to the prosodic and Nimai' rules, the poem is written in more "natural" words and incorporates a prose-like process without losing its poetic distinction. Sepid poetry is a developing branch of Nimai' poetry built upon Nima Youshij's innovations. Nima thought that any change in the construction and the tools of a poet's expression is conditional on his/her knowledge of the world and a revolutionized outlook. Sepid poetry could not take root outside this teaching and its application.

According to Simin Behbahani, Sepid poetry did not received general acceptance before Bijan Jalali's works. He is considered the founder of Sepid poetry according to Behbahani. Behbahani herself used the "Char Pareh" style of Nima, and subsequently turned to ghazal, a free-flowing poetry style similar to the Western sonnet. Simin Behbahani contributed to a historic development in the form of the ghazal, as she added theatrical subjects, and daily events and conversations into her poetry. She has expanded the range of traditional Persian verse forms and produced some of the most significant works of Persian literature in the twentieth century.

A reluctant follower of Nima Yushij, Mehdi Akhavan-Sales published his Organ (1951) to support contentions against Nima Yushij's groundbreaking endeavors. But before long he realized that Nima and the modernists emulating him had more to offer than a just a change in rhythm, rhyme, and the general application of the classical Arabic meters. In Persian poetry, Mehdi Akhavan Sales has established a bridge between the Khorassani and Nima Schools. The critics consider Mehdi Akhavan Sales as one of the best contemporary Persian poets. He is one of the pioneers of free verse (new style poetry) in Persian literature, particularly of modern style epics. It was his ambition, for a long time, to introduce a fresh style to Persian poetry.

Forough Farrokhzad is important in the literary history of Iran for three reasons. First, she was among the first generation to embrace the new style of poetry, pioneered by Nima Yushij during the 1920s, which demanded that poets experiment with rhyme, imagery, and the individual voice. Second, she was the first modern Iranian woman to graphically articulate private sexual landscapes from a woman's perspective. Finally, she transcended her own literary role and experimented with acting, painting, and documentary film-making.

Fereydoon Moshiri is best known as conciliator of classical Persian poetry with the New Poetry initiated by Nima Yooshij. One of the major contributions of Moshiri's poetry, according to some observers, is the broadening of the social and geographical scope of modern Persian literature.

A poet of the last generation before the Islamic Revolution worthy of mention is Mohammad-Reza Shafiei-Kadkani (M. Sereshk). Though he is from Khorassan and sways between allegiance to Nima Youshij and Akhavan Saless, in his poetry he shows the influences of Hafez and Mowlavi. He uses simple, lyrical language and is mostly inspired by the political atmosphere. He is the most successful of those poets who in the past four decades have tried hard to find a synthesis between the two models of Ahmad Shamloo and Nima Youshij.

Among the prominent Persian poets of the younger generation is Mana Aghaee and Ziba Karbasi. Mana Aghaee is a female poet who combines the form of the previous generation (especially Farrokhzad and Sepehri) with new topics and metaphors relevant to the 21st century.

2

DEVELOPMENTAL PHASE

HISTORICAL PERSPECTIVE

In the course of the seventh century Persia was overrun by victorious Muslim armies, and the Sassanian Empire (AD 226-652), fabled for the splendor of its court, crumbled. The conquest proved to be far more than military, for it introduced a new religion into Persia and opened an entirely new chapter in Iranian history. The country whose soldiers had subdued faraway Yemen, captured Jerusalem, and marched to the gates of Constantinople only a few decades earlier, now came under the aegis of the caliphs and was ruled by Arab governors for some two hundred years before it could assert its identity again. In the meantime the majority of the Persians, particularly in urban centers, converted to Islam. With conversion came a new spirit and a new social order. As the unity of the overwhelming and transcendent Allah was impressed upon the converts, the characteristic belief in the dualism of the Iranian religion disappeared. Gone too, were the class distinctions, which had been the backbone of Sassanian social and political organization. The powerful Zoroastrian church was reduced to a marginal institution catering to the spiritual needs of a declining community....

....The Islamization of Persia brought about such deep and enduring transformations in the life and culture of the country that some Persians began to regard their pre-Islamic past as a pagan era which had ended with the fall of the Sassanian Empire . The advent of Islam indeed marked a unique turning point in the life of the Persian people; however, it would be an error to view the change as too drastic. There were powerful links between the pre- and post-Islamic eras of Persian history. Changes which appeared radical at first, proved to be less trenchant as the old habits and traditional modes of thought returned in a new guise. Many of the old religious beliefs and practices found a home within "Iranian Islam," to borrow Henry Corbin's phrase. Popular religion, in particular, preserved many aspects of old religious thought and practice, albeit with different terminology. People continued to expect a savior who would rise one day, punish the wicked, and fill the world with justice....

....The most effective link between the two periods of Persian history, however, was a linguistic one. Most of the countries that were conquered by the Arab armies in the first century of Islam, when the new religion was at the height of its drive, lost their language to Arabic and eventually shed their previous identities, becoming "Arab." Such was the case with Iraq, Syria, Egypt, and much, of North Africa. Persia was a notable exception: although conquered completely and absorbed inextricably into the Muslim world, it nonetheless retained its language and its identity. The Sassanians had strongly promoted the language of their homeland Persis (Fars), making it the official tongue of their Empire. This language, called Middle Persian in modern scholarship, continued to be used in Iran after the Islamic conquest; it underwent some gradual changes and emerged in the ninth century as the language of a "renaissance" in Persian literature. In the process, its grammar had become simpler, it had borrowed some vocabulary from Arabic, and it had shed a number of words with Zoroastrian connotations or else adapted such words to the prevailing Islamic environment. It is through this later language, called New Persian (or simply Persian) that the literary gifts of the Iranians found their major channel of expression.

The term "renaissance" implies an earlier period of literary activity, and indeed the early Persian poets and writers owed much to the literature which had, flourished in pre-Islamic Iran. The greatest monument of Persian language and literature, the Shah-nama (Book of kings) by Ferdowsi (completed ca. AD 1000), although the work of a literary genius, is in substance the reworking of the national saga compiled and committed to writing in Middle Persian toward the end of the Sassanian period....

DEVELOPMENT

We have few literary remains from the ancient Persians. Most of these consist of the royal inscriptions of the Achaemenian kings, notably Darius I (522-486 BC) and his son Xerxes. Old Persian, the language of these inscriptions, is an inflected tongue like Greek and Latin and shares many linguistic features with its close relatives, Avestan and Sanskrit. Old Persian inscriptions were engaged chiefly to record the deeds of the "king of kings" or to commemorate the foundation of a building. They have a declaratory, direct and unadorned style, and are laced with repetitive set-phrases, a style common to the genre in the entire ancient Middle East. A typical opening statement of longer Achaemenian inscriptions can be seen in the inscription of Darius I at Naqsh-e Rostam in Persis. It tells us something about this monarch's faith, as well as his pride in his ancestry and race:

"A great god is Ahura Mazda, who created the earth, who created the sky, who created man, who created happiness for man, who made Darius king ... I am Darius, the Great King, the King of Kings, king of countries containing all kinds of men, king of this great earth far and wide, son of Hystaspes, an Achaemenian, a Persian, son of a Persian, and Aryan, having Aryan lineage."

In another inscription we have an instance of Darius's comments on his rule, his temper, and his moral objectives:

"Says Darius the King: by the favor of Ahura Mazda I am such a man who is friend to right; I am not a friend to wrong. It is not my wish that the weak man should have wrong done to him by the mighty; nor is it my wish that the mighty man should have wrong done to him by the weak. What is right, that is my wish. I am not a friend to the man who follows the lie; I am not quick tempered; things which develop in my anger I hold firmly under control by my thinking power. I am firmly in control of my own [impulses]. The man who co-operates, I reward him according to his cooperation. He who does harm, him I punish according to the damage. It is not my wish that a man should do harm; nor is it my wish that he who does harm should go unpunished."

The same theme is expressed toward the end of Darius's Great Inscription at Bistun. The most interesting story that Darius tells concerns the episodes which led to his killing the pretender Gaumata and assuming royal powers - events which, in effect, transferred the line of kingship from Cyrus to a parallel Achaemenian line. The story is related in greater detail by Herodotus, who essentially agrees with Darius's presentation. We hear it from the mouth of Darius himself as a specimen of the Achaemenian recording of history:

"Says Darius the King: This is what was done by me after I had become king. Cyrus's son, Cambyses by name, of our family, was king here. Cambyses had a co-parental brother by the name of Smerdis. Cambyses slew Smerdis. When Cambyses slew Smerdis it did not become known to the people that Smerdis had been slain. Then Carnbyses went to Egypt. When Cambyses had gone off to Egypt, the people became evil. Then the lie waxed great in the country, both in Persia and in Media and in the other provinces."

"Says Darius the King: Then there was a man, a Magian, Gaumata by name, who rose up from Paishiyauvada....He lied to the people thus: "I am Smerdis the son of Cyrus, brother of Cambyses." Then all the people rebelled against Cambyses and went over to him, both Persia and Media and the other provinces. He seized the kingdom....After that Cambyses died by his own hand. Says Darius the King: This kingdom which Gaumata the Magian took away from Cambyses from long ago belonged to our family....Then Gaumata the Magian took it from Cambyses, he took to himself both Persia and Media and the other provinces.... He became king."

"Says Darius the King: There was not a man, neither a Persian nor a Mede nor anyone of our family, who might deprive Gaumata the Magian of the kingdom. The people feared him greatly, [thinking that] he would slay in numbers the people who had previously known Smerdis. He would slay people "lest they know me, that I am not Smerdis son of Cyrus". No one dared say anything about Gaumata the Magian until I arrived. Then I besought help of Ahura Mazda; Ahura Mazda bore me aid; of the month of Bagayadi ten days were past when I, with a few men, slew Gaumata the Magian and those who were his foremost followers. A fortress by name of Sikayauvati [in] the district of Nisaya in Media - there I slew him. I took the kingdom from him. By the favor of Ahura Mazda I became king; Ahura Mazda bestowed the kingdom upon me."

We have no direct record of the myths, legends, and stories of the ancient Persians, or of their poetry, since this literature was orally transmitted and was eventually lost or absorbed by the oral literature of eastern Iran. So, too, was the literature of the Medians, the erstwhile masters of the Persians. The case is different with the Avestan people 1, who produced the most notable religious and literary monument that we have in writing from ancient Iran, namely the Avesta. Frequently displaying a remarkable poetic quality, the Yashts (hymns) describe with moving eloquence lofty mountains, rolling rivers, refreshing rains, and green pastures, as well as radiant, all-powerful deities (yazatas, izads) and virtuous, brave heroes.

OLD PERSIAN LITERATURE

The most significant literary heritage of ancient Iran, however, is the heroic poetry which eventually evolved into the Iranian national epic. The core of this poetry belongs to a heroic age of remote antiquity, that of the Kayanians. Under this dynasty, whose history is wrapped in legend, the ancestors of the Avestan people offered worship and sacrifice to a broad range of deities who often symbolized the forces of nature. Grappling with the hazards of a cold, frost-stricken climate, beset by demons of drought, and harassed by marauding neighbors, they struggled to overcome the physical and social challenges of their environment. The institution of kingship had already developed among them; the worship of tribal gods and ancestral spirits had given way to a common worship of universal gods and the spirits of protective, departed heroes.

The first adumbration of the major legends of the Iranian epic are found in the Yashts of the Avesta, where Kayanian kings offer sacrifice to the gods in order to earn their support and gain strength in the perpetual struggle against their enemies, the Turanians. As the major concern of the Kayanians, this bitter, never-ending feud with the Turanians constitutes the main theme of the Iranian epic. Zoroastrianism adopted these legends of the past and extended its blessing to their protagonists.

Transmitted by professional minstrels, the legends were inherited in turn by the Parthians, who lived close to the Avestan regions and had become Zoroastrian. During the long reign of the Arsacids (247 BC-AD 226) these legends spread to the rest of Iran and overshadowed the local ones. In the process, the memory of the Medes and the Persians, who did not figure in the eastern epics or in Zoroastrian literature, faded into oblivion; when the Sassanian scribes (dabirs) eventually attempted the compilation, and systemization of an Iranian history, all they could find for the ancient periods were the cycles of legends and stories that had come down from Parthian times, reaching back into Kayanian memories.

The Parthian period itself saw the resurgence of a second heroic age, and the Arsacid princes and some of their vassal lords became the focus of a number of adventure tales; in the hands of the minstrels (gosans) these tales eventually became legend. The gosan was a poet-musician, "privileged at court and popular with the people; present at the graveside and at the feast, euologist, satirist, storyteller, musician; recorder of the past achievements, and commentator of his own times," who performed at courts and among the people, entertaining them with his repertoire of tales of heroism, love, and adventure to the accompaniment of musical instruments.

As time went by and the history of the Arsacids was also lost to the people, their legends, together with other myths and legends of eastern Iran (notably those of the house of Rostam of Seistan) were mingled with Kayanian legends and woven into the fabric of the national saga. Parthian figures, such as Godarz, Giv, Bizhan, Milad (Mehrdad), and Farhad generally appear as warrior nobles at the court of the Kayanians. It is hard to say to what extent the linear systematization of the heroic cycles was created by the gosans, guided by their narrative instincts, and to what extent created through a conscious effort of the Sassanian compilers. The compilation toward the end of the reign of Khosrow II (590-628) in the form of the Khwaday-namag (Book of lords) may have been subconsciously prompted by a perception of the deteriorating national spirit and a need for boosting national pride by recalling past glories. The result, in any event, was a long history of the Iranian nation from the first world-king, Gayomart, to the reign of Khosrow II, with events arranged according to the perceived sequence of kings and queens, fifty in number. Although the legends have been skillfully reconciled and read as a progressive history, some incongruities traceable to the independence of different cycles remain.

The fierce struggle with the Turanians, symbolic of the recurrent menace and destructive invasions of the Central Asian nomads, runs through the mythical and legendary parts of the epic almost as a connecting thread. Naturally the heroic legends of the past did not reach the compilers in their original purity. With each major social and religious reform the legends had to be adjusted to comply with new sensibilities. Heroic ages, in which the warrior class stands out are generally succeeded by periods of predominantly moral and spiritual concerns, when the seer, the saint, and the prophet outshine the warrior, and the literature reflects the change. Such literature, be it magical, didactic, or apocalyptic, is often superimposed on or mixed with the heroic tales, as is most noticeable in the Indian epic Mahabharata. The Iranian legends too, were augmented by a considerable number of religious postulates and moral and moralizing comments. Accordingly, the Middle Persian Khwaday-namag, as seen through the pages of the Shah-nama, was studded with royal words of wisdom, priestly discourse, moral precepts, philosophical observations, and testaments and enthronement speeches extolling justice, religiosity, and honesty. Thus the Khwaday-namag, rather than being the work of a single genius, was a compendium of Iranian epics and morals, elaborated and refined throughout the ages. As such it constitutes the most important literary heritage of ancient Iran.

Admittedly, the Khwaday-namag was regarded primarily as a book of history, but we must remember that "history" did not mean the factual, dispassionate investigation and recording of events as expected from modern scholarship....

....If the subject was historical, the method was literary, and ample use was made of metaphors, hyperbole, and other rhetorical devices to enhance the effect of the narrative. Action, pageantry, scenes of battles, hunting, banquets, and drinking bouts were depicted with relish, but logistics, dates, and circumstantial details were mostly ignored. The emotional force of the narrative, moreover, was kept at a high level: warriors' conceits were cited with dramatic impact, and the miraculous was conjured up without reservation. Thus the Khwaday-namag was indeed also a work of artistic merit and literary effect.

It is sometimes suggested that Middle Iranian did not produce great works of imaginative literature. This judgment ignores two basic facts: that the secular literature of Iran prior to Islam was essentially oral, and that much of the early New Persian literature was in fact only a new recension or direct rendering of Middle Persian and Parthian creations.

PARTHIAN AND MIDDLE PERSIAN

Written Literatures

The remains of Parthian writings, mostly inscriptions from the early Sassanian period and Manichaean hymns, are few, but renderings into other languages from Parthian testify to the existence of genres other than epic. One such work is the love story of Vis and Ramin of which there exists a versified Persian version by the eleventh-century poet, Fakhr al-Din Gorgani (based on a Persian prose translation of a Middle Persian model), as well as a thirteenth-century Georgian translation. It describes the ardent love between Ramin and the bride of his brother, King Mobad. Its remarkable resemblance to the story of Tristan and Isolde has often been pointed out. The story, set in a feudal society, is embroidered with various episodes, tender love scenes, subterfuges, intrigues, escapades, wars, sieges, chivalrous deeds, and feminine resourcefulness, all blended in a meandering series of events framed by a loose plot. An example of a different genre is afforded by Draxt i asurig (The Babylonian tree), extant in a Middle Persian verse rendition. It concerns a contest of merit between a palm tree and a goat, and provides a precursor of the monazara or contest poems in Persian. The Manichaean hymns in the Parthian language are valuable remains from pre-Islamic Iran and give us an idea of the religious poetry of this Middle Iranian language.

More works are preserved in Middle Persian than in Parthian; these include inscriptions, books, tracts, and epistles. The bulk of the material, however, consists of religious books which were revised and edited in the ninth and tenth centuries, when the mobads of the diminished and enfeebled Zoroastrian community made an effort to defend their religion and instruct the faithful in the face of Islamic inroads.

A few poems also survive; in fact, the Ayadgar i Zareran (The memorial of Zarer) and the Draxt i asurig are both metrical, if somewhat corrupt in the extant manuscripts. From the little written poetry that remains it is clear that Middle Persian meter, like the Parthian, was governed by stress, the quantity of syllables being flexible within limits. Poems were generally sung or chanted, with instrumental accompaniment. The Sassanian court extended generous patronage to its poet-musicians, and Bahram V is said to have promoted their rank to one of the highest in the courts. Minstrel poetry continued into Islamic times, particularly in the countryside, which was less susceptible to Arabic influence and court formality. Shams-e Qays, the famous thirteenth-century prosodist who knew nothing but the quantitative prosody of the aruz, expressed bewilderment that some cultivated Persian poets of high literary standing could not see the flaw in the meter of their dialect poems, the fahlaviyyat.

Elsewhere, however, he concedes that no poems could move even the literary elite as these fahlaviyyat did. Among the varieties of Sassanian poems one may count the sorud (ode), used for celebration and panegyrics; the chakama, for narration; and the tarana, for light poetry, generally in quatrains. Unfortunately, few original Sassanian works have survived. Many were lost in the course of the Muslim invasion and other foreign conquests, and others were lost because of the religious zeal of the Muslim Persians themselves; but, mostly, their loss is due to the neglect of these works after the change of script from Aramaic to Arabic. Judging by their Arabic and Persian translations and adaptations, and by bibliographical notices, Middle Persian literature (apart from clerical writing) included historical, geographical, didactic, and astronomical works; books on land survey and travel; rules of conduct and etiquette; law books, historical novels, romances, folktales, and fables.

THE RISE AND DEVELOPMENT

When (New) Persian literature finally found royal patronage, and social and political circumstances made possible the tenth-century renaissance, Persian society had undergone far-reaching transformations. Persia was now part of the Muslim world, a world in which Arabic was the lingua franca. Middle Persian script had been given up for the Arabic alphabet and a number of Arabic words had entered the language. It was now fashionable to write poetry, like the Arabs, in quantitative meters (based on the number and length of the syllables) and the adaptable Persians proceeded to apply the rules of Arabic prosody to their favorite meters, making them even more strictly quantitative than Arabic ones. Blossoming first in Greater Khorasan (an area which is now part of Iran, Afghanistan, and the Central Asian Soviet Republics of Turkmenistan, Uzbekistan, and Tajikistan), Persian poetry soon evolved into a pervasive literary force.

Far exceeding the geographical boundaries of the Iranian plateau in its dominance, it provided a literary model for the entire eastern half of the caliphate. This penetration was accelerated, and became particularly widespread after 1258, when the Mongol armies occupied Baghdad and put an end to the long-lived Abbasid caliphate. For some five centuries the caliphate in Baghdad had provided a focal point of religious and cultural unity in the Islamic world. With its disappearance, Muslim countries were left practically free to go their separate ways and cultivate their own idiosyncrasies. In the western half of the Islamic world, namely Arabia, the Levant, Egypt, and North Africa, Arabic continued as the cultural and administrative language. In the eastern half, however, including Iran, Afghanistan, Central Asia, and India (as well as Anatolia), Persian performed the same function, and its literature benefited from a great many talents nurtured in these countries....

....Persian was introduced into India in the tenth century by Mahmud of Ghazna, who led many raids into the subcontinent and occupied the Punjab. His descendants continued to rule in northwestern India until 1168. They were followed by other Muslim houses, mostly of Turkish or Afghan origin: the Ghorids, the sultans of Delhi, Kashmir, Gujarat, and Bengal; the Bahmanids of North Deccan, and others. They extended Muslim rule, and with it Persian language and culture, to most parts of the subcontinent, as far east as Bengal and as far south as Hyderabad. Although for the most part these dynasties were not ethnically Persian, they were so culturally and therefore became propagators of Persian language, literature, and way of life. In the meantime a large number of dedicated Muslim missionaries from Persia and Central Asia, as well as other Islamic lands, were active in India. Most notable among these were Persian or Persian speaking Sufi mystics, whose saintly bearing and passionate preaching were important elements in the conversion of many Indians to Islam and in the spread of Persian language and culture.

They also laid the foundation for a number of Sufi orders. Persian lyric poetry has always been popular with the Sufis as a symbolic expression of their love of the divine and their longing for union with God. Therefore the Sufi brotherhoods and their hospices also became instruments for cultivating Persian poetry among the Muslim Indians. The patronage of Persian literature in India reached its culmination with the Mogul emperors (1526-1858), whose reign constituted a golden age of Indo-Persian literature. Some of the emperors, like

Homayun and Jahangir, as well as many Mogul princes and princesses, governors, nobles, and high officials, were not only enthusiastic sponsors and promoters of Persian letters but they wrote Persian poetry themselves. The court of Akbar (1556-1605) was studded with a large number of poets who wrote in Persian. An indication of the extent and popularity of Persian poetry in India may be seen in the notices of poets by Qane Tatavi and Khalil Tatavi, who mention 719 Persian poets in Sind province alone. Indeed, under the Moguls, India (rather than Persia) became the center of Persian literature.

A large body of Persian poetry, historical works, mystical treatises, literary criticism, biographies of poets, works of theology and Koranic literature, and numerous Persian grammars and lexicons were produced in India during this period, many of these works still unpublished.

In Turkey, Persian was first sponsored by the Seljuks of Rum (1077-1307), who introduced Persian culture into Anatolia. When the Ottoman Turks penetrated Asia Minor in the thirteenth century, they found that "Persian literature and Persian culture ruled supreme."

The Ottomans soon absorbed the Seljuks into their ranks and readily embraced this culture; they even took Persian models as their guides when they encouraged the creation and growth of Turkish poetry. Thus, in the words of E. J. W. Gibb, they "forthwith appropriated the entire Persian literary system down to its minute detail." For five and a half centuries the Ottoman sultans, like the Ghaznavids, the Seljuks, and many other ruling Turkish houses before them, were patrons of Persian letters.

Between the fifth and the nineteenth centuries, Persian was the literary and cultural language of most of the Islamic countries east of the Tigris and north of the Fertile Crescent. More important, its influence was such that poems written in the native languages of these regions - Turkish, Urdu, Azeri Turkish, and Chagatai - were modeled after Persian poetry in form, outlook, and imagery. Such poems are similar to their Persian counterparts in sentiment, concepts, and content, and differ in language only; even so, they are replete with words and phrases borrowed from Persian and, by extension, from Arabic.

Thus in the vast regions where Persian literature was patronized, it was a mere ethnic or linguistic accident whether the poet wrote in Urdu, Sindi, Turkish, Chagatai, Pashto, or Persian; the poetic ideas and images were the same, and the characteristics of the poetry of any of these languages, except the folk idioms, are the same. In other words, Persian poetry was written not only in Persian, but in Turkish, Urdu, and Chagatai as well. Therefore, in a discussion of Persian letters our scope extends beyond what was written in the Persian language to encompass works by those who thought in Persian when it came to literature, irrespective of their native tongues and ethnic origins.

GENERAL FEATURES OF PERSIAN LITERATURE

At this point we may consider some of the general characteristics of this literature.

i. *Preponderance of Poetry*: A fairly extensive prose literature, mainly of a narrative, anecdotal, and moralizing kind also flourished, but it is overshadowed by poetry in terms of quality and quantity alike. In fact, poetry is the art par excellence of Persia, and her salient cultural achievement. Despite their considerable accomplishments in painting, pottery, textiles, and architecture, in no other field have the Persians succeeded in achieving the same degree of eminence. Whereas the scope of the other arts remained limited, poetry developed into a vehicle for the most refined thoughts and the deepest sentiments. Contemplative and passionate at the same time, poetry speaks the language of the Persian heart, mind, and soul, fully reflecting the Persian world view and life experience.

ii. *"Tangential" Structure and Organization*: The literatures of Persia generally tend to be descriptive rather than dramatic, expressionistic rather than naturalistic, organic rather than architectural. This does not mean that Iranian literatures lack dramatic or well-constructed stories. The Shah-nama contains some powerful stories with considerable dramatic effect. The episodes of Rostam and Sohrab, Siyavosh and Sudaba, and Rostam and Esfandiyar, are not only effective in themselves, but are also told with commendable structural cohesion-as are a number of events reported by the eleventh-century historian Bayhaqi. From their Persian renditions, it is clear that the Middle Persian historical novels based on the lives of Mazdak and Bahram Chobin were dramatic and well-constructed. One need only refer to the epigrammatic quatrains of Omar Khayyam and his imitators to show that dramatic technique was not alien to Persian literary taste. Many writers and poets excelled in driving a point home effectively by the judicious use of contrast, emphasis, paradox, and irony, but most of all by a fitting illustration (which is frequently used in Persian didactic literature to dramatize an abstract point or dictum).

And yet it is the creation of moods and effects and the description of scenes and sentiments that have remained the chief concerns of the writers and poets of Persia. Literary constructions of an architectural nature, where all details are subordinated to the requirements of an overriding theme or idea, have seldom been the compelling aim of Iranian literary works. Structural frames as, they are understood in the West, with dramatic tension resulting from their development of characters and their contrived interaction do not preoccupy the Persian literary mind.

Rather than following a planned development from initial premises to climax and resolution, the Persian writers allow themselves to explore, often at a leisurely pace, the scenes and details that excite their own imagination, and to share these with the reader. This, unfocused, meandering type of literary construction finds its supreme example in Rumi's Mathnavi, where mystical ideas and preachings are illustrated by stories within stories, with no clear structure between rambling sermons and philosophical comments....

....It is also revealing that in the present century, when fiction writing has become popular, it is the short story (mostly descriptive) and not the novel that has attracted the best talents. And in Afghani's Showhar-e Ahu Khanom and Dowlatabadi's Kelidar, two significant post-World War II novels, frequent peregrinations, delight in exploiting the ramifications of their subjects, and branching off into side alleys are typical of the same centrifugal tendency that we notice in the works of Nezami or Attar.

On the other hand, Persian poets and writers are proven masters of vignettes, aphorisms, pithy remarks, proverbial sayings, felicitous formulations, pregnant allusions, illustrative anecdotes, and imaginative short descriptions; almost all of these techniques are exemplified in the pages of the most celebrated Persian prose work, Sadi's Golestan (The rose garden), composed in the thirteenth century. Persian and Middle Persian possess a rich store of wisdom literature, consisting mainly of detached or loosely connected moral maxims and ethical observations from which one can hardly deduce a coherent system of ethical philosophy. It is symptomatic of the Persian mode of thinking and literary predilection that the true unit of Persian poetry is the line (distich or bayt). The best Persian poets often succeed in expressing profound thoughts or impassioned sentiments within the confines of a single couplet.

iii. *Decorative Tendency*: A third feature of Persian literature is its taste for the use of rhetorical devices and ornament. It has often been observed that Persian art has a marked decorative tendency. This is clearly seen in the visual arts: architecture, book illustration, wall painting, bookbinding, calligraphy, and textiles, as well as in music. In modern Persian criticism this tendency, an integral part of artistic expression in Persian letters, has been somewhat deprecated, partly as a result of changes in literary values and partly because the critics have usually focused on excessive examples. Such a view, however, ignores the standards of taste prevailing in medieval Persia and its spheres of cultural influence, and it misses, as well, the true nature and function of

> ornament in Persian literature. Far from being a mere addition or embellishment, ornament is a vital element of literary expression. It is one of the major devices writers or poets use to display their ingenuity, imparting elegance and sophistication to their products, and rousing the reader's admiration. If in treatises on rhetoric the embellishing devices occupy such a conspicuous place, it is because they were seen not as marginal but rather as essential parts of the craft.

In early Persian poetry, ornament is minimal, partly as a result of the poetry's youth and partly because it was modeled on Sassanian poetry. In pre-Islamic Persia, as we have seen, poetry and music went hand in hand, and the minstrels usually sang their poems to the accompaniment of instruments. Poetry, to judge by our few remaining examples, was fairly simple in composition since the music was there to help deliver its emotional impact. Many early Persian poems were, in fact, conceived as songs and were sung by the poet or a ravi (Arabic rawi, reciter) as instanced by Rudaki's famous poem on Bukhara, which reportedly made his patron king abandon Herat and rush to his capital without even taking time to put on his riding boots.

It was not long, however, before poetry achieved a totally separate existence from music and its own tradition was established with a repertory of conventional themes, motifs, and imagery. Since the free play of imagination was somewhat limited by the restraints of this tradition, embellishment and decoration became a primary means of exhibiting literary dexterity and of impressing one's audience. Stylistic mastery and rhetorical craftsmanship gradually became a hallmark of good writing. Even the writers of informative prose who mastered the craft were considered practitioners of literary art.

Embellishments enjoy a wide scope and variety in Persian letters. Sometimes they have to do with the sound and the music of the word and include such devices as alliteration, homophony (jenas), internal rhyming, double rhyming, and the addition of a radif (refrain) to the rhyme. At other times the embellishment takes place at the semantic level and plays on the associative meanings of words or metaphors and their connotations; these devices include amphibology (iham), antithesis (tazadd), congruence (mora'at-e nazir), and various types of allusion. Again, it may concern the arrangement of words and their messages in some pleasing or impressive pattern such as laff o nashr (involution and revolution), in which a number of words in a hemistich or line find correspondences normally in the next hemistich or line. Embellishment also results, though less frequently, from playing on the shape of the letters or the presence or absence of dots. And finally, ornament may be brought to bear on the metaphorical plane by means of statements, similes, and tropes that enhance and elaborate the effect of the basic metaphor or expression.

In the hands of masters like Hafez, who use ornament aptly and with discretion, poems become contrapunctal designs in which the substance and ornament interact with considerable aesthetic effect. In the hands of less-endowed writers, however, meaning often becomes overshadowed or obscured by excessive ornamentation....

iv. *Conventionality*: A fourth feature of Persian literary tradition is the conventionality of its themes and imagery. The major themes and forms of Persian poetry were set in the first century of its appearance; they are seen as early as the works of Rudaki (d. 940-41). Furthermore, the different genres of Persian poetry generally correspond to specific forms: the qasida (ode), a long mono-rhyme, for panegyrics; the ghazal, a shorter mono-rhyme of about seven to fourteen lines, for lyrics; the mathnavi or couplet, for narrative themes; the roba'i or quatrain for epigrammatic poems; and the qet'a (piece or fragment) for casual themes. These forms and their corresponding genres have remained fairly constant for nearly a thousand years.

Traditional poets have always composed their works within the requirements of formal canons and thematic and imagistic conventions. If this framework has made the poet's task of achieving originality more difficult, it has also made it more impressive once accomplished. Such originality is often achieved not by deviating from the norm but by improving upon it: development in Persian literature consists mostly of the refinement of existing techniques, not bold or unsettling innovation.

Since the merit of Persian literature rests largely on its poetry, we shall address ourselves to it in more detail. We may begin with a brief sketch of the periods and styles of Persian poetry and then consider its development....

THE DEVELOPMENT OF PERSIAN POETRY

Basing a chronological division of Persian poetry on radical changes, we can distinguish no more than two periods of Persian poetry: one traditional, from the tenth to nearly mid, twentieth century; the other modernist, from about World War II to the present. Within the long period of traditional poetry, however, four periods can be traced, each marked by a distinct stylistic development.

The first of these, comprising roughly the tenth to the twelfth century, is characterized by strong court patronage, a profusion of panegyrics, and an exalted style (sabk-e fakher). One may define this style (generally known as Khorasani, from the association of most of its earlier representatives with Greater Khorasan) by its lofty diction, dignified tone, and highly literate language.

The second, from the thirteenth to the fifteenth century, is marked by the prominence of lyric poetry, the consequent development of the ghazal into the most significant verse form, and the diffusion of mystical thought. Its style is generally dubbed Eraqi because of the association of some of its earlier exponents with central and western Persia (even though its two major representatives, Sadi and Hafez, were from the southern province of Fars); it is known by its lyric quality, tenderness of feeling, mellifluous meters, and the relative simplicity of its language.

The third period, which extends from the fifteenth well into the eighteenth century, is associated with the Indian style of Persian poetry (sometimes called Isfahani or Safavi). It has its beginning in the Timurid period and is marked by an even greater prominence of lyric poetry, although it is somewhat devoid of the linguistic elegance and musicality of the preceding period. The poets of this period often busied themselves with exploring subtle thoughts and far fetched images and elaborating upon worn-out traditional ideas and metaphors. The fourth period, from approximately the eighteenth to the mid-twentieth century, is known as the Literary Revival (bazgasht-e adabi).It features a reaction against the poetic stagnation and linguistic foibles of the late Safavid style, and a return to the Eraqi style of lyric poetry and the Khorasani style of panegyrics. One can certainly make a case for dividing this period into two parts: before and after the Revolution for the Constitution (1906-11). The latter part saw many attempts at modernizing Persian poetry by the introduction of new themes, colloquial language, patriotic subjects, and political and social satire; nevertheless, the formal aspect of Persian poetry resisted change, and major poets continued writing in the traditional styles.

The current phase of Persian poetry, which dates from World War II, is characterized by a radical break with the literary tradition of the past and by the introduction of fresh imagery and poetic forms.

Court Poetry

Recorded Persian poetry began under court patronage, a continuation of the Sasanian and Abbasid practice. As a result, much of the earliest classical poetry is court poetry. The poets were to compose for formal occasions: major festivals, the birth of a son, deaths, conquests, and the like. Eulogy constituted the principal part of the panegyrics, but the poet was also expected to be entertaining. Therefore great attention was paid to the lyrical or descriptive preludes of the panegyrics The favorite form of panegyrics was the qasida, but occasionally narrative or didactic works in couplet form contained praise of the patron in their introductions, particularly when such works were commissioned by or dedicated to a ruler or grandee.

The ambiance of the court imposed a certain formality on its poetry. Diction was lofty, language elegant, and grammar impeccable. Much of its imagery, taken from battle scenes, banquets, palaces, gardens, flower beds, hunting scenes, polo, chess, drinking parties, and weaponry, mirrors the milieu of the court. The earliest poets also show a remarkable love of nature and acquaintance with flowers, trees, and birds, and their descriptions of nature are refreshing.

The earliest period of Persian poetry is marked by a hopeful and resilient spirit, and although its contemplative pieces betray age and experience, its lyric lines display a youthful and joyous mood. The deep-seated sense of melancholy that characterizes later lyrics is absent. The poet sings of his rather mundane love in a light-hearted manner, seeking pleasure where beauty lies. The chief representatives of this happy lyricism are Rudaki, Farrokhi (d. 1037-38), and Manuchehri (d. 1040-41); their lyrics appear generally as introductory preludes (tashbib or taghazzol) to their panegyrics.

Rudaki, attached to the court of Nasr b. Ahmad (913-43) of the Samanid dynasty, was (like the Sasanian minstrels) a poet-musician who wrote songs as well as qasidas. The first major Persian poet, he is generally considered the father of Persian poetry. Farrokhi, for his part, is the most readable of the court poets. His poems are lively and abound in descriptions of nature, be it the arrival of Spring or the onset of Autumn, garden flowers, clouds, or rain. He wrote his lyrics, one imagines, with a twinkle in his eye. Manuchehri, too, excels in descriptive poems. His fertile imagination, which poured out original images and metaphors, has given us some of the most attractive poems on vineyards, wine, and wine-making.

Epic Poetry

With Ferdowsi's immortal poem, the Shah-nama, epic poetry rose to the height of its achievement almost at its beginning. Hailed as the greatest monument of Persian language and one of the major world epics, it consists of some fifty thousand couplets relating the history of the Iranian nation in myth, legend, and fact, from the beginning of the world to the fall of the Sassanian Empire. Ferdowsi, who belonged to the landed gentry (dehqan) and was well versed in Iranian cultural heritage and lore, fully understood the sense and direction of the work he was versifying. His approximately thirty years of labor produced a magnificent epic of tremendous impact. By glorifying the Persian past in heroic and high-minded poetry he presented the Persian nation with a source of pride and inspiration that has helped to preserve its sense of identity over the centuries. Ferdowsi set the model for a host of other poets who followed his meter and style, but whose works never reached similar heights.

Lyric Poetry

Important as epics are, the heart of Persian poetry is its lyrics. In the poems of the tenth and eleventh centuries, lyrics appeared mostly in the introductory parts of panegyrics, as we have noted. But lyric poetry can be found in several forms; many romances, for instance, contain numerous lyric sections or lines, and quatrains have been frequently used to express the pains and passions of love. There are even qasidas, most notably by Sadi, given to lyrical themes. But the form par excellenceof Persian lyric poetry became the ghazal, which in some ways resembles the sonnet. In the twelfth century a number of poets, notably Sana'i (d. 1130-31), Khaqani (d. 1199), Nezami (d. 1209), and Attar (d. ca. 1220), were writing independent ghazals. By the thirteenth century, with major lyricists like Rumi (d. 1273), Eraqi (d. 1289), and Sadi (d. 1292), the ghazal had become indisputably the most favored form of Persian poetry.

With the passage of time, the spirited and youthful poetry of the earlier lyrics gained in tenderness and depth of sentiment. It was poets such as Anvari, Nezami, Khaqani and Attar who, although better known for other genres of poetry, contributed to this development of the ghazal into a heartfelt, intimate poem of love and its afflictions.

From about the twelfth century, lyric poetry was enriched with a spirituality and devotional depth not to be found in earlier works. This development was due to the pervasive spread of mystical experience. Sufism (Islamic mysticism) developed in all Muslim lands, but its literary expression reached its zenith in the countries located within the sphere of Persian cultural influence. As a counterpoise to the rigidity of formal Islamic theology and law, mysticism sought to approach the divine through acts of devotion and love rather than through mere rituals and observance. Love of God being the focus of the Sufis' religious sentiments, it was only natural for them to express it in lyrical terms, and Persian mystics, often of exceptional sensibility and endowed with poetic verve, did not hesitate to do so. The famous eleventh-century Sufi, Abu Sa'id of Mehna, for example, frequently used his own love quatrains (as well as others) to express his spiritual yearnings, and with the appearance of a vowed mystic poets like Attar and Eraqi, mysticism became a legitimate, even fashionable subject of lyric poems. Furthermore, as Sufi orders and hospices (khanaqahs) spread, mystical thought gradually became so much a part of common culture that even poets who did not share Sufi experiences ventured to express mystical ideas and imagery in their poems.

Mystical lyrics culminated in the ghazals of Rumi. Fired by an irresistible love of the divine and endowed with unusual poetic gifts, he wrote lyrics of extraordinary passion and musicality. The ecstatic fervor, explosive spontaneity, and rich but unconventional language of Rumi's lyrics place him in a class all his own. His Mathnavi, generally considered the greatest literary monument of Islamic mysticism, is a long poem of twenty-seven thousand couplets designed primarily to expound and preach his dynamic mysticism. His method is anecdotal, his tone frequently lyrical. The complexity of Rumi's mystical thought, wedded to a loose, "centrifugal" treatment, and his indifference to polishing his language do not make the Mathnavi easy reading, but the work contains many charming stories, moving passionate lines, and well-expressed profound thoughts that account for its great popularity.

As time went by, a set of poetic conventions began to crystallize, and the world of Persian lyrics became recognizable by a repertory of conventional themes, motifs and images. We meet stock characters and types such as the Lover, the Beloved, the Wine-Seller, the Shaikh, the Sufi, the Judge, the Mohtaseb (supervisor of religious observances), the Blamer, and the Rival; their behavior is predictable to a certain extent. The beloved, for example, becomes more disdainful and inaccessible than before, and the joys of union rarer than ever. Songs of love become mostly fervent laments of a spurned but dedicated lover who, afflicted by the pains of love and tormented by a fickle fate, has to endure interminable nights of separation. He sees his plight in the candle's silent and tearful burning, in the moth's perishing in the consuming flame of the candle, and in the nightingale's outpouring of love to the inconstant rose. The sorrow of love becomes his constant companion; he flouts the counsel of the wise, who advise him to abandon his unavailing passion. He is ready to give up his faith and sell out the two worlds for a fleeting sign of favour from the beloved; wandering aimlessly and suffering the heartless blame of both friend and foe, his best solace is wine and his favourite refuge the tavern. He abhors the tedious company of the self-righteous and those who pretend to virtue as much as he treasures the society of carefree drinkers, the rends, and those who flout social decorum. In today's terms he would be called an anti-establishment advocate of a counter culture, who prefers the free and sincere atmosphere of the tavern to the cant-ridden precincts of the madrasa and mosque. To exult in the liberating effects of wine and the virtues of wine-sellers and tavern buffs becomes as much a theme of the lyrics as love and beauty. The major representative of this poetry is Hafez (d. 1390), who perfected the paradigm of themes and imagery and provided the model for all the lyric poets who followed him.

It must be pointed out that the subject of Persian love poems, from the period of court poetry through later lyrics, is not always the woman but often a young man. Since the Persian language does not distinguish between genders, even in pronouns, this goes mostly unnoticed, but much of the imagery and many of the conventions of Persian lyrics become understandable only by appreciating this point. Young slaves, bought at markets or captured in wars, were often the subject of amorous feelings. They were trained for a variety of courtly professions, including playing musical instruments, serving wine at banquets as saqi, and of course also serving as pages, bodyguards, and soldiers. Some grew into accomplished companions (nadims), and others rose to high ranks. Ayaz, a favorite of Sultan Mahmud of Ghazna, ended as one of his major generals.

It is not surprising, therefore, if the beloved is sometimes pictured carrying a sword, commanding a company, serving wine at an all-male party, being himself drunk or obstreperous, or surrounded by a host of eyeing admirers. Many of the metaphors and similes that describe the beloved in terms of weapons and soldiery is derived from this situation; so too is the fact that saqi passes practically as a synonym for ma'shuq or the beloved. The typical image of the beloved that emerges is an epitome of beauty beset by a host of lovers to whom he is indifferent; when importuned by them he flies into a rage, abuses them, and is liable to draw his sword or bend his bow. On the other hand, we see him occasionally as a sweet companion reciting poetry and playing music for his lover.

In order to better appreciate Persian lyrics one should take into account some of their other features. While a ghazal has a stringent formal frame, using the same strict meter and rhyme throughout, its content need not observe any thematic unity. In fact a ghazal often consists of a set of distinct themes or ideas, each expressed in a distich (bayt). Sometimes a common mood governs the lines of a ghazal, and less frequently a theme is pursued in several lines or throughout the poem, but the norm tends toward disparity. This situation also explains the fact that a number of traditional anthologies consist mostly of single lines.

It is this thematic disunity that has made it possible for the poet to juxtapose amatory, satirical, mystical, and didactic themes in the same ghazal. Of course, there is an ultimate connection among the ideas of a ghazal; it derives from the conventional repertory of themes and basic images that are already known to the reader, in the same way that the episodes and themes of passion plays are known to the audience in advance. Thus, although the ideas in a ghazal may appear disparate, the reader can always recognize them as belonging to a familiar "master design" that, in its totality, displays the unity of a coherent outlook. The poet, one might say, uses fragments of a mosaic; the reader, already familiar with the whole picture, is capable of recognizing its pieces from the total context....

....A new height in Persian lyric poetry is reached in the thirteenth century with Sadi, a versatile poet and writer of rare passion and eloquence. He holds a position in Persian literature, in terms of the power of expression and the depth and breadth of his sensibilities, comparable to that of Shakespeare in English letters. His sparkling ghazals display a youthful love of life and passion for beauty, be it natural, human, or divine. Sadi's dexterous use of rhetorical devices is often disguised by the beguiling ease of his locution and the effortless flow of his style; his masterly language has been a model of elegant and graceful writing.

Sadi is also the author of the best known work of Persian prose, the Golestan, a collection of moralizing and entertaining anecdotes and aphorisms written in elegant rhymed prose and interspersed with fitting lines of verse. Sadi's ideas, observations, moral convictions, and social comments, which appear in the Golestan in a lively, world-wise, and witty fashion, find a fuller expression, in a more sober and mature vein, in his Bustan (The orchard). Didactic in content, lyrical in tone, and anecdotal in composition, this poem is one of the masterpieces of Persian literature. It is probably the best expression of the humanitarian outlook on life and its moral dimensions that evolved in Islamic Persia among enlightened preachers as a result of the interaction between religious precepts and Sufi teachings; it embodies an ethical philosophy emphasizing moderation, justice, contentment, humility, detachment, and compassion for the weak and needy. An admirer of the ethics and the tolerant attitude of the venerable Sufis, Sadi often draws on the lives and sayings of Islamic mystics to illustrate moral virtue. His humanitarianism, however, avoids the pantheistic and ecstatic excesses of some of the extreme Sufis. His approach remains one of the applications of ethical and devotional principles to common circumstances and problems. Sadi manages to infuse his moral teachings with such lyrical charm that much of the Bustan reads like a moving ghazal in couplet form.

The culmination of Persian lyric poetry was reached about a hundred years after Sadi with Hafez, the most delicate and most popular of Persian poets. His ghazals are typical in their content and motifs but exceptional in their combination of noble sentiments, powerful expression elegance of diction and felicity of imagery. His world-view encompasses many Gnostic, mystical, and stoic sentiments, which were the common cultural heritage of his age. While Hafez's satirical lines against pretense and hypocrisy lend a biting edge to his lyrics, his philosophical outlook and Gnostic longings impart an exalted air of wisdom and detachment to his poems. But he is above all a poet of love who celebrates in his ghazals the glory of human beauty, the passion of love, and the exhilarating qualities of wine....

....It is true that some lines of Hafez's poetry, as with many other ghazal writers, are capable of being understood on two different planes, the sensuous and the spiritual. But these instances are relatively few, and there is no reason to believe that every time the word "cup" or tresses" occurs, a mystic meaning lurks behind it. Belief in a mystical "inner meaning" of Hafez's poetry represents the application of a bateni, or esoteric principle, which distorts his meaning and flies in the face of his poetic sense. Again, Hafez's satire of fanaticism and pretension in general, and of the pseudo-religious authorities in particular, hardly ever lends itself to mystical interpretation. This aspect of his poetry, although often mentioned, is not sufficiently stressed. Zakani's deserved fame notwithstanding, Hafez is the most notable satirist Persia has produced. Poignant gibes at the hypocritical shaikhs, judges, professional Sufis, and other pretenders to virtue form an integral part of his ghazals and (following his model) are a common theme of Persian lyrics. The liberal Hafez strongly felt the sting of pretense and cant; to express his outrage was as much a motive for his writing as were his aesthetic and amorous sentiments. But his subtle wit and his magnanimity keep his lyrics from being indignant or bitter. Siding with sinners and tavern dwellers, championing the Fends and the kharabatis - the "hippies" of his time - are essentially his protests against the narrow views and bigotry of the establishment, and part of his satirical thrust. To read mystical meanings into all this is to miss the intent and the sense of Hafez's poetry to the detriment of his real worth.

The ascent of Persian poetry ends with Hafez. Jami (d. 1492), a many-faceted poet of note, continued the tradition of the ghazal, as did many poets of the Safavid period (1502-1722) and the Mogul court in India. Vahshi (d. 1583), Naziri (d. 1612-13), Kalim (d. 1651-52) and Sa'eb (d. 1676-77) all wrote dainty lines and explored subtle poetic ideas, but by the time the Safavids rose to power, Persian poetry had lost much of its freshness and vigor and was becoming entangled in a web of farfetched ideas and images.

The virile tones and clipped rhythms of early Persian poetry (the Khorasani style), which had given way to the passionate tenderness and fluent language of the lyric writers (the Eraqi style), now fell into languid rhythms, abstruse imagery, and often less-than-felicitous constructions (the Indian style). The outstanding example of these traits is the otherwise profound mystical poet Bidel (d. 1720), whose, lyrics frequently present a real challenge for decipherment.

Didactic Poetry

There are fewer themes less poetic or more tedious than the didactic, and yet wisdom (andarz) literature has long been associated with Iranian literary creations. Its roots are found in the gnomic writings of the priestly class of ancient Iran, and Middle Persian already possessed a good deal of andarz literature in the form of testaments, epistles, and collections of precepts. Judging from the Shah-nama, the Khwaday-namag must have also contained a good dose of didactic writing. Sassanian wisdom literature continued its existence after the advent of Islam in the form of Arabic and Persian recessions and adaptations and thus found its way into adab literature. Fortunately, in Persian didactic writings the tedium is generally relieved by illustrative anecdotes. Good examples of early didactic literature are Sana'i's Hadiqa and Nezami's Makhzan al-asrdr. Attar's mathnavis also belong essentially to this genre, as does Rumi's major work, although their mystical intent and passionate tones give them a lyrical quality. On the other hand, the high-minded odes of the Ismaili poet and moralist Naser-e Khosrow (d. 1061) are engaging by virtue of the poet's noble thoughts, elevated diction, and original imagery. The true gem in this field is Sadi's Bustan, already mentioned.

Satire

Social satire, distinct from invective, has had limited scope in Persia, no doubt largely because of the oppressiveness of autocratic rulers and fanaticism of the religious establishment. What satire exists is often characterized by ribald or abusive language, both shunned in polite society. Three figures, however, stand out as master satirists: Obayd-e Zakani (d. 1371), Hafez, and Iraj (1874-1925).

Zakani's satire is essentially based on humorous parody or sarcastic and derisive irony, often dressed in ribald language. His ribaldry, however, does not detract from his being one of the masters of prose style as well as one of the wittiest and most readable Persian writers. Hafez's satire appears in succinct and poignant lines in the course of his lyrics and is directed for the most part against those who abuse religion or religious offices through their selfishness and hypocrisy. The sharpness, wit, and impact of his satire are based primarily on mocking irony, paradox, and sarcasm. He is the only major satirist whose language remains invariably pure, polished, and courteous.

Iraj, a rather casual poet and yet a satirist of high standing, belongs to the post-Constitutional period. He normally focuses his satire on situational incongruity in order to reveal the weaknesses and ills of a society stricken by ignorance, superstition, and corrupt religious and secular leadership. With an acute sense of humor his language draws successfully on colorful colloquial idioms.

Most other satire in modern times has been published in humorous papers. Among the better known humorist-satirists of the present century are Dehkhoda (d. 1956), whose political, social, and anti-clerical satires in prose and verse won him considerable renown, and Zabih Behruz (d. 1971), whose one-act play, jijak 'Ali Shah, is a farcical satire on the Qajar court.

His "Me'raj'-nama" (The book of the ascension [of the Prophet]) and "Gand-e badavard" (The wind-blown stinks), parodies of classical mathnavis, were quite popular for many years before they were finally published in 1983 in West Germany.

THE LITERARY REVIVAL AND MODERN POETRY

It was about the mid-eighteenth century that a group of poets in Isfahan, conscious of the impasse to which the belabored Safavid poetry had come, sought to restore the relative simplicity and more elegant diction of the old masters, thus initiating a revival in Persian letters.

Among the early exponents of the movement were its articulate spokesmen, Lotfi 'Ali Azar, Asheq, and Hatef. The last is the author of the famous Tarji' band (Stanzaic poem); this lyrical poem of mystical purport, divided into five sections on the unity of being and the pantheistic view of the world, counts among the most noteworthy of Persian poetic compositions.

The poets of the Qajar period (1795-1925) remained faithful to the principles of the Literary Revival and maintained the linguistic clarity and eloquence associated with the old masters. Lyric poetry followed the style of Sadi and Hafez; panegyrics, which flourished as a result of court patronage, followed the Khorasani style (chiefly poets of the Ghaznavid and Seljuk courts). The creative energy of the poets, however, fell short of originality and was satisfied with emulating the poets of the past, grinding their worn-out clichés in well-composed and highly polished poems.

The conscious effort to return to the style of the old masters was symptomatic of a social phenomenon: a semiconscious realization of the weakness in the spirit and body politic of the nation, and a desire to counter it. The Shaikhis, and the attraction of the Babi movement for many intellectuals and patriots, may all be viewed as manifestations of a gradual social awakening, which eventually led to the reformist Constitutional Revolution.

With the winning of a constitution from the Qajar king Mozaffar al-Din in 1906, the way was opened for Western-style modernization and concomitant mild changes in literary outlook and style. The pendulum of Persian history had swung once more to the west, only to reverse itself in 1979 with a vehement reaction against things alien in an attempt to remedy a social malaise, the root of which lay elsewhere.

Modern Persian poetry, which essentially continues the Qajar style, may conveniently be dated from the beginning of this century until World War II. Whereas the poets of the Qajar period produced sturdy and well composed but unoriginal poems, the twentieth-century poets proved more receptive to fresh ideas, new forms, and original imagery.

Three poets, of this period are worthy of particular note in terms of originality and attractiveness, one in the Indian subcontinent and two in Iran. Iraj (who has already been mentioned as a satirist) soon abandoned his earlier Khorasani style for a more intimate and idiomatic language, in which he wrote mostly casual and satirical poems, but also delectable lyrics. Parvin (1910-41), who remains, with Iraj, one of the two most popular poets of the period, is an eloquent writer of passionate humane feelings and ethical outlook. She is best known for her tender, fable-like moqatta'ats (pieces) written in moving tones with moralizing intent.

The third is Iqbal of Lahore (1877-1938), an admirer of Rumi, who sought in a series of impassioned poems to expound his vision of Islam as a dynamic faith and a panacea for the social and political ills of the Muslim world. An intellectually endowed poet of fertile mind and reformist ambitions, his lively imagination is matched by his emotive intensity and mastery of expression. Iqbal may well be considered the most significant poet in the classical Persian tradition since Hafez. The present century also saw the last of the poets of note to write in the grand style of the Khorasani school, M.T. Bahar (1886-1951).

MODERNIST POETRY

Modernist poetry, namely, a poetry which departs radically from the traditional school of the old masters, began to emerge only after World War II, when the deep social changes which had been developing for some time finally challenged the venerable literary tradition in a drastic fashion and eroded its foundations. It not only dispensed with the necessity of rhyme and consistent meter, but it also rejected the imagery of traditional poetry and departed noticeably from its mode of expression.

Nima Yushij (1897-1960), the father of modernist poetry, died in relative obscurity, but after World War II a number of young poets took up his cause, fighting against the shackles of literary conventions and writing free verse, sometimes with a vengeance. The vogue gathered momentum, and by the late 1950s it had become the dominant mode of avant-garde Persian poetry. Most of the contemporary literary movements in the West, from the Symbolist to Letterist to Imagist schools, have found exponents among modernist Persian poets.

In modernist poetry, all formal canons, thematic and imagistic conventions, as well as mystical dimensions of the traditional school are by and large abandoned, and the poets (taking their cues from the West rather than from native traditions) feel free to adapt the form of their poems to the requirements of their individual tastes and artistic outlooks. Hence the great variety of styles among modernist poets.

N. Naderpour, whose well-crafted poems are distinguished by a rich imagery no less than by the felicity of his polished language, has produced poems of considerable elegance and appeal since the mid-forties. He is also among the few modern critics who have not confused artistic integrity and achievement with commitment to definite sociopolitical views. A. Shamlu (Bamdad), who, prompted by his innovative urge, has experimented with a variety of styles, has remained a major influence among the modernist poets. An outstanding poet of this school is F. Farrokhzad, a female poet who casts her challenge against the shackles of social convention and marital morality, and the expression of her soul's search for love and fulfillment, in impassioned poems of remarkable sensuality and daring. Akhavan-e Thaleth, also a follower of the Nima school, has produced among others, long poems of veiled protest and of epic quality. In Sepehri, a poet of serene simplicity but overweening imagery, we find an original poet singing in praise of the simple pleasures of life and basking in the contemplation of nature. Lyric poetry has found able representatives in H. Ebtehaj ("Saya") and Simin Behbehani. Many other poets, mostly beginning their careers in the 1950s, have become well known in the modernist school. It is a fact, however, that practically no new major poet has come to the fore since the mid-sixties. While the core of modernist poetry remains romantic, many poets of a liberal or radical bent have been preoccupied with protest against the establishment as well as with promoting their social and political ideas. Poems of protest, however, are mostly couched in allegory, symbolic language and muffled terms, as open criticism of sensitive issues could be perilous.

Modernist poets have, no doubt, produced works of considerable freshness and beauty, more in concert with the contemporary cultural climate of Iran than traditional poetry, but the new freedom and the continuing absence of well-defined and universally accepted criteria have also led to much inept and even nonsensical writing.

PROSE

Literature

Until this century, literary achievement in Persian prose was distinguished more by the style of writing than by creative aspects of the content or construction. Literary fame was garnered by imaginatively embellishing and crafting one's prose, whether informative or recreational.

The stylization of prose was frequent in works on the humanities but more particularly in historiography, where the narrative lent itself easily to this form of writing; in history books the author could draw on rhetorical devices in order to heighten the praise of the patron, obfuscate his shortcomings, or gloss over his defeats. Some early histories, such as Bal'ami's

Tarikh-e Tabaii and (more notably) Bayhaqi's Tarikh-e Mas'udi, however, display considerable literary merit and dramatic force in many of their episodes without recourse to ornamentation.

With the passage of time, the style of writing became even more ornate, so that sometimes considerable skill is needed to extract the meaning from under a heap of rhetorical flourishes and turgid verbosity. An attractive balance between sense and artifice is struck in Sadi's Golestan,, only to be lost again in the contentious and florid style favored in later periods before the Revivalist Movement returned a new balance to prose.

This is not to say, however, that belles lettres as a genre was not cultivated. It might be better described as the literature of entertainment. Middle Persian knew tales of adventure (e.g., Hazar Afsan) and books of fables (e.g., Kalila and Demna, translated from the Indian Panchatantra). These varieties continued in Islamic times, with others, such as "stories of the prophets" and works of adab, which consisted mostly of interesting tales, witty remarks, curious observations, and attractive quotations. It was only in modern times that prose literature began to assume a distinct status rivaling that of poetry. At the turn of the century, journalism became an instrument of social change and political reform, paving the way for the judicious use of simple, unadorned prose for fiction. The first dramas, novels, and short stories written in this prose style were all aimed at social criticism and satire and played a considerable role in raising the national consciousness and promoting social reform.

Fiction

After an inept and hesitant beginning with Ebrahim Beg's Siyahat-nama (Travelog [Istanbul, 1888; first published a few years earlier in Cairo]), modern Persian prose fiction had a splendid second beginning with Jamalzada's Yeki bud, yeki nabud (Berlin, 1921; English trans. Once upon a time, New York, 1985), a collection of six satirical stories and sketches in engaging and colorful colloquial language.

During the reign of Rezi Shah (1925-41) a number of novels were published, mostly maudlin works with pious social postures and weak techniques. Mohammad Mas'ud's first novel Tafrihdt-e shab (Night entertainments) made a stir by openly exposing the frustrations of the educated classes and urban civil servants with a mixture of humor and tragedy. It was followed by several others of the same kind. Hedayat, a gifted and sensitive writer, whose frustrated latent nationalism and morbid sense of doom often led to mocking flippancy, emerged after World War II as the most outstanding fiction writer and the undisputed leader among his younger contemporaries. Although essentially a short-story writer, his short novel the Buf-e kur (Blind owl) has outshone by far all his other works and has exerted an enormous influence on Persian fiction. A number of his admirers, notably Al-e Ahmad, Chubak, and Behazin, distinguished themselves in depicting the lives and circumstances of the poor, the oppressed, the ignorant, and the superstitious in a veiled or openly critical vein.

In 1952 B. Alavi produced Chashmhayash (Her eyes), a well-constructed novel of psychological insight and oblique political protest. The rather sagging and undernourished literary scene of the 1960s was enlivened for a while with M. A. Afghani's Showhar-e Ahu Khanoum (Ahu Khanom's husband), a voluminous novel of love and betrayed loyalty, in which the circumstances of a provincial baker and his wife, mistress and children receive realistic and at the same time moving treatment. The 1970s saw the emergence of M. Dowlatabadi as a leading novelist. A writer of considerable verve and imagination, he writes mostly of the harsh life in southern and eastern deserts and oases of Persia. In his major work, Kelidar, a roman fleuve in ten volumes (1979-84), he writes about the life and times of a large array of characters, mostly poor villagers and semi-nomadic peasants and herders at the foot of the Kelidar mountains north of Nishapur. The spectrum of experiences reflected in the pages of this marathon novel, the rich and original language, and the narrative dexterity of its author make it the most impressive Persian novel to date.

In the course of the 1970s and early 1980s, the novel, compared to the short story, has been gaining ground and increasing in number, even though well-constructed novels of merit, such as J. Mirsadeqi's Badha khabar az taghyir-e fasl midadand (The winds presaged the changing of season, Tehran, 1984) have been few.

Drama

Satirical drama began brilliantly with Akhundzada's plays; although written in Turkish, they were conceived in the Persian cultural climate of the Caucasus and were aimed primarily at Azerbaijani readers. Some of them were translated by Ja' far Qarachadaghi who also wrote a number of plays in a similar vein. The reformist and satirical zeal exhibited in these early plays abated with the success of the Constitutional Movement in Iran and later with the restrictions imposed by autocratic rule. After World War II experiments were made with different kinds of plays, from poetical to symbolic to absurd. However, with the exception of Gholam Hosain Sa'edi ("Gowhare Morad," 1930-85), Persian drama has not been blessed with writers of the same caliber as poetry and fiction. Sa'edi, a prolific dramatist, short-story writer, and essayist of strong liberal convictions, wrote a number of socio-political and psychological dramas and has remained a strong literary influence for the past three decades.

It should be noted that Shi'ite passion plays or ta'zia are in verse which is generally of inferior quality and hardly rises to the level of literature.

Prose Style

The prose style of post World War II period has been subject to several influences and constraints. Nationalism, westernization and claims of the colloquial language have been the main forces affecting modern prose. Three different styles may be mentioned here.

The polite style of writing which finds its best representatives in books on the humanities and essays and articles in social criticism has evolved from the style of the Literary Revival. Its chief characteristic, compared to Safavid and Qajar prose, is clarity. At its best, it is also elegant. By "elegant" I mean a style of writing which is not only free from vulgarisms, verbosity, pretence, and adheres to correct grammar, but also uses apt words and phrases, is pleasing to the ear, and is informed by a quality of mind which results in firm constructions and attractive expressions. Symptomatic of the continued importance attached in Persia to this style are anthologies of essays, articles and excerpts chosen by the virtue of their stylistic qualities". The practitioners of the polite/formal style generally have a good foundation in Persian classics, often revealed in their borrowings from and allusions to the old masters' writings.

This style has been generally resistant to the influence of the West and continues the classical linguistic, heritage. On the other hand it has been affected by nationalistic feelings since the turn of the century, particularly after the Constitutional Revolution. An outcome of this has been a tendency to opt for words of Persian origin rather than Arabic, and to reduce or abandon some morphological Arabic features used also in Persian, such as feminine adjectives with broken plurals (e.g. marakez-e 'elmi for the earlier marakez-e 'elmiyya "scientific centers") and of Arabic plural suffixes (e.g. mo'allefan instead of the now less frequent mo'allefin "authors"). This tendency, which has gained steadily, can be seen clearly in the writings of M. A. Forughi (d. 1949), A. Bahmanyar (d. 1955), and S. Nafisi (d. 1966). The Persian Academy (Farhangestan), in which some ardent nationalists wielded considerable influence was inaugurated by Reza Shah in 1935, and coined or proposed words of only Iranian origin.

The second type is the style which has prevailed in fiction. Whereas some writers like M. Hejazi (d. 1973), Ali Dashti (d. 1982), and T. Modarresi (in his Yakoliya va tanhay i-e u [Yakoliya and his loneliness], Tehran, 1964) have used polished, even mellifluous prose, the general tendency has been increasingly to use idiomatic and colloquial language, and this is now, by and large, the kind of prose which prevails in dialogue. In the hands of an able writer, the medium is colorful and effective. The use of slang and dialectical forms in fiction has been an offshoot of this tendency. The third is the journalistic style which is more difficult to define in view of its variety, but which has played a major role in the development of contemporary language. Journalists have been less constrained by the canons of literary usage and more influenced by the necessity of forging new expressions and coining novel words in order to deal with the immediacy of publishing international news and concommittant situations or ideas. An invasion of expressions based on foreign idioms characterized journalistic writing of the less conservative papers and magazines in the 1970s, when the alien-sounding editorials of some "progressive" journals and newspapers reflected a galloping Westernization and an ever-diminishing familiarity with the literary heritage of the past. The revolution of 1979 with its reaction against Western cultural elements has attempted to check this tendency.

TRANSLATING PERSIAN LITERATURE

Several features of traditional Persian poetry make life difficult for its translators. One is its rhythmical musicality, which cannot be rendered satisfactorily in Western languages. Another is its ornamental aspect, often dependent on the sound and shape of words, all of which is lost in translation. A third feature is the rhyming pattern of the qasida and ghazal, where the same rhyme is employed throughout the poem. Yet another is the tendency of Persian poets to play on the associative meaning of words and their overtones, impossible to reproduce in a different idiom. With good fortune one might find a translator who can absorb the original and express it in his or her own language as genuine poetry. Such is the case with Edward Fitzgerald's translation of Omar Khayyam, Omar Pound's translation of Zakfini's The Gorbi and the Mouse, and to some extent Ruckert's German translations of Sadi. Even Matthew Arnold's "Sohrab and Rustum" (although much abridged and not entirely following Ferdowsi's plot) is, in the absence of a satisfactory translation of the Shah-nama, a treasure to be valued.

Many have tried their hand at translating Hafez, but we must perhaps despair of ever finding an adequate translation for the rich arabesque of his thought and the music of his lines. Even Sadi's Golestan, despite several translations, awaits one comparable to Arthur Ryder's translation of Kalidasa's Shakuntala. The Shah-nama is an excellent candidate for an effective translation in verse, perhaps on the model of Dorothy L. Sayer's translation of Le Chanson de Roland.

Modern Persian literature, on the other hand, having eschewed the formal and stylistic features of traditional writing, lends itself easily to translation, and some good translations of both poetry and prose are available in English and some other languages.

While few of the literary products of ancient Iran remain in their original form, Persian literature on the whole offers a vast corpus of poetry and prose written in Persia, Afghanistan, India, Central Asia, Turkey, and elsewhere. Persian poetry exhibits a distinct character, reflecting a distinguished literary culture; its form, its conventions, and above all its imagery impart to it a flavor all its own. Once we have acquainted ourselves with its modes of expression, a new vista of literary delight opens before us. We can enjoy the noble sentiments, passionate feelings, and profound thoughts that Persian poets and writers have been able to express so well.

The One Thousand and One Nights

One of the most famous collections of ancient tales is Alf Layla wa Layla, the Arabic name of One Thousand and One Nights, commonly known in English as The Arabian Nights. The original Arabic compiler is reputedly the 9th century storyteller Abu abd-Allah Muhammed el-Gahshigar.

These stories came to Europe during the Middle Ages, but were not written down in a European language until the beginning of the 18th century, when Antoine Galland a French orientalist, translated them into his own language. Translations into English by Edward Lane and Sir Richard Burton followed in the 19th century.

Sources dating to the 10th century AD which mention this collection allude to the existence of a Persian book called Hezar Afsaneh (The Book of a Thousand Tales), the story of a king, his vizier, and the vizier's daughters Shahrazad and Dinazad.

These same characters appear in the story that frames One Thousand and One Nights, though here the main plot is built around two brothers, the Sassanian kings Shahzaman and Shahriyar, one of whom rules in Samarkand and the other in India and China. Both find out that their wives have been unfaithful, and all the women and slaves involved in their affairs are beheaded.

Shahriyar, then gives his vizier (meaning minister in Persian) an order to find him a new wife every night (in some versions, every third night). After spending one night with his bride, the king has her executed at dawn. This practice continues for some time, until the vizier's clever daughter Shahrazad (better-known in English as "Scheherazade") forms a plan to become Shahriyar's next wife. She persuades her father to let her go to the king, taking her younger sister Dinazad with her. After their marriage, she instructs Dinazad to ask her for a story every night. She spends hours telling her sister and the king stories, and each time she stops by dawn, at a crucial point, thereby arousing the king's interest in hearing the rest of the story the following night. She is then able to make them last for one thousand and one nights.

During this period Shahrazad gives birth to three male children by the king, and when her storytelling finally ends he offers to grant her a wish. She asks the king to spare her life for the sake of their young children, which he willingly agrees to do, and they live happily ever after.

The names of Shahriyar (holder of a kingdom; prince or king), Shahrazad (of noble lineage) and Dinazad (exalting the goddess Den) are Iranian, and the name of Shahriyar's brother Shahzaman consists of the Persian shah (king) and Arabic zàman (time). It is believed that the frame story of One Thousand and One Nights is of both Persian and Indian origin.

The tales vary widely; they include historical tales, love stories, tragedies, comedies, poems, burlesques and Muslim religious legends. Some of the famous stories Shahrazad spins in many western translations are Aladdin's Lamp, Sindbad the Sailor, and the tale of Ali Baba and the Forty Thieves; however

Aladdin and Ali Baba were in fact inserted only in the 18th century by Antoine Galland, who had heard them in oral form from a Maronite story-teller from Aleppo.

Among the tales in the collection which are believed to be of Persian origin are love stories and fairy tales, which often include div (demon) and pari (fairy), as well as magical animals and birds. Other stories, such as The Ebony Horse, although beginning with a description which fits perfectly into the Persian tradition, are nevertheless believed to be of Indian origin. The Ebony Horse, also known as The Magic Horse, is about a magical horse presented as a gift to the king of Persia. The king's young heir sits on the ebony horse to test the magic and flies into the sky. He visits another country (Yemen), falls in love with a princess, and after a series of adventures returns to his father's court and marries the princess.

Numerous stories depict djinns, magicians, and legendary places, which are often intermingled with real people and geography; the historical caliph Harun al-Rashid is a common protagonist. Sometimes a character in Shahrazad's's tale will begin telling other characters a story of his own, and that story may have another one told within it, and so on, adding to the fantastic texture.

PERSIAN CLASSICAL POETRY

"Ibrahim Fakhr-od-Din Iraqi"

One of the greatest Persian mystic, Sufi poets of 13th Century AD. He was born in Hamedan and was educated there in literature and the sciences of the time. He started travelling to other countries from the age of eighteen. In Multan (then in India, and now in Pakistan) he studied under Sheikh Baha-od-Din Zakkaria one of the greatest Sufi masters. In Konya (ancient Iconian, now in Turkey), he attended the lectures of Sheikh Sadr-od-Din of Konya who was one of the followers of Ibn-al-Arabi the famous Sufi poet. He wrote his book entitled Lama-at (Illuminations) under the influence of Ibn-al-Arabi's Fusus al-Hikam (The Gems of Wisdom). His travels then took him to Egypt and Syria, and he died there. He was buried near Ibn-al-Arabi's tomb in Damascus. His most famous poems are his ghazals, which are mystical love poems and Ushshaq-Nameh (The Song of Lovers). Hafez was one of the many poets to be influenced by him.

"Grace of Love"

O Sweetheart, of spirit your body is created,

With the black disbelief of your hair faith is created.

Have you ever heard about the beauty of Joseph of Egypt?

Your beauty with twice more grace is created.

From the garden of your cheeks one rose was picked;

With that rose the eternal paradise was created.

A cloud of dust rose in the road to your abode;

With that dust the spring of eternal life was created.

The anguish of your love shed the blood of men of heart and mind;

With that blood ruby and coral were created.

May my body and my soul be sacrificed for you,

Because your body with pure soul is created.

I wonder how can I succeed to be one moment with you,

For, to watch you, a hundred demons are created.

How long should I drink the wine of the anguish of your love?

Intoxicated and unconscious

I am created.

By the grace of your love

Iraqi has a wondrous breath

With which the image of man was created.

"My Beloved's Face"

Every moment my Beloved's face in a new look shows itself;

Under each twist of her curls she has a thousand tricks!

With one coquettish glance she traps a thousand hearts;

That is why in this world lonely are the hearts of lovers.

If my heart is gone and lost, tell it be gone and lost forever,

For, instead of heart, I have in my hands the musky curls of my Beloved.

Since a Beauty from the Tavern robbed my heart from me,

I have been all, nothing but a desire for the Tavern, Wine and the Harp.

With the wine of love I am so far away from soberness and reason

That no care is left in me for the wonders of name and fame.

Bring, O cup-bearer, a goblet of that wine for me

That with the reflection of Your face it takes a new colour every moment!

Shed Iraqi's blood in the dust but renew our friendship,

For, now and always, friendship is and will be better than separation.

"Kamal-od-Din Khajoo Kermani"

A 13th Century AD poet and a contemporary of Hafez. He was influenced by other poets such as Sana'i, Attar, Mowlavi, and Saadi. In addition to a collection of ghazals (lyrical poems), he wrote five narrative poems (sn tories in verse), similar to Nezami's Khamsa, of which "Homay and Homayoon" is the most famous.

"The Gem and The Mine"

Of thee I tell thee secrets in a wordless language;

From thee I ask the way to thee on a traceless trace.

In vain thou concealest thyself from the eyes, for thy sun-like face Beams through heavenly veil like the light of day.

What a delicate concept thou art, far above reasoning!

What a divine Verse thou art, needless of interpretation

How can I close my eyes to thee?

Thou art the lamp inside the eye.

How can I part with thee?

Thou art the resident in the soul.

We are all rays and thou art the candle;

We are all substance and thou art the spirit;

We are all raindrops and thou art the ocean;

We are all gems and thou art the mine.

I have never seen a face like thine, so graceful point by point;

I have never seen a scripture like thee, so meaningful verse by verse.

So mercilessly injuring Khajoo's heart with the arrow of thy coquettish glances

Is far from the way of friendship and against the rules of affection.

"Hunting the Hunter"

Reason is a bird from our nest;

Galaxies are some dust risen from our doorstep.

The world-illuminating sun, the sovereign of the East,

Is an ornamental image on the ceiling of our hall of mirrors.

The blood you see in the eye of the horizon at sunset

Is the sips of our nocturnal wine.

What we hunt is no one but the hunter;

Our trap is the same as our bait.

Our arrow pierces through the armour of the firmament,

For our target is the heart of the universe.

No charm can lure us away from the path

Since the two worlds are full of our fascinating tale.

Though with the people of the time we are not happy,

Happy are those who live in our time.

If there exists a paradise, it lies in the dust of his doorstep,

Where we have our eternal abode.

Khajoo, now our songs are sung All over the world with the music of our fame.

PEOPLE AND THEIR HEROES

Iranian people have had a rich memory of their past history since the invasion of their country by the Arabs in early 7th century AD. Although they were, compulsorily or voluntarily, converted to Islam, they did not want to let their culture and their language - the living memory of their spiritual identity - be destroyed by the will or the influence of foreign conquerors.

Long before their defeat by the Arabs, they were also defeated by Alexander the Great in 331 B.C. This defeat led to the rule of the Seleucids, Alexander's successors, first over the whole of the Achaemenid empire and then, when the Parthians began to gradually come to power, over some parts of the country for more than two centuries. Yet the collective memory of the Iranian peoples first called the foreign conqueror Alexander the Wicked or the Accursed Alexander the Roman, and later made a story about his real ancestry through the marriage of Darab (Darius), the Iranian King, to Philip's daughter, who became pregnant, but because of the repugnant smell of her mouth she was soon sent back to her father. She gave birth to Alexander, but Philip, who had kept his daughter's pregnancy secret, declared Alexander as his own son.

Therefore, the collective memory presumed Alexander as an Iranian royal son from a Macedonian woman. As a historical fact, Alexander himself married the daughter of the defeated and slain Achaemenid king. Thus, that long alien rule lost its disgraceful poignancy and was shelved in the museum of history among the unpleasant but forgettable events.

In the case of the conquest of Iran by the Arabs, the fighting missionaries of a new religion, the threat was so disastrous that nothing would be left of national culture and heritage if the Iranians did not make every possible effort to defy it. They preserved almost all their beliefs, traditions and customs in the guise of the principles of the victorious faith. Two elements essential to this achievement were the language and the national identity. Therefore, in the collective memory of the Iranian peoples, their history was mixed with legends and myths in order to revive the past in a new appearance not manifestly incompatible with the faith of the conquerors. From the early 9th century AD, most of the regional governors were Iranian and, although they were either appointed by the Arab caliphs, or they ruled with their consent, many of them founded their own regional dynasties.

To back their right to rule, and to win the loyalty of the people, many of them showed nationalistic zeal by reviving and promoting the Iranian culture and traditions. One of these enthusiasts was Abu Mansour Abd-ur-Razzaq, the governor of Tus in Khorassan, by whose order his vizier commissioned a group of historians and scholars to compile a book of authentic as well as legendary history of Iran from the prehistoric times to the fall of the Sassanid dynasty. Their sources were Pahlavi texts, especially Khudaynmneh (Book of Kings) as well as oral epic stories and myths. This book which was written in prose, and today only its "Introduction" is extant, was later used by Ferdowsi as his main source for the versification of the Shahnameh, the Book of Kings. His other sources, like the compilers of the prose version of the Shahnameh, were the narrative traditions, mostly memorized by the dehgans, or the noble landowners, who were the real preservers of the culture and the Persian language.

Ferdowsi who himself was a dehgan, by versifying the Shahnameh, not only safeguarded the epic stories and myths against oblivion, but also by limiting the use of Arabic words to a minimum gave a new power and glory to the Persian language, a pride-inspiring, vivid testimony to the Iranians' nationhood and independence. Now that Avesta, the Zoroastrian sacred writings, was replaced by the Holy Koran and the Fire-temples by the Mosques, it was the Shahnameh, the embodiment of the Iranian worldview, culture and history, which people came to regard as the document of their national identity. Prior to the Iranians' access to the printing machine in the 19th century, of books copied by calligraphers, the Holy Koran and the Shahnameh were on the top of the list, with the difference that the former remained completely safe from the slightest change or even error in the text, but the latter went through every kind of change, such as misreading of the archaic and unfamiliar words and replacing these words with some understandable but corrupted ones; many legends, which Ferdowsi had not deemed to be appropriate to the epic structure of his book were inserted into the Shahnameh, and here and there, some couplets expressing certain ideas and thoughts dictated to the scribes by either the political conditions of the time or by personal preference.

With the development of the printing industry in Iran the need arose for choosing the oldest and the least corrupted scripts and editing them through comparative and critical studies. For decades many Iranian academics and scholars worked diligently and sincerely in this field, and even in the time of Mohammad Reza Shah Pahlavi a foundation was established under the supervision of Professor Mojtaba Minovi for the publication of an authentic and critically edited copy of the Shahnameh. But few attempted to open doors to the Shahnameh's epic, historical, mythical and philosophical world. However, in the past few decades a new generation of Iranian scholars, inspired by the systematic and enlightening studies of a number of foreign scholars and orientalists, began to take remarkable steps in this field. They not only have presented the results of their own studies of the different aspects of the Shahnameh, but have mentioned, with an appreciative attitude, the misunderstandings, incorrect interpretations, and other shortcomings they have observed in the foreign scholarship about the Shahnmneh...

Rostam & Kaveh

We know that in the Shahnamneh, besides Rostam there are many heroes or Pahlavans, but only Rostam is called Jahan-Pahlavan, meaning Champion of the World. These heroes, who served the kings, were in fact the generals or commanders of the army and at the same time, the heads or members of the noble and powerful families of the country. The greatest of them, in the time of Key Kavus, was Tus, son of Novzar, who had no choice but to acknowledge the power and the position of Rostam. Tus could not help resenting Rostam's glorious popularity and, particularly, the Shah's respectful reliance on him. The reason for the uniqueness of Rostam's position among all the other Pahlavans, especially those who officially served in the king's army, can be something more than his being the guardian of farr, the divine right of kingship of the Keyanids...

There are essential differences between the relationship of the people with God and King on the one hand and with their heroes, on the other. God is omnipotent and beyond comprehension and kings, considering the non-democratic aspect of kingship, were His shadows on earth and ascended the throne through His divine will. Benevolent or evil the kings did whatever they liked, and when a king was an "evil oppressor " like Zahhak, who fed the serpents grown on his shoulders with the brains of teenage boys, the people had to suffer in their vengeful silence and to wait for the miraculous rise of a simple blacksmith, like Kaveh from amongst themselves, a hero of the people, with no farr, who made a banner of his leather apron in his uprising against Zahhak. It is that piece of leather which becomes, as Edward G. Browne describes, "by a patriotic apotheosis", the Iranian national flag or their "standard of national liberty", and remains flying in the Shahnameh from the reign of Faridun, the Pishdadi king, to the fall of the Samanid dynasty. Even though many of the Iranists convincingly explain that the standard called Darafsh-e Kaviyani in the Shahnameh is not related to Kaveh the Blacksmith and Kaviyani means Keyani or imperial, yet the people, whose imagination creates their realities, want to believe that the national flag in the Shahnameh is the same leather apron of their own hero and it is not related to kingship. Rostam in the Shahnameh is the people's hero of heroes. He is the preserver of the country's independence and the protector of the people against all their enemies...

It is true that he serves the kings unreservedly, even when a king like Kavus does not personally deserve such a service, but in performing his duty, Rostam is molded by the mythological principle to regard the king as the divine symbol of independence and national sovereignty. Therefore, in a study of the mythical character of a hero like Rostam, the relation between the people and their hero is as important as the hero's devotion to his duty, which, in its turn is perceived and determined by the people, i.e. the mythmakers.

Ferdowsi's Sources

Although Ferdowsi owes most of the materials of the Shahnameh to the oral poetic traditions, he himself was not something of a gosan, a minstrel, an oral poet, a performer of legends and myths, but a well-educated, intellectual member of a rather wealthy social class called dehgan (dehqn). He was a poet of the post-Islamic era who had learned the art of New Persian poetry like all his other contemporaries. He versified the Shahnameh as a pure literary work to be read and appreciated by educated people. As a consequence of this, reading and understanding his book has never been easy for ordinary people...

As Jalal Khaleqi Motlaq, a well-known scholar of the Shahnameh, has said in one of his essays about Ferdowsi's Shahnameh, in a book entitled The Flower of the Past Toils, - "the Khudaynamehs, compiled or written by the historians and the Zoroastrian priests (mobads) in the time of the Sassanian dynasty, consisted mainly of historical records about the kings and of dry reports of wars, with some differences, such as Keyumars (Gayumarth) being introduced by the Zoroastrian priests as the first man (Adam) and by the court historians as the first king. These Khodaynamehs did not include many of the epic stories, which we know through the Shahnameh or other sources; and these stories, especially the Sistan (Saka) narratives (about Rostam and his family), were independently narrated, or translated (from Pahlavi) by the Iranian dehgans, and later incorporated in the Shahnameh... Therefore, the epic narratives were primarily prevalent among and developed by the ordinary people who gathered round and listened to the gosans (minstrels), and also by the aristocratic dehgans, who had remained away from the effects of urban life and the influences of the Sassanian court. After the fall of the Parthians, (the most important promoters of the Persian epic literature), they preserved these narratives with faithfulness to the past and its traditions, basically a characteristic of rural life."

However, in comparison to dehgans, the Zoroastrian priests or mobads were more interested in scriptures and religious literature, and did not place much value on non-religious or worldly literature.

Because of this, after the emergence of Islam in Iran, they remained loyal to their own religion and preserved their language and alphabet, through many Pahlavi texts, but saved almost nothing of the worldly literature. Yet, in the time of Ferdowsi nearly four centuries later, in addition to some of dehgans, these mobads were the only people who had broad knowledge of the Zoroastrian scriptures, and could also read the Pahlavi texts still in existence. Consequently it was obvious that Ferdowsi, for anything that he could not find in the Khodaynameh, had to turn to either a dehgan or a mobad; and this fact is mentioned by Ferdowsi whenever in the Shahnameh he versifies their version of a story...

Ferdowsi wants to be known as a poet who, in his versification of the legends, myths and historical accounts, has been thoroughly faithful to the original sources. Therefore, many times, especially at the beginning of the stories, he has emphatically stated that he simply "versifies" what is written in the Nameh-ye Khosrovan, or the Book of Kings (Khodaynameh) and what the learned, wise, honest, noble dehgans have related to him. We also know that Ferdowsi did not know the Pahlavi language. Therefore, if any of his sources had been in syllabic verse, it must have been translated into the conversational New Persian language...

SHAMS-OD-DIN MUHAMMAD HAFEZ

A Classic Poet from Shiraz (c. 1320 - 1389)

Shams-od-Din Muhammad Hafez was born in Shiraz between 1317 and 1326.

He is known under his pen name Hafez (Koran-memorizer) because he was well-versed in theological studies and knew the Koran by heart. Although Hafez's poetry contains some eloquently worded attacks against the Sufis and ascetics who feign piety, it is said that he himself belonged to a Sufi order.

Little is known about Hafez's life; however, through his poetry we can deduce that he was married and had lost both his wife and a son. He lived during the reign of Abu Eshaq Inju (1343 - 53), Mobarez-od-Din (1353 - 58), and Shah Shoja the Mozaffarid (1358 - 85). There are few if any facts regarding Hafez's relations with the rulers of his time. Abu Eshaq and Shah Shoja were cultured rulers with a love for literature, but Mobarez-od-Din was a bigoted ascetic responsible for many executions under the guise of religion. He is often indirectly referred to by Hafez as mohtaseb the much-hated censor who indulged in controlling not only the business in the bazaars, but also the morals of the people:

"Though wine incites to jocund mirth, and winds through flowers are sighing,

While drinking, let the harp be mute; the mohtaseb is prying.

If e'er thy genial lot bestow a mate and flagon cheery,

With prudence to the goblet turn; the days of life are dreary."

The prohibitions introduced by Mobarez-od-Din came to an end with Shah Shoja's ascension to the throne, which was a time of celebration for Hafez. Nevertheless, for a short period the relations between the new ruler and the poet seem to have been somewhat strained.

After Shah Shoja's death, there followed a period of confusion, with the advance of Timur's armies in the eastern lands of the Muslim world and the conquest of Persia. One of Hafez's ghazals1, has given birth to a famous anecdote that tells of the meeting between the cruel, and yet artistically-minded Timur, and the ageing poet.

Hafez passed away shortly after in 1389.

***

As far as Hafez's poetry is concerned, although he was initially declared a heretic, he was soon to be acknowledged as the leading master of lyrical poetry with the brilliance, energy and originality of his poems shining through. In addition, his verse was given a mystical interpretation and his small divan2 became not only the source of joy for lovers of poetry, but also a mystic and prognostic treasure. Hafez's mausoleum is to this day one of the most important monuments in Shiraz, and is frequented by many visitors, who like to open there the poet's divan to find out what the future may hold.

The real meaning of Hafez's verse has been a matter of dispute. Among all the commentators, the great poet and thinker Goethe stands out, as one of the few who managed to penetrate his psyche. In his Westostlicher Divan, Goethe expresses that for him Hafez's song is "turning like the starry spheres", with the beginning, centre, and end mysteriously united by the same movement.

Today Hafez is considered the undisputed master of the ghazal, and his poems reflect a richness and subtlety unequalled even by that other great talent Saadi. His poems convey something far beyond their external meaning, and thus enable the reader to sense things that transcend the simple statements found in a verse.

The world to me has been a home;

Wherever knowledge could be sought,

Through differing climes I loved to roam,

And every shade of feeling caught

From minds, whose varied fruits supply

The food of my philosophy.

And still the treasures of my store
Have made my wanderings less severe;
From every spot some prize I bore,
From every harvest gleaned an ear,
but find no land can ever vie
With bright shiraz in purity;
And blest for ever be the spot
Which makes all other climes forgot!

"Of Will and Immortals"

They came just before dawn, as in grief I did plead;
I drank life's elixir and watched darkness recede.
They turned me ecstatic in the brightness of soul,
gave me wine from cup of the awakening seed.
Such a blessed dawn and such a time to rejoice-
that moment divine they handed down my fresh deed.
Henceforth I'll search mirror of beloved's image
where they did appear and my new essence decreed.
I'm cheered, it's no mystery my desires are fulfilled;
they found me worthy and my starvation did feed.
That angelic voice told me of riches to come
through patience in the face of suffering and need.
All this sweetness and nectar that flow from my words
are enduring rewards given me by that weed.
Through the will of Hafez and souls of immortals
emerges liberation-from slavery I'm freed.

"A Tale Of Love"

In the garden at dawn I sought for a rose when night-
ingale's voice broke the peace with her prose.

Like me, she was mad for love of a flower and woke up
the garden by trilling her woes.

I strolled round the garden moment by moment, eyeing songbird's affair with flower she chose.

Sweet flower did swoon while the nightingale wooed; this one's yet to age, that one's caught in love's throes.

As nightingale's song penetrated my heart, it erased all desires my mind could compose.

In garden where so many roses abound,to pick even one is to learn where thorn grows.

Hafez, seek no comfort from life's wheel turning, for its one thousand squeaks create no repose.

SAADI - THE GENIUS OF SHIRAZ

The lifetime of Saadi (also known by the name: Mosleh al-Din Saadi Shirazi) falls in a period of major political and social change in Iran and the whole of the Middle East (the decline of the Abbasid Empire with the invasion and subsequent wanton destruction by the Mongols). As a result of this, little is known about his life apart from what he wrote in his "so called " autobiographical works.

One of his nicest autobiographical stories, in the Golestan, tells the story of his release from slavery:

... He was imprisoned by the Crusaders and had to dig trenches in Tripoli until a Muslim merchant bought and freed him; but then his previous form of slavery was replaced by another, since he had to marry his benefactor's daughter....

What we know for sure is that he was born in Shiraz in the late 12th century AD (this is even questioned by some scholars who believe he was born in 1210) and began life as a student of the Koran, which he later exchanged for Sufism. During his life he travelled widely and returned to his native town some time around 1256. One usually assumes that Saadi travelled for some thirty years, and it was his experiences and his gift of acute observation that made him such a wonderful storyteller. In 1257 he dedicated his Bustan, a book on moral virtues in the form of moralising anecdotes in verse, to Abu

Bakr b. Sa'd (ruled Shiraz between 1226-60), and in the following year he completed the Golestan. The Golestan is mainly written in prose and contains stories and personal anecdotes. In it he contrasts the fate of those who depend on the moods of kings to the freedom of the dervishes. Its text is interspersed with a variety of short poems containing advice and humorous reflections.

Copies of both works were often penned by the masters of calligraphy and sometimes decorated with miniatures of great beauty.

Saadi displays great wisdom in all his works with an understanding of the human mind, and many of his lines and sayings have been frequently quoted.

He is also remembered as a great panegyrist and lyricist. He wrote many qasidas (long panegyrics) in Persian and Arabic, mystic ghazals (love poems) and satirical poetry.

Saadi is said to have died in 1290 and his tomb in Shiraz is a shrine. He remains the master of love poetry and one of the greatest poets that Persia has produced.

THE GOLESTAN (THE ROSE GARDEN)

On Love and Youth

I remember that in my youth I was passing along a street when I beheld a moon-faced beauty. The season was that of the month of July, when the fierce heat dried up the moisture of the mouth, and the scorching wind consumed the marrow of the bones. Through the weakness of human nature I was unable to support the power of the sun, and involuntarily took shelter under the shade of a wall, waiting to see if any one would relieve me from the pain I suffered, owing to the ardour of the sun's rays, and cool my flame with water. All of a sudden, from the dark portico of a house, I beheld a bright form appear, of such beauty that the tongue of eloquence would fail in narrating her charms. She came forth as morn succeeding a dark night, or as the waters of life issuing from the gloom. She held in her hand a cup of snow-water, in which she had mixed sugar and the juice of the grape. I know not whether she had perfumed it with her own roses, or distilled into it some drops from the bloom of her countenance. In short, I took the cup from her fair hand, and drained its contents, and received new life.

"The thirst of my heart cannot be slaked with a drop of water, nor if I should drink rivers would it be lessened."

Most blest that happy one whose gaze intense

Rests on such face at each successive morn;

The drunk with wine at midnight may his sense

Regain; but not till the last day shall dawn

Will Love's intoxication reach its bourne.

On Decrepitude and Old Age

One day, in the pride of my youth, I had travelled hard, and at night stopped, much fatigued, at the foot of a mountain. An infirm old man, who followed the caravan, said to me, "Arise! This is not a place to slumber in." I replied, "How can I proceed, when I have not the power to stir a foot?" He rejoined, "Hast thou not heard that they have said, 'It is better to walk and rest, than to run and be oppressed?' "

Thou who wouldst reach the halting-place, haste not;

Be patient! and my counsel hear aright:

Two courses may be sped by charger hot;

The mule goes slowly, but goes day and night.

On the Effect of Education

A philosopher was advising his children as follows:

"Dear to me as life! acquire knowledge; for there is no reliance to be placed in worldly possessions, either of land or money. You cannot take rank abroad with you; and silver and gold on a journey occasion risk, and either the thief may carry it off at one swoop, or the owner will gradually expend it: but knowledge is an ever-springing fountain, and a source of enduring wealth, and if an accomplished person ceases to be wealthy it matters not, for his knowledge is wealth existing in his mind itself. Wherever the accomplished man goes he is esteemed, and is seated in the place of honour, while the man without accomplishments has, go where he will, to pick up scraps and endure raps.

'Tis hard t' obey for those who have borne rule,

Or fortune's minions in rough ways to school.

In Syria once commotions so arose

That discord shook each person from his hearth.

Eftsoons the king his vazirship bestows

On peasants' sons, wise, though of lowly birth:

The vazir's dullard children in their stead,

Through town and hamlet humbly beg their bread.

Learn what thy father knew, if thou wouldst hold

his place. In ten days thou wilt spend his gold.

On the Manners of Kings

... They relate that once, during a hunting exhibition, they were preparing for Nushirwan the Just some game, as roast meat. There was no salt; and they dispatched a slave to a village to bring some. Nushirwan said, "Pay for the salt you take, in order that it may not become a custom, and the village be ruined." They said, "What harm will this little quantity do?" He replied, "The origin of injustice in the world was at first small, and everyone that came added to it, until it reached this magnitude."

On the Qualities of Derwishes

They asked Luqman, "of whom didst thou learn manners? He replied, "From the unmannerly. Whatever I saw them do which I disapproved of, that I abstained from doing."

Not e'en in jest a playful word is said,

But to the wise, 'twill prove a fruitful theme.

To fools, a hundred chapters may be read

of grave import; to them they'll jesting seem.

***

A certain pious man in a dream beheld a king in paradise and a devotee in hell. He inquired, "What is the reason of the exaltation of one, and the cause of the degradation of the other? For I had imagined just the reverse." They said, "That king is now in paradise owing to his friendship for derwishes, and this recluse is in hell through frequenting the presence of kings."

On the Excellence of Contentment

An African mendicant, in the street of the mercers of Aleppo, said, "O wealthy sirs! if you had but justice and we contentment, the custom of begging would be banished from the world."

Contentment! do thou me enrich; for those

Who have thee not are blest with wealth in vain.

Wise Luqman for his treasure patience chose:

Who have not patience wisdom ne'er attain.

***

A thief said to a beggar, "Art thou not ashamed to hold out thy hand for the smallest particle of silver to every contemptible fellow?" He replied,

"Better hold the hand for coin, though small,

Than lose, for one half a dang (1), it all."

On the Duties of Society

- "Riches are intended for the comfort of life, and not life for the purpose of hoarding riches"

They asked a philosopher, 'Who should be called fortunate, and who unfortunate?' He replied, 'He is to be called fortunate, who sowed and reaped; and he must be reckoned unfortunate, who died and left [what he possessed without enjoying it.]'

- A learned man who does not restrain his passion is like a blind man holding a torch; he guides others but not himself.
- He that has acquired learning and nor practised what he has learnt, is like a man who ploughs but sows no seed.
- Do not reveal to a friend every secret you possess.

How do you know if at some time in the future he may become an enemy?

Nor inflict on your enemy every injury that is in your power, as he may someday become your friend.

Tell no one the secret that you want to keep, although he may be worthy of confidence; for no one will be so careful of your secret as yourself.

- Anger that has no limit causes terror, and unseasonable kindness does away with respect. Be not so severe as to cause disgust, nor so lenient as to make people presume.

1) A dang is the sixth part of a dirham and is equal to about one penny.

JALAL AL-DIN RUMI

Persian Sufi Sage and Poet (1207 - 1273)

Jalal al-Din Rumi, was born in Balkh 1 on the 30th September, 1207. His proper name was Mubammad, title Jalal al-Din and later "Khudawandagar", "lord". In his poetry he used the pen-name "khamush" (meaning "silent") and from the 15th century came to be known as Mawlawi, the term deriving from his earlier title of Mulla-yi rum, "the learned master of Anatolia". His disciples, such as Ahmad Aflaki called him "The Greatest Mystery of God" (sirr Allah al-a'zam), while the Persian speaking world usually refers to him as Mawlana. In the West where his fame has spread steadily since the 19th century he is usually known as Rumi, (meaning from Roman Anatolia).

Rumi's father Muhammad ibn Hussain Khatibi, known as Baha' al-Din Walad (entitled Sultan al-'ulama'), was an outstanding Sufi in Balkh. He is the author of the Ma'arif 2, a masterpiece of Sufism, which left its mark upon Rumi's Mathnawi.

When Rumi was about twelve or thirteen years old (around 1220), Baha al-Din Walad left the eastern provinces of Persia with his whole family and a group of disciples and travelled westward. This may have been as a result of the threat of invading Mongol armies. It is said that in Nayshapur he met the renowned Persian Sufi poet Farid al-Din 'Attar and presented Jalal al-Din to him. Apparently Sheikh 'Attar was very impressed by the young Rumi, and told Baha' al-Din Walad, 'soon this son of thine shall set the spiritual aspirants of this world afire'.

From Nayshapur Baha' al-Din Walad and his entourage set out for Baghdad where they were highly respected, meeting many of the scholars and Sufis of the city. From there they went to the Hejaz and performed the pilgrimage at Mecca. It was after this journey that most likely as a result of the invitation of 'Ala', al-Din Kayqubad, the ruler of Anatolia, Baha' al-Din came to Asia Minor and finally settled in Konya, a city associated with his family to this day. The family of Baha' al-Din Walad was welcomed warmly in Konya, which was witness at this time to many immigrants from the eastern cities of Persia, since Anatolia offered a peaceful haven in the Islamic world during the turbulent years of the Mongol invasion. Baha' al-Din rapidly gained fame as a religious scholar and Sufi and died with honor when Rumi was 24 years of age.

Around a year after his father's death, Rumi met Burhan al-Din Muhaqqiq Tirmidhi, a Sufi master of high quality who was himself a disciple of Baha' al- Din Walad. It was through Burhan al-Din that Rumi inherited the spiritual heritage of his father and became initiated into the mysteries of Sufism. For nine years Rumi practiced Sufism as a disciple of Burhan al-Din until the latter died in 1240-1. During this period Rumi also travelled to Damascus and is said to have spent four years there.

Having become a master of both the Shari'ite sciences and Sufism, Rumi established a circle around him in Konya, and from around 1240 to 1244, he was occupied with teaching, meditating, helping the poor, and other activities of a religious scholar. It is said that he was a popular teacher and that as many as four hundred students attended his formal classes. In 1244 Rumi's life was transformed through his encounter with Shams al-Din Tabrizi, who had entered Konya that year after spending some time in Baghdad. Shams was a mysterious and powerful Sufi, who fled social connections. Even his death remains a mystery and he has several tombs which have remained sites of pilgrimage, to this day.

There is no doubt that Shams al-Din Tabrizi was not just a Sufi master for Rumi. Jalal al-Din had already practiced Sufism for many years before meeting Shams al-Din. It seems, rather, that Shams al-Din had a spiritual influence on him. Rumi was the type of Sufi who needed spiritual companionship in order to express himself in words. The companionship that Shams al-Din provided, was so powerful that it transformed the sober teacher Rumi, into an ecstatic poet. The first poem ever written by Rumi is in a letter to Shams, and from the time of their encounter until Rumi's death, the latter never ceased to compose poetry. The spiritual, friendship between these two towering figures is rare in the history of Sufism and has become proverbial in the East.

Harassed by some of the disciples, who had become jealous of the fact that Jalal al-Din spent all of his time with Shams, the latter left Konya. Rumi became so distressed that he sent him many letters and messages containing his first poems in Persian and Arabic and finally, after having discovered that he was in Damascus, sent his own son Sultan Walad after him. Shams finally accepted to return to Konya, he stayed at Rumi's home and again the mystical conversation began, leading to a renewed jealousy among some of Rumi's disciples. On the night of December 5, 1248, as Rumi and Shams were talking, Shams was called to the door. He went out, and was never seen again. It is believed that he was murdered. The mystery of his absence engulfed Rumi's world and he searched for him for two years travelling as far as Damascus, but to no avail. It was there that he came to the following realization:

Why should I seek? I am the same as he.

His essence speaks through me.

I have been searching for myself!

Rumi returned to Konya, began his open instruction of Sufism and devised the spiritual dance (sama), for which the Mawlawi order has been famous for the past seven centuries.

The rest of Jalal al-Din's life from 1249-50 to 1273 was the period of dissemination of Sufism and the esoteric sciences contained in it. He trained numerous disciples, some of whom like Salah al-Din Zarkub Qunyawi and Husam al-Din Chalabi were themselves spiritual guides. According to Rumi, Husam Chelebi was the one who understood the vast, secret of the Mathnawi, that great work that shifts so fantastically from theory to folklore to jokes to ecstatic poetry. For the last twelve years of his life, Rumi dedicated the six volumes of this masterwork to Husam.

In December 1273, Jalal al-Din fell ill. He knew that the moment of encounter with the Beloved was near, a moment which for him could not but be the most joyous moment of life. He predicted his own death and composed the well-known ghazal, which begins with the verse:

How doest thou know what sort of king I have within me as companion? Do not cast thy glance upon my golden face, for I have iron legs.

He died on the 17th December 1273 in a state of joy and peace surrounded by his spiritual progeny, which also included his closest family. Sadr al-Din Qunyawi, the other great master of Sufism in Konya at that time, read the prayer of the dead before the body and the earthly remains of the greatest Sufi poet of the Persian language was laid to rest in Konya. His tomb remains to this day, is one of the most important sites of pilgrimage in the Islamic world, a second Ka'ba for the Sufis and the spiritual centre of Turkey.

An Insight into Rumi's Works

The writings of Rumi are unique in Persian literature because of their quality and immense richness. His works reflect nearly all earlier works from Koranic commentaries to the Sufi treatises of Sana'i, 'Attar and Ibn 'Arabi, and his writings have found their echo in countless works written from Bengal to present day Turkey.

Rumi's most extensive work is Diwan-i Shams-i Tabrizi, consisting of some thirty-six thousand verses in most ghazals1, in which Rumi uses the name of Shams al-Din at the end instead of his own, as if Shams had written them. This fact displays the special relation that existed between the two men and the role that Shams played in the composition of this vast work. Most of these verses were written in the state of ecstasy and have a musical and rhythmic quality that is unique in Persian literature. The dance and music of the Mawlawi order is in a sense crystallized in these verses of unmatched ecstatic power. The meaning dominates so much over the form that in many instances the ghazals break the laws of traditional prosody and metrics. It is a case of the spirit remolding its material form and breathing into the formal order a new life, thereby creating a new yet totally traditional artistic form.

The Diwan has been celebrated throughout the eastern lands of Islam since its composition, and several lithographed editions were printed in both India and Persia before its critical edition appeared under the care of B. Forouzanfar in ten volumes in Tehran. It is also partially known in the West thanks to the selections translated by Nicholson and Arberry. The Diwan-i Shams along with the Diwan of Hafez, is perhaps the work that lends itself least to translation from the point of view of the orchestration of words and the harmony of sounds and the effect that its very rendition creates in the soul of a Persian speaker.

Rumi's most famous work is without doubt the Mathnawi, dubbed by Jami as the "Koran of the Persian language". It was composed at the request of Husam al-Din Chalabi, who asked the master to write a work on the mysteries of gnosis2 based upon the model of the Hadiqa of Sana'i or the Mantiq al-tayr of 'Attar. The Mathnawi is so celebrated that although the term refers to any poem of rhyming couplets it has come to mean the Mathnawi of Jalal al-Din Rumi. This unmatched masterpiece of Sufism is more didactic3 than the Diwan. It consists of a prelude in Arabic or Persian for each volume, in the first of which the author calls his work the "principles of the principles of the principles of religion", followed by six volumes of poems in Persian. It was begun between 1259 and 1262-3 and its composition continued to nearly the end of Rumi's life. In fact it was never completed. Some have referred to a seventh book of the Mathnawi and have even tried to "complete" the work with a seventh volume. The original work of the master is without doubt in six volumes, which have been published many times in Persia, India and Turkey with the most critical edition to date being that established by Nicholson in his monumental eight volume text, translation and commentary upon the work.

In nearly twenty-six thousand verses of poetry, Rumi unravels in the Mathnawi the vast ocean of the world of the spirit and man's journey to and through that world. Drawing from sacred history, simple tales, earlier Sufi writings, learned discourses of predecessors, lives of saints and many other sources, Rumi discusses nearly every aspect of Islamic metaphysics, cosmology and traditional psychology. Few mystical works in any language combine such mastery of pure metaphysics with insight into the intricate structure of the human soul and the pitfalls which face the man who awakens, through initiation, to his own spiritual possibilities and who begins the journey towards the One.

The Mathnawi is also well known to the Western world thanks to the efforts of Nicholson, who made the whole text available in English and also presented selections of it in a highly readable form. Students of the Mathnawi are also indebted to A. J. Arberry for his masterly translations of the stories within that book in clear prose as well as his other studies of the text.

The Mathnawi has received continuous attention since its composition. Several special musical forms have come into being in Sindh, Persia, Turkey and other regions simply for the chanting of the Mathnawi, and numerous commentaries have been written in Persian, Turkish, Arabic and some of the languages of the Indo-Pakistani sub-continent. Commentaries continue to be written on this work to this day; more recent ones include the Persian works by J. Homa'i, B. Forouzanfar and M. T. Ja'fari.

The third poetical work of Rumi is the Ruba'iyyat. Although it possesses quatrains4 matching the powerful verses of the

Diwan and the Mathnawi, altogether the Ruba'iyyat has never gained the fame of Rumi's other two poetical masterpieces. This work has again been made known to the English-speaking world thanks to the translation of a selection by A. J. Arberry.

Of the prose works of Rumi the most important is the Fihi ma fihi, a unique work reflecting Rumi's most intimate discourses on various aspects of the spiritual life assembled from his "table talks" during Sufi gatherings by his son and other disciples. This work, whose critical edition appeared first under the care of B. Forouzanfar and which is now well known in the West thanks to the selective translation of A. J. Arberry, discusses in an intimate and direct manner many of the most subtle aspects of Sufism. It is a precious companion as a practical guide for the "Way", and it reveals an aspect of Rumi's personality not reflected so directly in the poetical works.

Closely related in content to Fihi ma fihi is the Makatib, or "collection of letters" written by Rumi to his close associates such as Salah al-Din Zarkub and his own daughter-in-law. The letters, like the discourses in Fihi ma fihi, reveal the more personal and intimate aspects of the master's life, while at the same time containing doctrinal passages and instruction concerning the practical aspects of the "Way".

Finally the Majalis-i sab'ah, is another prose work, which consists of a number of Rumi's sermons and lectures delivered from the pulpit. The sermons are mostly in the form of advice and counsel and reflect in style the background in which they were delivered.

These works are the written legacy of the "master from Rum". They complement the oral transmission and the particular type of grace or barakah, which issued from the being of Rumi and resulted in the foundation of the Mawlawi order, that vastly extended Sufi order which has survived to this day. Jalal al-Din has remained alive through his works and his order to our own times. His spirit continues to resurrect those who are capable of following the spiritual life. Rumi's message which issues from the world of the Spirit is as pertinent today as when it was first spoken, for his words come from a world which is ancient while being young, and young, while being ancient, a world, which encompasses man in his journey from eternity to eternity.

Examples of Rumi's Works in English Translation

Rumi came to the attention of European scholars in the late 18th century and has been translated since then into various European languages such as English, German, French, Dutch, Russian, and Swedish. In this way Rumi has entered into the literary life of Western man and has gained a home for himself in Western languages. Rumi has received most attention in German and English.

Thanks to the efforts of such scholars as Sir William Jones, Sir James Redhouse, E. H. Palmer, C. E. Wilson, E. H. Whinfield, E. G. Browne, R.A. Nicholson and A.J. Arberry, the name of Rumi has become practically a household word in English, and it is not just the Orientalists who read and study the works of this supreme poet of the spirit; his admirers come from almost every walk of life.

The following are a selection of English translations of Rumi's poetry:

The Song of the Reed

From the Mathnawi, Book I

(Translation by: Sir William Jones)

Hear, how yon reed in sadly pleasing tales
Departed bliss and present woe bewails!
'With me, from native banks untimely torn,
Love-warbling youths and soft-ey'd virgins mourn.
O! Let the heart, by fatal absence rent,
Feel what I sing, and bleed when I lament:
Who roams in exile from his parent bow'r,
Pants to return, and chides each ling'ring hour.
My notes, in circles of the grave and gay,
Have, hail'd the rising, cheer'd the closing day:

Each in my fond affections claim'd a part,
But none discern'd the secret of my heart.
What though my strains and sorrows flow combin'd!
Yet ears are slow, and carnal eyes are blind.
Free through each mortal form the spirits roll,
But sight avails not. Can we see the soul?
Such notes breath'd gently from yon vocal frame:
Breath'd said I? no; 'twas all enliv'ning flame.
'Tis love, that fills the reed with warmth divine;
'Tis love, that sparkles in the racy wine.
Me, plaintive wand'rer from my peerless maid,
The reed has fir'd, and all my soul betray'd
He gives the bane, and he with balsam cures;
Afflicts, yet soothes; impassions, yet allures.
Delightful pangs his am'rous tales prolong;
And LAILI'S frantic lover lives in song.
Not he, who reasons best, this wisdom knows:
Ears only drink what rapt'rous tongues disclose.

From the Diwan

(Translation by: R.A. Nicholson)

O Thou who art my soul's comfort in the season of sorrow,

O Thou who art my spirit's comfort in the bitterness of dearth!

That which the imagination hath not conceived,

that which the understanding hath not seen,

Visiteth my soul from Thee; hence in worship I turn toward Thee.

By Thy Grace I keep fixed on eternity my amorous gaze,

Except, O King, the pomps that perish lead me astray.

The favour of him who brings glad tidings of Thee,

Even without Thy summons, is sweeter in mine ear than songs.

If the never-ceasing Bounty should offer kingdoms,

If the Hidden Treasure should set before me all that is,

I would bow down with my soul, I would lay my face in the dust,

I would cry, "Of all these the love of such an One for me!"

From the Ruba'iyyat

(Translation by: A.J. Arberry)

Be just: confess
In love is ample righteousness;
The fault lies in
Thyself, that thou art prone to sin.
If thou dost claim
For human lust Love's holy name,
Then know, and prove
The way is far from lust to Love.

***

Down a flowing stream
A barque borne fast.
To the mind it may seem
The rushes hurry past.
Every moment thus
From this world we fly,
And it seemeth to us
The world goes by.

***

We are the treasury
Of God's great mystery;
The sea wherein doth dwell

His pearl incalculable.
From end to farthest end
Of being we extend,
Yea, we sit upon
God's imperial throne.

***

The heart is a secret garden
Its trees unseen;
A hundred hues it blossoms Unchanged, serene.
The heart's a boundless ocean Illimitable;
Its waves break unnumbered In every soul.

***

I am drunk with the love of Thee,
Not with wine, or opium;
I am mad; dost Thou look to see
In a madman decorum?
A hundred torrents rise
From the surge my soul within;
The heavens in glad surprise
Stand still to behold me spin.

***

Of the book of God
Thou art a copying,
A mirror wherein showed
The beauty of the King.
All God ever wrought
Dwelleth not apart;
All thou hast ever sought,
Find it in thy heart.

THE LEGEND OF "LAYLI AND MADJNUN"

The story of Layli and Madjnun is one of the most popular legends of the Middle East.

Its original version dates back to around 7th Century AD, and can be found in Arabic literature.

The Persian version written by the 12th Century poet Nezami (part of the set of stories known as the "Khamsa") is not just a classic love story, but a profound spiritual allegory. Folk versions of Layli and Madjnun have been told from North Africa to India.

THE ORIGINAL LEGEND

In Arabic Literature

This romantic love story can be dated back in its original form to the second half of the 7th Century. The content of the romance, insofar as it can be extracted from the ancient versions, is relatively simple. However, from the start there have been two different versions:

In one, the two young people spent their youth together tending their flocks; while in the other, Madjnun [meaning madman] whose actual name according to the narrators was Qays, meets Layla, [commonly named Layli in Persian] by chance at a gathering of women, and the effect on him is devastating...

He kills his camel as a contribution to the feast, and Layla falls in love with him from the start. Subsequently he asks for her hand in marriage, but her father has already promised her to another. Gripped by the most violent anguish, Qays loses his reason and sets out to wander half-naked, refusing nourishment and living among wild animals. His father tries to make him forget Layla, by taking him on a pilgrimage , but his madness only intensifies.

He does, however, show moments of lucidity in his poetry about his lady-love, and while talking about her to those curious people who have come to see him...

He dies alone, only meeting Layla one more time.

The origins of this story is difficult to establish. It is thought that it may have been a young man of the Umayyad clan who, under the pseudonym of Madjnun, circulated some stories designed to introduce verses in which he sang of his love for his cousin. This identification is, however, isolated and in any case, the poet is anonymous. The fact that historical individuals such as Nawfal ben Musahik, governor of Medina (702 AD) are mentioned in the traditions relating to the adventures of Qays, suggests that the latter version came to existence at about this period. The author, or rather authors of the verses attributed to this Madjnun and the introductory or explanatory tales, will always be unknown, which makes the legend more mysterious and intriguing.

3

EARLY INSCRIPTIONS OF PERSIAN LITERATURE

THE PERSIAN LANGUAGE

The Old Persian of the Achaemenian Empire, preserved in a number of cuneiform inscriptions, was an Indo-European tongue with close affinities with Sanskrit and Avestan (the language of the Zoroastrian sacred texts). After the fall of the Achaemenians the ancient tongue developed, in the province of Pars, into Middle Persian or Pahlavi (a name derived from Parthavi - that is, Parthian). Pahlavi was used throughout the Sassanian period, though little now remains of what must once have been a considerable literature. About a hundred Pahlavi texts survive, mostly on religion and all in prose. Pahlavi collections of romances, however, provided much of the material for Ferdowsi's Shahnameh.

After the Arab conquest a knowledge of Arabic became necessary, for it was not only the language of the new rulers and their state, but of the religion they brought with them and - later - of the new learning. Though Pahlavi continued to be spoken in private life, Arabic was dominant in official circles for a century and a half. With the weakening of the central power, a modified form of Pahlavi emerged, with its Indo-European grammatical structure intact but simplified, and with a large infusion of Arabic words. This was the Modem Persian in use today.

Arabic continued to be employed in Iran, though on a decreasing scale, as Latin was used in Europe -that is, as a language of the learned. As such it was employed by Avicenna, al-Biruni, Rhazes, Al Ghazali and others; indeed, many of the most famous names in Arabic literature are those of men of Persian birth. But in general the use of Arabic declined; Persian developed rapidly to become the vehicle of a great literature, and before, long spread its influence to neighboring lands. In India, Persian language and poetry became the vogue with the ruling classes, and at the court of the Moghul emperor Akbar Persian was adopted as the official language; spreading thence and fusing later with Hindi, it gave rise to the Urdu tongue. To the west of Iran, Persian heavily influenced the language and literature of Turkey; Turkish verse was based on Persian models as regards form and style, and borrowed an extensive vocabulary.

A notable feature of Persian is the small extent to which it has changed over the thousand years or more of its existence as a literary language. Thus the poems of Rudaki, the first Persian poet of note, who died in the year 940 A.D., are perfectly intelligible to the modem reader. Persian literature too has a number of noteworthy characteristics, the most striking of which is the exceptional prominence of poetry. Until quite recently there was practically no drama, and no novels were written; prose works were mostly confined to history, geography, philosophy, religion, ethics and politics, and it was poetry that formed the chief outlet for artistic expression. Classical Persian literature was produced almost entirely under royal patronage whence the frequency of panegyric verse. An influence of at least equal strength was religion, and in particular Sufism, which inspired the remarkably high proportion of mystical poetry.

PERSIAN POETRY

Classical Persian poetry is always rhymed. The principal verse forms are the qasida, masnavi, ghazal and ruba'i. The qasida or ode is a long poem in monorhyme, usually of a panegyric, didactic or religious nature; the masnavi, written in rhyming couplets, is employed for heroic, romantic, or narrative verse; the ghazal (ode or lyric) is a comparatively short poem, usually amorous or mystical and varying from four to sixteen couplets, all on one rhyme. A convention of the ghazal is the introduction, in the last couplet, of the poet's pen name (takhallus). The ruba'i is a quatrain with a particular metre, and a collection of quatrains is called "ruba'iyyat" (the plural of ruba'i). Finally, a collection of a poet's ghazals and other verse, arranged alphabetically according to the rhymes, is known as a divan.

A word may not be out of place here on the peculiar difficulties of interpreting Persian poetry to the western reader. To the pitfalls common to all translations from verse must be added, in the case of Persian poetry, such special difficulties as the very free use of Sufi imagery, the frequent literary, Koranic and other references and allusions, and the general employment of monorhyme, a form highly effective in Persian but unsuited to most other languages. But most important of all is the fact that the poetry of Persia depends to a greater degree than that of most other nations on beauty of language for its effects. This is why much of the great volume of "qasidas in praise of princes" can still be read with pleasure in the original, though It is largely unsuited to translation. In short, the greatest charm of Persian poetry lies, as Sir E. Denison Ross remarked, in its language and its music, and consequently the reader of a translation "has perforce to forego the essence of the matter".

In the following brief sketch of the vast field of Persian literature we cannot hope to do more than mention a few of the most eminent authors, and to devote a paragraph or two each to the most famous of all.

EARLY LITERATURE

Though existing fragments of Persian verse are believed to date from as early as the eighth century A.D., the history of Persian literature proper begins with the lesser dynasties of the ninth and tenth centuries that emerged with the decline of the Caliphate. The most important of these were the Samanids, who established at Bokhara the first of many brilliant courts that were to patronize learning and letters. Here Abu

Ali Sina, better known in the west as Avicenna, developed the medicine and philosophy of ancient Greece, and wrote numerous works that were to exercise considerable influence not only in the East but in Europe -where, translated into Latin, they were in use as late as the seventeenth century. Avicenna wrote mostly in Arabic, but composed an encyclopaedia -- the Danish Nameh-ye Ala'i - in Persian.

The most famous of the court poets were Rudaki and Daqiqi. Rudaki, generally regarded as the first of the great Persian poets, wrote a very large quantity of verse, of which but little has survived. His style direct, simple and unadorned - was to appear unpolished to some of the over-elaborate versifiers of later ages, but appeals more to modem tastes. Daqiqi, a composer of epics, was commissioned to write a work on the ancient kings of Persia, but only completed a thousand couplets before his death. Some of these were later incorporated in the celebrated Shahnameh.

THE GHAZNAVID AND EARLY SELJUQ PERIODS

It is said that four hundred poets were attached to the court of Sultan Mahmoud; of these, the most notable were Unsuri, the greatest of Mahmoud's panegyrists, followed by Farrukhi, Manouchehri and Asadi. Of the prose writers, the most celebrated was Biruni, author of the "Chronology of Ancient Nations", who wrote exclusively in Arabic.

The Seljuq era, regarded as the second classical period of Persian literature, is one rich both in prose and poetry. Famous prose works include Ghazali's influential Revivification of the Religious Sciences in Arabic and its Persian summary entitled Kimiya-ye Sa'adat (The Alchemy of Happiness); Baihaqi's History of the Ghaznavids: the Siasat Nameh, a treatise on the art of government by Nizam ul-Mulk, vizier to Alp Arslan and Malik Shah; the entertaining Qabus Nameh of Kai Ka'us, translated by Professor Levy as "A Mirror for Princes"; the collection of animal fables of Indian origin entitled Kalila va Dimna by Nasr Ullah; the charming Chahar Maqala or Four Discourses of Nizami Aruzi; the Fars Nameh of Ibn al-Balkhi, and the noted treatise on poetics of Rashid-i Vatvat. Four of the above works - the Chahar Maqala, the History of Baihaqi, the Qabus Nameh and the Siasat Nameh - are considered by the poet Bahar as the four great masterpieces of early Persian prose.

A number of authors of this period wrote both prose and poetry. One of the most brilliant of these was Nasir-i Khosrow, writer of some fifteen works in prose and 30,000 verses, of which less than half have survived. His best known prose work is the Safar Nameh, an account of his journey to Egypt. Most of Nasir-i Khosrow's poems are lengthy odes, mainly on religious and ethical subjects; they are noted for their purity of language and dazzling technical skill. In the opinion of the scholar Mirza Mohammad Qazvini, the name of Nasir-i Khosrow should be added to those of the six poets - Ferdowsi, Khayyam, Anvari, Rumi, Saadi, and Hafez - whom "practically all" agree to consider the six greatest Persian poets, each in his special field. Other famous poetry of the period includes the work of the mystics Ansari, Abu Sa'id and Baba Tahir of Hamadan; the odes of Qatran; Gurgani's romantic epic Vis o Ramin, and the Divans of the two Indian-born poets Mas'ud-i Sa'd-i Salman and Runi. Seven other poets of the period are of outstanding fame and brilliance; these are Khayyam, Sana'i, Mu'izzi, Anvari, Khaqani, Nizami and Attar.

The versatile Khayyam - "the only man known to me", says Bertrand Russell, "who was both a poet and a mathematician" - is still perhaps the best known and most appreciated Persian poet in Europe and America. There was for long considerable skepticism as to whether he was in fact the author of all or any of the quatrains attributed to him, but the discovery recently of manuscripts more ancient than any of those previously known has removed these doubts.

Khayyam's poetry was largely neglected in Iran until the end of the nineteenth century, mainly no doubt owing to the censure of orthodoxy. When Fitzgerald's translation made him suddenly popular in the west the Iranians began to reassess his merits as a poet, and as we have seen, some native critics are now ready to accord him a place in the poetic Pantheon. Since he uses imagery common to the Sufis, Khayyam has often been hailed as a Sufi himself; but while some of his quatrains can be made to bear a mystical interpretation, the general impression of his work is one of hedonism tinged with a gentle melancholy, born of acceptance of the tragic transience of life, the power of destiny and man's ultimate ignorance. The attitude is that of a materialist rather than a deist; indeed, he has with some justice been compared to Lucretius.

Sana'i, who wrote in a style similar to that of Nasir-i Khosrow, was the author of two great Sufi epics, the prototypes of the later masterpieces of Attar and Rumi, as well as of a huge divan. Mu'izzi, hailed by 'Abbas Ighbal as "one of the artistic virtuosi of the Persian language", wrote mainly panegyric verse in a highly elaborate style. Anvari, author of numerous poetical works, mostly panegyric, wrote in a difficult style, sometimes requiring a commentary; he is regarded by some as one of the greatest Persian poets. The poetry of Khaqani is even more mannered. The last three poets mentioned - Mu'izzi, Anvari and Khaqani - are all famous in Iran, mainly for their technical brilliance; but, being particularly difficult to translate, they are less appreciated in the west. This is not the case with the next two poets to be mentioned.

Nizami, born at Ganja in the Caucasus in 1140, was a prolific writer famous especially for his Khamseh or Quintet, a series of five great romances and epics. These consist of the Makhzan al-Asrar or Treasure House of Secrets, a mystical epic inspired by Sana'i; the popular romances Khosrow o Shirin and Laila o Majnun; the Iskandar Nameh or Story of Alexander, and the Haft Paikar, the life story of Bahrain Gur. Nizami's style is original and, colorful; his works enjoyed great popularity, and episodes from his romantic poems were favorite subjects for miniature painters.

Farid ud-Din Attar, who was born possibly around 1136, was a great and an original poet who produced numerous religious and didactic works. He was essentially a mystic, and as such exercised a great influence on Rumi. The best known of his works, the Mantiq ut-Tair (translated by Fitzgerald as the Bird Parliament) , is a mystical allegory in which the birds all set off in search of the mythical Simorgh, whom they wish to make their king. The story, which symbolizes the quest of the soul for union with God, ends with their discovery that they have no existence separate from the object of their search.

The Simorgh then addresses them thus:

Pilgrim, Pilgrimage and Road
Was but Myself toward Mvself, and Your
Arrival but Myself at my own Door.....
Come, you lost Atoms, to your Center draw
And be the Eternal Mirror that you saw:
Rays that have wandered into Darkness wide
Return, and back into your Sun subside.

THE THIRTEENTH CENTURY

The Thirteenth century produced two poetic geniuses of the first rank, Sa'adi and Rumi. It is also particularly notable for histories, of which many were inspired by these singularly troubled times. Hamdullah Mostofi produced notable works both of history and geography, as well as an epic, the Zafar Nameh or Book of Victory, in 75,000 couplets, and Nasir ud-Din Tusi wrote on philosophy and logic. Three notable poets of the period are Iraqi, author of the mystical Lama'at or Flashes; Amir Khosrow, known as "The Parrot of India" and author of no less than five divans, and Zakani the satirist.

Foremost in the ranks of historical works are Juvaini's Tarikh-i Jahan Gusha, an account of the Mongol conquests; the history of Juzjani, an important source book for the history of Moslem India; Rashid ud-Din's great Jami' ut-Tawarikh or Universal History, and the History of Vassaf. The style of the period tended to over-ornateness; Juvaini, according to Arberry, was "the most accomplished exponent of the prized art of verbal arabesque", while Vassaf "modeled his style on Juvaini at his most intricate and verbose." Of the writings of this school Levy remarks that it was "so filled with metaphor, allusion, and assonance, that the meaning was often lost in a tangle of verbiage". By contrast, the work of the conscientious Rashid ud-Din, considered by Browne to be the best of all the Persian historians, is a model of clarity.

THE FIFTEENTH CENTURY ONWARDS

The fifteenth century produced a number of notable historians - Nizam ud-Din Shami, author of the Zafar Nameh (a history of Timur); Yazdi, who wrote a work of the same name; Hafiz-i Abru, Khafi, Dowlatshah and Mir Khand, author of the immense Rozat as-Safa or Garden of Purity. Other prose writers of note , include Davvani, author of the Akhlaq-i Jalali, and Kashefi, who produced an elaborate prose paraphrase of Kalila va Dimna known as Anvar-i Suhaili (The Lights of Canopus). Fifteenth century poets include the Sufis Maghribi and Qasim-i Anvar, Katibi, the saintly Ni'mat Allah Vali, and Jami.

Jami, "universally regarded as the last eminent figure in the history of classical Persian literature" (Arberry) was born in 1414. A man of considerable erudition as well as of poetic genius, Jami produced some forty-five works, of which the best known are the Baharistan, the Divan, and the Haft Aurang or Seven Thrones, a series of four didactic works and three romances (Salaman o Absal, Yusuf o Zulaikha and Laila o Majnun) which he intended to rival the work of Nizami.

After Jami, who died shortly before the rise of the Safavis, Persian poetry is generally considered to have fallen into decline. There were indeed no poets of the very first rank after the fifteenth century, yet in this long period there was no lack of writers and poets of talent, some of them of great eminence.

Of the poets immediately following Jami, his nephew Hatif was a noted writer of romantic and historical epics; also famous were his pupils Asafi, Fighani (who earned himself the title of "The Little Hafiz"), Ahli and the Sufi poet Hilali. Later in the sixteenth century came the poets Hayrati, Kasimi, Kashi the panegyrist, Shani, Fasihi and Shafai.

Sa'ib (born 1677), the greatest literary figure of the seventeenth century, is considered by some to be the best Persian poet after Jami. In early life he spent some time in

India as court poet to the Moghul emperor Shah Jahan, and returned to Iran to become poet laureate to Shah Abbas II. Sa'ib was a vivid and original poet who infused fresh life into the old forms and founded a new school. Also of note was his contemporary Fayyaz. A famous prose writer of the eighteenth century was Azar, author of the Atesh Kadeh (a biographical dictionary containing the lives of over 800 poets) as well as of a divan and a romantic epic.

The prolific writer Hazin produced histories and an autobiography, as well as four divans. Also worthy of note is the poet Nejat.

In the nineteenth century Saba, poet laureate to Fath Ali Shah, composed a divan and an epic called the Shahanshahnameh; as a poet he was excelled by Neshat, also author of a divan. Qa'ani (died 1853), the best writer of the nineteenth century and perhaps the most outstanding since Jami, was one of Iran's most brilliant and melodious poets. Well known prose works of the period include Nasir ud-Din Shah's diaries of his three journeys to Europe and the literary biographies of the poet Reza Quli Khan. This period was marked by the increasing influence of European literature, noticeable in the works of the poet Shaybani and others.

The real revival of Persian letters came in the early twentieth century, when the growing desire for reform inspired numerous satires. One of the most outstanding figures of this period was Iraj Mirza (died 1926), a poet of great talent and champion of the emancipation of women. Other noted poets were Adib, Bahar, Lahuti, Shahryar, Aref and the poetess Parvin E'tesami. Poets of more recent decades include Nima, Ra'di, Khanlari, Islami, Gulchin, Shamlu, Akhavan Salis, Mas'ud Farzad and the poetess Foroogh Farrukhzad., Some of these poets have introduced verse forms new to Persian literature.

Iranian history represents a rich blend of legend, mythology, recorded fact and living tradition. Several civilizations have risen in various parts of the country at different times, each leaving its own impression on the subsequent development of Iranian history.

The oldest known civilization in Iran is that of Elam in the 10th century B.C. and the Assyrians in the 8th century B.C. Other major Iranian civilizations are Media, Achaemenids, Parthians and Sassanians. Unfortunately, most of the landmarks of these civilizations were demolished during the Arab and subsequent Mongol and Tatar invasions. The 16th century Safavids civilizations that has the most lasting number of monuments has inherited from both Persian civilization and its invaders. Many other dynasties and monarchies succeeded the country until the Pahlavi, that was once again demolished by the Islamic Revolution under the leadership of Imam Khomeini, in a way similar to its predecessors.

Iran has a long history of almost 7,000 years since the Aryans emigrated to the Iran Heights. Aryans gave their name to this land and called it "land of Aryans" or Iran. Achaemenid appeared in the 550 B.C. was the first unified dynasty and until it was conquered by Alexander of Macedonia (Eskandar e Maghdooni) in 330 B.C., Iran prospered as "The Great Persian Empire" for more than two centuries.

Contributions of the Achaemenians to the worlds culture are numerous. Cyrus (Xerxes) The Great (550 B.C.) was the first emperor who conquered Elam and gave Jews freedom. He was also the first one who declared and practiced human rights.

In the Great Persia Empire from East China to Libya, many nations were coexisting and all were declared free to pactice their own religion and follow their own traditions and customs. Daryush The Great (500 B.C.) was the first emperor who commited to digging the ancient Suez Channel, joining the Red and Mediteranian sea. There are many landmarks left from the Achaemenian period mostly in Persepolis and Naghshe-rostam near present Shiraz.

A BRIEF HISTORY OF IRAN:

~750 BC

The Medes era. Deioces (728 to 675 BC) was the founder of the Median knigdom. The Median capital Ekbatane or Hegmatane (Hamedan) was founded in this era.

~600 BC

The Achaemenids era. The capital of Achaemenids was located in Fars in southwestern Iran. Many present day landmarks, such as Takhte-jamshid and Persepolis are from this era.

329 BC

Defeat of the Achaemenids by Alexander. Aryo-barzan, a brave Persian commander fought to death with all his personnel and couldn't stop Alexander to invade and destroy the capital.

~250 BC

The Parthians era began by defeating the Greeks.

226 AD

The Sasanid era. The Sassanians overthrow the Parthians and established a vast and wealthy empire that included the Central Asia, Middle East, Turkey and North Africa.

570-632 AD

The birth and death of Muhammad (S.A.), the prophet.

642 AD

The Arab invasion. The Sassanid emperor Yazdgerd III was defeated by the Arabs at the Battle of Nahravan. Bisotoon, the capital of the Sassanian was destroyed. The palace and library hosting more the 20,000 old books and scripts were set on fire.

~800 AD

Uprising of the Shi'ite movement in Khorasan (Northeastern Iran) by Abu Moslem Khosasany who fought the Arabs and established the first independent Persian state in Khorasan.

867 AD

The birth of the Saffarid dynasty by Yaqub Saffar who was the first leader to unite Persians under the Shi'ite flag.

874 AD

The rise of the Samanid dynasty in Northeastern Persia. Eventually, Samanid overthrow the Saffarids in 900 AD.

962 AD

Ghaznavid dynasty established in eastern Iran. The capital was Ghazneh located in present day Afghanistan. The Ghaznavids could defeat the Samanids in the early 11th cent and established a vast kingdom from India to Syria.

1040 AD

The Seljuqians era began by defeating the Ghaznavids at the Battle of Dandanqan, near Marv. Seljuqians' reign ended with the death of Sanjar, the last king of this dynasty around 1160 AD.

~1160 AD

The rise of Kharazmshahian in Northeastern Iran.

1220 AD

The Mongol invasion. The Mongols captured nearly all Persia except the Fars. In Bukhara and Samarkand, they ruined and killed more than one million residents. Later the Il-Khanid dynasty was established in central Persia.

1380-87 AD

The Tatar invasion under the command of Timur and the reign of the Timurid rulers started.

1502 AD

Safavid dynasty was established by Shah Ismail.

1729 AD

Nader Shah established the Afsharian dynasty by driving the Afghans out of Persia. He also captured Dehli and North India.

1751-1794

Zandian dynasty.

1796-1925

Qajarian dynasty. Nehdzat Mashrooteh or the Constitutional Movement happend in this era and the first constitutional government was established.

1925-1979+

Finally Pahlavi dynasty, a constitutional monarchy ...

Concentrating on modernization, education and establishing close diplomatic relations with the Western countries were among the main objective of the King Reza and Mohammad Reza Pahlavi. The gap between the government and people's will, mostly due to corruption, ultra-speed modernization of the society and what was called unfair diplomatic relations, led to the Islamic movement in 1979, that established a kind of republic called Islamic Republic.

1979- today

The Islamic Republic ...

ECONOMY

The government of Iran practices the so called Islamic economy, based upon three sectors: public, cooperative and private providing the most essential needs: housing, food, clothing, public health, medical treatment, education and the necessary conditions for establishing a family for all. Respect for freedom of choice in selecting one's occupation and refraining forcing people to a particular job and preventions of the exploitations of the work of others. Private property acquired through legitimate means, is respected. The relevant criteria shall be determined by law.

The main economic wealth of Iran is, of course, petroleum. It is the fourth among the countries of the World, after Saudi Arabia, Russia and Kuwait, and is ranked second in the world in view of its natural gas reserve, after Russia's, totaling seven hundred trillion cubic feet. Almost one-tenth of the world's oil and one-fifth of the world's natural gas reserve are in Iran. Besides this, Iran has large mineral deposits and considerable amount of forest wealth, in addition to zinc, lead, chromite, iron ore, copper, red oxide and manganese, nickel, cobalt, tungsten, uranium, gold and silver.

In the past few years there has been a series of development plans initiated by the Iranian government to rehabilitate the country, and in spite of decrease in national revenues because of swift changes in global oil prices, the first 5 year plan for Economic and Social development was carried out and the economic institutions as well as the infra-structure of the national economy were reconstructed or strengthened. The Iranian government reports mention that although there have been some consequences of such plans to daily life of the people, such as inflation, they are supposed to be of short-term in nature and are not that much significant compared with accomplishments made in energy, transportation, ports, general and higher education, social welfare, agriculture and industrial strategic productions.

The realistic politics adopted to privatize economy have been instrumental in economic growth and prosperity. The G.D.N.P. has been increased during a period of 4 years from 10,664.9 billion Rials to 13,464 billion Rials, and the average growth rate during the first four years in agriculture sector was 6.3%. The value added in the industrial sector during the first Five-Year Economic Development Plan was 9.2 percent at constant prices and the share of income from this sector in the GDP rose from 10.5% in the beginning to 16.5 at the end of the plan.

According to the Central Bank of Iran (CBI) Iran's economy shows a 5.5% increase in fiscal year 1996-97 as compared to 4.5% increase in the previous fiscal year. Apart from the oil sector, the economy in the 1995-96 fiscal year registered growth of 19.5% in foodstuff industries, 17.1% in paper production, 22.5% in chemical products and 11.4% in non-metallic mineral products.

The Iranian government has been imposing restrictions on foreign-exchange movements in an effort to check inflation. The national currency, rial, has been fixed at 3,000 Rials to one U.S. dollar, as compared to 70 Rials in 1978-79, before the Islamic Republic was established. CBI report shows that Iran's foreign debt has dropped to $20.36 billion on Sep. 21, 1996, compared with $22.56 billion at end of fiscal 1995-96. It should be noted that Iran had more than $40 billion trade surplus and foreign reserves in 1978-79, before the Islamic Republic. The inflation rate in the first half this fiscal year declined to 27%, compared with 53.6% in the same period a year earlier.

Iran has about 4,847 kilometers of network of main roads and about 1,184 kilometers of secondary commercial and industrial roads that traverse 16 provinces. Presently, 3706 kilometers of main roads are also under construction. In the past four years, road cargo transportation has increased from 19.4 million tons to 19.8 million tons, and passenger transportation has claimed from 8.7 million to 9.16 million person during last year. Presently, about 2,000 kilometers of railways are under construction and plans for 8,000 kilometers of railways throughout the vast area being studied. Bafq-Bandar Abbas and Sarakhs-Mashhed railway projects link East Asian and independent Certral Asian republics to Iranian railways network which will connect European network to Asia, and the East Asian network will link with the sea of Oman and the Persian Gulf. This rail road network revives the ancient Silk Road and benefits not only Iran but also the Central Asian countries that are linked to international and free waters conveniently.

Iran has established free trade zones in Persian Gulf and Caspian Sea and offers incentives for investment and distribution of good in the domestic and regional market.

There is a shift from oil consumption to natural gas in households and industries. More than 265 cities in Iran are connected to the country's gas pipeline network. The number of cities on the network is expected to reach 300 by the end of the five-year development plan in 1999. Iran's domestic gas consumption is around 40 billion cubic meters. Iran also has gas-export facilities and annual revenue of $3 billion from gas exports to neighboring countries and Europe is expected.

The capacity of installed electrical power has reached 17,863 megawatt during past five years. Furthermore, projects for construction of 19 additional power plants with the capacity of 14,163 megawatt are under construction.

Iran has a population around 62 million. It had an odd population growth rate of 3.2% during the early 1980s. However, the population growth rate has declined from 3.2% to 1.8% in the recent years.

AGRICULTURE

The support of agriculture and the achievement of self-sufficiency in this sector was placed at the top of the government's policies it was announce the agriculture should be the main axis of economic activities and that the promotion of the other economic sectors should be conducted in relation and to support that sector.

During the first development plan, 4.2 billion dollars were spent in agriculture sector. Iran's agriculture sector grew by 1% in 1996 and 4.5% in 1997. The gross value of products in Iran's agricultural sector reached $25 billion in 1997. While 28% of the countries man power are engaged in agriculture, agricultural productions comprise 30% of non-oil exports of the country. According to the report of the ministry of industries more than 237 food processing industries with the capacity of 1.5 million tons a year will be commissioned.

About 11 percent of the country's total land area of 163.6 million hectares is cultivated. Still 63% of the cultivable lands have not been used, and given the fact that 18.5 million hectares of the present farms are being used with 50 to 60% utility, and about one-seventh of the total cultivated land is sufficient to meet domestic demand.

HANDICRAFTS

The carpet weaving industry in Iran is as old as time itself. Iran is the world's leading carpet producer. Persian carpet with its fast colors, fine designs and unique texture, has always been the most tangible manifestation of Persian art for other nations and yearly a considerable number of Persian carpets are exported all around the world. A good quality carpet is generally distinguished by its pile material and construction, design and color composition, border design, foundation threads and knot density. In spite of tight challenges in the global carpet market, Persian carpets have a superior quality from every aspect.

Unlike the figural arts of the Western culture, in Persian art, words and shapes are important means to convey artistic messages. The art of carpet weaving takes the most of the shape aesthetism. The Iranian carpet weaver in her enchantingly beautiful designs penetrates deep into human emotions. Carpet weaving is a well established traditional form of art in most parts of Iran. The best Persian carpets are usually produced in Tabriz, Kashan, Qom, Isfahan, Mash-had, Naiin, Kerman and Hamedan. Carpets of a region have design and colors specific to that region. For example, carpets woven in Kashan generally display a center medallion in an open red field with delicate scrolls in the border. The colors used in Kerman carpets are usually light pastel shades in an open field of ivory, cream, or blue and the large center design stands out as a paramount feature.

The inlaid wood working and embossed work of Isfahan also has world wide lovers.

Rug weaving, silver making, sculpturing, painting, woodworking, crockery making, ceramic and mosaic works are some of the Iranian handicraft skills. Among them, the art of ceramic is the oldest in the Great Persia and unearthed ceramic works dates back upto seven centuries B.C.

RELIGION

Before Arab invasion, the main religion of Persians was Zoroastrianism. Zoroaster, or pronounce his name in his ancient Iranian language Avesta Zarathushtra, gave the world a universal message, meant for all humanity without any discrimination. Good Thoughts, Good Words, Good Deeds were first propounded by him. This meant that a thought, word or deed which is beneficial to one's own self as well as to all others. It should benefit the living world of human beings, other animals, plants, in fact, the entire human environment. Zarathushtra says that the entire living world is a single unit, a Fellowship and every man and woman should endeavor to promote it through Good Thoughts, Good Words and Good Deed. This can be achieved through good education to train people who "radiate happiness to others, whoever they be, and in turn feel the happiness themselves." With the advent of Islam, a monotheistic faith regarded as revealed through Muhammad as the Prophet of Allah (700 A.D.), the history of Iran blended with the history of Islam for some centuries and the majority of Iranian people accepted the religion of Islam either at will or by force. Presently, about 95% of Iranians are Shiah Muslim. There are also minority Sunni Muslims (Kurds and Turks on the western periphery and the Baluchs along the eastern borders of Pakistan and Afghanistan). Christians are mainly concentrated in Djolfa near Isfahan and Urumieh and a minority of Jews are concentrated in Hamedan and Isfahan. Ismaili and Baha'i are other religious sects/groups that can be mentioned.

As for Iranians, religion has always been regarded as a way for breaking from "self" and unification with Allah (asceticism and mysticism) as displayed by Sufi asceticism. It has also been a catalyst for concentration and political movement, such as Abu-moslem movement in Khorasan (8th century), Sarbedaran movement (13th century), tobacco boycott and Constitutional Movement (18th century).

During the Qajar dynastic rule (18th century), Iranian history witnesses two Islamic fundamentalist events. During the reign of Nasseruddin Shah Qajar the tobacco monopoly was given to an English company. This deed was interpreted as adverse to the country's independence by some of the religious leaders such as Mirza Shirazi who gave a fatwa (Religious Decree) to abstain and boycott the consumption and use of tobacco. From economical point of view, this movement finally led to the cancelation of the contract concluded by the government of that time and the English company. However, from the political point of view, it was understood that the religious leaders with the support of people can possibly adverse the dynastic law and pursue democratic reforms. This later became a handy weapon in the hand of some religious leaders to fight against constitutional laws in the name of Islam.

The other event was called Nehdzat Mashrooteh or the Constitutional Movement. This movement came about during the reign of the Qajar dynasty in order to limit the powers of the monarchy and restrain the self-interests of the household and involve the people in the country's administration and affairs through the formation of a National Consultative Assembly (Majlis Shooraye Melli). However, the first and second World War postponed the emergence and growth of a true constitutional system in Iran during the Pahlavi dynasty. This led to the turbulances in the present day political structure of Iran that overturned the Pahlavi dynasty and pursued breaking away from the alignment to all the countries and restricting economic ties with the so called foreign conspiracies and putting faith only in the so called Islamic teaching.

PILGRIMAGE CENTRE

A considerable amount of pilgrimage centers abound in Iran. These pilgrimage centers are mostly the last resting place or mausoleum of the family members of the Prophet of Islam Mohammed (S) and every year these pilgrimage centers are host to millions of Iranian and non-Iranian pilgrims.

The important pilgrimage centers of them all are: the mausoleum of Imam Reza (AS) the eight Imam of the Shiites of the Islamic world in the city of Mash-had; the sanctuary of Hazrat Masumeh the beloved sister of Imam Reza (AS) in Qom; and that of Hazrat Ahmad Ibn Moosa, known as Shah Cheragh, the brother of Imam Reza near the city of Shiraz.

Besides the above mentioned mausoleums in Iran there are also many great and beautiful mosques and churches. These majestic and imposing buildings which were built in past times are of great historical importance. They appear beautifully decorated, and contain many precious mosaics and works of art. They are daily visited by lots of visitors who deeply appreciate them.

ART AND LITERATURE

The history of Persian art and literature goes back to many thousands of years and its specimens can be seen as manuscripts of writing carved on stone in Be-Sotoon near Kerman-shah and in Takhte-Jamshid near Shiraz where it still stands. Due to the extensive number of Iranian poets, philosophers and writers we are obliged to restrict ourselves in naming only a few of them here. The oldest literature available is from the Sassanid period (200 B.C.) by the name of Khodai-Nameh. Is reported that a great collection of Persian script was kept in the Library at Tees-fun which was the second biggest center of art and literature after the Athens. Unfortunately, during Arab invasion it was put into fire and that outstanding collection was destroyed. Now the oldest remaining Persian literature mainly pertains to the last decades of the 8th century of Hejira (1300 A.D.).

Persian poetry has been also translated into other languages, of which we can name Omar Khayyam's Rubayyat. and Ferdowsi's (940-1020 A.D.) epic The Shahnameh is one of the definite classics of the world. The epic poet worked for thirty years to finish this masterpiece. The Bustan and Gulistan of Sa'adi are world famous due to their eloquence of style, clear language, moral guidance and counseling through the art of poetry. The odes of Jami are among the greatest poetry ever written in Persian literature while the Gazal of Hafaz (1300 - 1389 A.D.) and the Mathnavi or Couplets of Moulavi are counted as among the great works of Persian literature. The book Canon and Therapy by the distinguished Persian philosopher and physician Ibn Sina, was thought in many European schools of medicine till 18th Century. The book Hawi is also the product of the famous philosopher and physician of Iran, Zakariah Razi who is well known for discovering alcohol.

Among the writers of note we see the first Iranian historian Dinevari who lived in the 15th century. His works were later continued by Tabari. Another Persian historian of repute is Atto-ul-Mulk Javini who compiled the book History of the World Conquests.

Contemporary Iranian writer Ali Akbar Deh-khodah whose everlasting work of compiling a Dictionary of the Persian Language deserves mention here. Other contemporary writers to note are Sadegh Hedayat, Samad Behrangi, Dr. Hashtroudi and Dr. Parviz Natel Khanlari. Among contemporary Persian poets one can name Shariyar, Parvin Ehtesami and poets laureate Bahar. Shariyar, the contemporary Persian poet has also written poems in Turkish language spoken in Azarbaijan and the works of Ehtesami and Bahar are available as complete works. Parvin Ehtesami is a symbol of Persian intellectual women.

The art of ritual drama, in the form of "Tazieh" "Parde-khani" and "Kheime-shab Bazi" is mostly unknown to the world. Tazieh and Parde-khani, inspired by historical and religous events, symbolize epic spirit and resistance. The common theme is the hero tales of love and sacrifice, and of resistance against the evil. Tazieh dates before the Islamic era and the tragedy of Saiawush in Shahnameh is one of the best examples. The main theme of Tazieh in the Islamic era is martyrdom of Imam Hosein A.S., the third Imam of Shi'a who was killed with his family and 72 followers in an unjust fight against the Khalifa Yazid.

Parde-khani's stage is generally a traditional tea shop, called "ghaveh-khaneh" where in the past men used to gather there after a day of hard work and sip a cup of black tea. In, Parde-khani the stage is covered by a picture of a heroic tale and the Parde-khan or naq'qal (story teller) tells the story of love and passion, nobility and sacrifice...

ARCHITECTURE

Menareh (Minaret): A tall building standing on both sides of the entrance to a mosque. There is a narrow path inside it leading to the top. In the past, A person in charge of announcing the prayer time (Muezzin) was used to climb this and invite prayers to the mosque with a loud voice.

Tagh: A kind of construction that besides its charm, was mainly used to distribute the weight of the roof among the columns. In this way very large round shaped buildings could be constructed without using concrete or iron bars. Great example of Tagh can be found in Imam Mosque and Vakil Mosque in Shiraz where 48 columns carry the weight of the building.

Kashi-kari: A kind of art work constructed of small pieces of colored ceramics, pieces of glass and mirror and golden bars blended with the art of calligraphy to scribe the verses of Koran, the Islamic Holy Book, and draw other religious events on the walls and ceiling. Many masterpieces of this kind have been preserved inside the mausoleums and mosques in pilgrimage centers.

CALIGRAPHY

Calligraphy has always been one of the most deared arts throughout the centuries of the Iranian history. These beautiful handwritings have been preserved in the form of about 15,000 copies of the Holy Koran and many other poems that blend together the art of painting and writing. Many of those hand written books are beautifully decorated and pages are often framed with precious golden characters. Many of Holy Scriptures are kept and well preserved at the museum of the Great Library situated in the city of Mash-had in North-East of Iran.

The history of calligraphy in Iran dates back to the pre Islam era. In Zoroastrianism beautiful and clear writings were always praised. With the advent of Islam, calligraphy got entered a new era. According to Islamic thought, figural arts and painting live objects has an idolatry implication, therefore words and shapes were chosen to convey artistic messages.

Becoming master of Persian calligraphy requires long and hard training together with self concentration. Training starts with practicing Mufradat, i.e., writing lone letters and proceeds to Javameh, i.e., writting a combination of letters and words. A piece of trimmed cane, called "ghalam" and ink, named "davat" are the only tools used. Ghalam is usually made of good quality cane, with around 5-10mm thickness. It is cut to around 20cm pieces. the calligraphers are responsible for trimming the nib and cutting the point. The nib should be split in the center to have equal halves. Among the various Iranian calligraphers we can name Abolfazl Savji and Mir Emad who were evidently the masters of this art. One of the most eminent students of Mir Emad by the name of Nuruddin Mohammed Lahiji another famous Persian calligrapher who was famous as Noora and nicknamed Khush-nevis.

In the painting world, of the Persian painters of repute one can name Reza Abbasi and Kamal-ul-Molk. Hussain Behzad the dextrous miniature artist is famous for his miniature works.

the works of this Persian artist can be seen in most of the museums of the world.

PRINCIPAL SITES

Iran is very wide and has many different geographical and cultural regions. Officially Iran has 25 provinces: Ardabil, Azarbayjan-e Gharbi, Azarbayjan-e Sharghi, Bakhtaran, Bushehr, Chahar Mahall va Bakhtiari, Esfahan, Fars, Gilan, Hamadan, Hormozgan, Ilam, Kerman, Khorasan, Khuzestan, Kohkiluyeh va Buyer Ahmadi, Kordestan, Lorestan, Markazi, Mazandaran, Semnan, Sistan va Baluchestan, Tehran, Yazd and Zanjan. Apart from Tehran (the capital of Iran), the visitor to Iran should at least see Isfahan, Shiraz (Persepolis), and Mash-had.

There are other cities and towns to be seen. Don't forget the Caspian Sea rim if you love the beauty of nature. If there is a gate to Paradise, you will certainly find it in Ramsar, Lahijan, Bandar Anzali and Amol. Visit Yazd and Kerman if you are interested in Islamic architecture. Also visiting Mash-had and Qom are recommended for those interested in pilgrimage centers. A trip to Hamedan is worth to visit the tomb of Avicenna and see Ali-sadr, one of the unique natural limestone caves in the world.

FOOD

Perhaps the most famous delicacy of Iran is khaviar. There are many other unique food items, such as mast (yogurt) khorma (dates), nan (bread), etc.

Breakfast

Generally, hot tea, cheese and local bread is found in every breakfast menu, no matter where in Iran you are. In the northern provinces of Mazandaran and Gilan, asal (honey) and occasionally, cooked cold rice and fish may be found on the breakfast spread. In central Iran mast (yogurt) and khameh (soft cream) is somewhat common for breakfast. In the mountainous provinces, butter, yogurt and cheese is quite popular. In the southern and humid regions (Khoozistan and the provinces along the coast of the Persian Gulf) cheese and khorma (dates) are on the menu.

In the cities and urban areas, breakfast foods are often industrially processed and packaged, much resembling the foods found in Western supermarkets. Iranians usually prefer to eat hot and readily made bread rather than the machine made ones. There are a lot of bread shops each specializing at a certain kind of bread, such as lavash, barbari and sangak, that provide hot bread from early in the morning. A typical breakfast in middle-class household in Tehran, consists of any combination of butter, jam honey, cheese, halva shekari (A kind of paste made of sugar, butter and sesame seeds) that is served together with milk, tea or coffee.

WRITING SYSTEM

Persian is a synonym for Farsi, and they both refer to an Indo-European language that was spoken in the old Persian Empire. It is spoken in today's Iran, parts of Afghanistan, and parts of the old southern Soviet states such as Tajikestan. There are numerous dialects of Persian language, such as Dari, Gilaki, etc. The standard and modern Farsi is spoken in today's Iran. Persian alphabet has 32 letters (as compared to 28 in Arabic and 26 in English) and is written from right to left. Some of the letters can be connected to from both left and right and some can only be connected from right. Therefore, each letter may have two or three different shapes based on connectivity and its occurence at the beginning, middle or the end of a word. It means that memorizing less than 100 visual icons is sufficient to read and write Persian words.

As compared to latin scripts, there is no limitation on the width of the letters and this brings a great variability in form and writing style. Letters can be expanded, curved and angled to fit the width.

Many have an image that Persian and Arabic alphabet are the same. Persian alphabet includes but not restricted to Arabic letters. Arabic alphabet belongs to the group of Semitic scripts in which the consonants are actually written and vowels are placed in between the lines. Arabic script is derived from the

Aramic Nabataean alphabet and has 28 letters derived from 18 shapes, distinguished by one (10 cases) or two dots (3 cases) placed above or below the letter or three dots place above the letter only (2 cases).

Persian has 32 letters derived from 18 shapes. Letters are distinguished by one (10 cases), two (3 cases) or three dots (5 cases) placed above or below the letter. Three long vowels, AA, EE and OO are also represented by letters. Short vowels for A, E and O have no letters and may be shown by small diagonal underbar stroke (for E) and overbar stroke (for A) or small comma (for O).

DRESS AND BEHAVIOURAL RULES

The government of Islamic Republic practices strict dress and behavioral code on females appearing in public. All Iranian and foreign females appearing in public should cover their hair and wear a dress that covers the body except the face, toes and hands!

Men are advised not to wear short sleeves and short trousers are strictly forbidden.

Unlike some other countries practicing Islamic law, women are allowed to drive vehicles in public. Females should use the "Women Only" services of the public transportation. There is also "Women Only" service in swimming pools, public beaches, ski slopes and other sport facilities. Jogging in public should not evade the dress rules.

All Iranians and foreigners if accompanied by members of the opposite sex in public should carry documents proving that their companions are their first degree (father, mother, childern, spouse) or second degree (brothers or sisters) relatives. Such documents should be shown upon request to the members of law enforcement task force (or Niroye Entezami, Formerly, Islamic Revolutionary Comittee).

LAWS AND RULES

According to the Islamic Republic law, all children born to an Iranian parent or parents are automatically granted the

Iranian citizenship no matter what shall be the naturalization law of the birth place. In case of individuals acquiring multiple nationalities, the only accepted one is Iranian. In other words, the government of Iran does not acknowledge individuals' right of selecting and/or switching nationality.

All male Iranians and those born to Iranian parents, with the age above 18 must complete a 2 years military service. Basic individual rights, such as granting a job, travelling abroad, may be denied from those who evade this.

According to the Islamic Republic law, all children born to a Muslim parent or parents are considered to be Muslim. Individuals cannot convert from Islam to any other religion, under any circumstances. However, believers of other religions may convert to Islam, freely.

According to the Islamic Republic law, Muslim Iranians are not allowed to marry non-Muslims unless the other part converts to Islam. This should be registered and certified by Iranian authorities. Children born to unregistered marriages under Islamic Republic law are not considered legitimate.

MASNAVI E MA'NAVI

THE SPIRITUAL COUPLETS OF MAULANA JALALU-'D-DLN MUHAMMAD RUMI

Jalal-e-din Rumi was born at Balkh (Khorassan) in 1207 A.D. The city at that time flourished under the rule of Muhammad the Shah of Khwarazm. The family to which our mystical poet belonged had been settled in Balkh for several generations; it was highly respected and, according to his biographers, had produced a notable succession of jurists and divines.

In 1219, Baha-e-din Walad, the father of Jalal-e-din Rumi, suddenly departed from Balkh with his family and journeyed westward. There can be no doubt that Baha-e-din fled before the terrible Mongol hordes which were already approaching his native city. Zarandeh was their first home in Rum (Turkey) and Konia, the capital of the western Seljuk empire, their final residence. Jalal-e-din, under the influence of Burhan-e-din Tirmidhi, became imbued with enthusiasm for the discipline and doctrine of Sufism. He devoted himself to imitation of his guide (pir) and passed through all the stages of the mystical life until the death of Burhan-e-din (1240). He in turn assumed the rank of shaykh and his ardent personality attracted disciples in Rum. In 1244, a wandering dervish, known to posterity by the name of Shams Tabrizi, arrived in Konia. Jalal-e-din found in the stranger that perfect image of the Divine Beloved which he had long been seeking. He took him away to his house and for two years they remained inseparable.

Meanwhile the disciples of Rumi, entirely cut off from their master's teaching and bitterly resenting his continued devotion to Shams alone, assailed the intruder with abuse and threats of violence. At last the dervish fled to Damascus but was brought back in triumph by the son of Jalal-e-din, Sultan Walad.

Jalal-e-din, deeply agitated by the loss of his bosom friend, sent out people in search of him. Thereupon the disciples repented (towbe) and were forgiven. Soon, however, a renewed outburst of jealousy on their part caused Shams to take refuge in Damascus for the second time and again Sultan Walad was called upon to restore the situation.

Finally, in 1247, the man of mystery vanished without leaving a trace behind. After the disappearance of Shams, Rumi composed an immense collection of mystical odes in the name of Shams and dedicated to his memory (Divan Shams Tabrizi).

The next period (1252 - 1261) in Rumi's spiritual life is a fainter repetition of the last. For many years, Jalal-e-din devoted himself to Salah-e-din Zarkub, who as his deputy (Khalifeh) was charged with the duty of instructing the Rumi's followers.

On the death of Salah-e-din, the poet's enthusiasm found a new and abundant source of inspiration in another disciple Husam-e-din ibn Akhi turk, whose name he has mystically associated with his greatest work, the celebrated Masnavi. During the last ten years of the poet's life this last beloved follower acted as his deputy, and upon his death in 1273 succeeded him as Head of the Mewlevi order.

We must note that a platonic type of mystical love had been cultivated by sufis long before Rumi declared that he and Shams Tabrizi were two bodies with one soul. In this union of loving souls all distinctions vanish: nothing remains but the essential unity of love in which lover and beloved have merged their separate identities.

In calling his lyrics the Divan of Shams, Rumi of course uses the name Shams as though Shams and himself had become identical and were the same person. The forms in which he clothes his religious philosophy had been fashioned before him by two great sufi poets, Sanai and Attar. Though he makes no secret of his debt to them both, his flight takes a wider range, his materials are richer and his method of handling the subject is so original that we can say the Rumi's literary works have a new style. In Jalal-e-din, the Persian mystical genius found its supreme expression.

The words used by Dante in reference to the Divine Commedia would serve excellently as a description of the Masnavi: The poem belongs to the moral or ethical branch of philosophy, its quality is not speculative but practical, and its ultimate end is to lead into the state of felicity, those now enduring the miserable life of man. Rumi's mysticism is not doctrinal but experimental. He appeals to the heart more than to the mind.

4

SADI'S MOST MEMORABLE GULISTAN

IN THE NAME OF ALLAH THE MERCIFUL THE CLEMENT

Laudation to the God of majesty and glory! Obedience to him is a cause of approach and gratitude in increase of benefits. Every inhalation of the breath prolongs life and every expiration of it gladdens our nature; wherefore every breath confers two benefits and for every benefit gratitude is due.

Whose hand and tongue is capable

To fulfil the obligations of thanks to him?

Words of the most high: Be thankful, O family of David, and but few of my servants are thankful.

It is best to a worshipper for his transgressions

To offer apologies at the throne of God,

Although what is worthy of his dignity

No one is able to accomplish.

The showers of his boundless mercy have penetrated to every spot, and the banquet of his unstinted liberality is spread out everywhere. He tears not the veil of reputation of his worshippers even for grievous sins, and does not withhold their daily allowance of bread for great crimes.

O bountiful One, who from thy invisible treasury

Suppliest the Guebre and the Christian with food,

How could'st thou disappoint thy friends,

Whilst having regard for thy enemies?

He told the chamberlain of the morning breeze to spread out the emerald carpet and, having commanded the nurse of vernal clouds to cherish the daughters of plants in the cradle of the earth, the trees donned the new year's robe and clothed their breast with the garment of green foliage, whilst their offspring, the branches, adorned their heads with blossoms at the approach of the season of the roses. Also the juice of the cane became delicious honey by his power, and the date a lofty tree by his care.

Cloud and wind, moon and sun move in the sky That thou mayest gain bread, and not eat it unconcerned. For thee all are revolving and obedient. It is against the requirements of justice if thou obeyest not.

There is a tradition of the prince of created beings, the paragon of existing things, the mercy to the inhabitants of the world, the purest of mankind and the completion of the revolving ages, Muhammad the elect, upon whom be blessing and peace:

Intercessor, obeyed, prophet, gracious, Bountiful, majestic, affable, marked with the seal of God.

What danger is there to the wall of the faithful with thee for a buttress?

What fear of the waves of the sea has he whose pilot is Noah?

He attained exaltation by his perfection. He disspelled darkness by his beauty. Beauteous are all his qualities, Benediction be on him and on his family.

The tradition is that whenever a sinful and distressed worshipper stretches forth the hand of repentance with hopes of acceptance to the court of heaven, God the most high does not notice him, whereon he continues to implore mercy with supplications and tears and God the most holy says: O my angels, verily I am ashamed of my servant and he has no other lord besides myself. Accordingly I have fully pardoned him.

See the generosity and kindness of God. The servant has committed sin and he is ashamed.

Those who attend permanently at the temple of his glory confess the imperfection of their worship and say: We have not worshipped thee according to the requirements of thy worship; and those who describe the splendour of his beauty are rapt in amazement saying: We have not known thee as thou oughtest to be known.

If someone asks me for his description, What shall I despairing say of One who has no form? The lovers have been slain by the beloved. No voice can come from the slain.

One of the devout who had deeply plunged his head into the cowl of meditation and had been immersed in the ocean of visions, was asked, when he had come out of that state, by one of his companions who had desired to cheer him up: `What beautiful gift hast thou brought us from the garden in which thou hast been?' He replied: `I intended to fill the skirts of my robe with roses, when I reached the rose-tree, as presents for my friends but the perfume of the flowers intoxicated me so much that I let, go the hold of my skirts.'

O bird of the morning, learn love from the moth Because it burnt, lost its life, and found no voice. These pretenders are ignorantly in search of Him, Because he who obtained knowledge has not returned.

O thou who art above all imaginations, conjectures, opinions and ideas, Above anything people have said or we have heard or read, The assembly is finished and life has reached its term And we have, as at first, remained powerless in describing thee.

PANEGYRIC OF THE PADSHAH OF ISLAM

The good reputation of Sa`di which is current among the people, the renown of his eloquence which has spread on the surface of the earth, the products of his friendly pen which are consumed like sugar, and the scraps of his literary compositions which are hawked about like bills of exchange, cannot be ascribed to his virtue and perfection, but the lord of the world, the axis of the revolving circle of time, the vice-gerent of Solomon, protector of the followers of the religion, His Majesty the Shahanshah Atabek Aa'zm Muzaffaruddin Abu Bekr Ben Sa'd Ben Zanki---The shadow of Allah on earth! O Lord, be pleased with him and with his kingdom---has looked upon Sa`di with a favourable eye, has praised him greatly, and has shown him sincere affection so that all men, gentle and simple, love him because the people follow the religion of their king.

Because thou lookest upon my humble person, My merits are more celebrated than those of the sun. Although this slave may possess all faults, Every fault pleasing the Sultan becomes a virtue.

A sweet-smelling piece of clay, one day in the bath, Came from the hand of a beloved one to my hand. I asked: `Art thou musk or ambergris? Because thy delicious odour intoxicates me.' It replied: `I was a despicable lump of day; But for a while in the society of a rose. The perfection of my companion took effect on me And, if not, I am the same earth which I am.'

O Allah, favour the Musalmans with the prolongation of his life, and with an augmentation of his reward for his good qualities and deeds; exalt the dignities of his friends and governors; annihilate those who are inimical to him and wish him ill; for the sake of what is recorded in the verses of the Quran. O Allah, give security protect his son.

Verily the world is happy through him; may his happiness endure for ever And may the Lord strengthen him and with the banners of victory. Thus the branch will flourish of which he is the root Because the beauty of the earth's plants depends on the virtue of the seed.

May God, whose name be exalted and hallowed, keep in security and peace the pure country of Shiraz until the time of the resurrection, under the authority of righteous governors and by the exertions of practical scholars.

Knowest thou not why I in foreign countries Roamed about for a long time? I went away from the distress of the Turks because I saw The world entangled like the hair of negroes; They were all human beings, but Like wolves sharp-clawed, for shedding blood. When I returned I saw the country at rest, The tigers having abandoned the nature of tigers. Within a man of good disposition like an angel, Without an army like bellicose lions. Thus it happened that first I beheld The world full of confusion, anxiety and distress; Then it became as it is in the days of the just Sultan Atabek Abu Bekr Ben Sa'd Zanki.

The country of Pares dreads not the vicissitudes of time, As long as one presides over it like thee, the shadow of God. Today no one can point out on the surface of the earth, A place like the threshold of thy door, the asylum of comfort. On thee is incumbent the protection of the distressed and gratitude Upon us and reward on God the creator of the world, As long as the world and wind endure.

THE CAUSE FOR COMPOSING THE GULISTAN

I was one night meditating on the time which had elapsed, repenting of the life I had squandered and perforating the stony mansion of my heart with adamantine tears. I uttered the following verses in conformity with the state of mind:

Every moment a breath of life is spent, If I consider, not much of it remains. O thou, whose fifty years have elapsed in sleep, Wilt thou perhaps overtake them in these five days? Shame on him who has gone and done no work. The drum of departure was beaten but he has not made his load.

Sweet sleep on the morning of departure Retains the pedestrian from the road. Whoever had come had built a new edifice. He departed and left the place to another And that other one concocted the same futile schemes And this edifice was not completed by anyone. Cherish not an inconstant friend. Such a traitor is not fit for amity. As all the good and bad must surely die, He is happy who carries off the ball of virtue. Send provision for thy journey to thy tomb. Nobody will bring it after thee; send it before. Life is snow, the sun is melting hot. Little remains, but the gentleman is slothful still. O thou who hast gone empty handed to the bazar, I fear thou wilt not bring a towel filled. Who eats the corn he has sown while it is yet green, Must at harvest time glean the ears of it. Listen with all thy heart to the advice of Sa`di. Such is the way; be a man and travel on.

The capital of man's life is his abdomen. If it be gradually emptied there is no fear But if it be so closed as not to open The heart may well despair of life; And if it be open so that it cannot be closed, Go and wash thy hands of this world's life. Four contending rebellious dispositions Harmonize but five days with each other. If one of these four becomes prevalent, Sweet life must abandon the body Wherefore an intelligent and perfect man Sets not his heart upon this world's life.

After maturely considering these sentiments, I thought proper to sit down in the mansion of retirement to fold up the skirts of association, to wash my tablets of heedless sayings and no more to indulge in senseless prattle:

To sit in a corner, like one with a cut tongue, deaf and dumb, Is better than a man who has no command over his tongue.

I continued in this resolution till a friend, who had been my companion in the camel-litter of misery and my comrade in the closet of affection, entered at the door, according to his old custom with playful gladness, and spread out the surface of desire; but I would give him no reply nor lift up my head from the knees of worship. He looked at me aggrieved and said:

`Now, while thou hast the power of utterance, Speak, O brother, with grace and kindness Because tomorrow, when the messenger of death arrives, Thou wilt of necessity restrain thy tongue.'

One of my connections informed him how matters stood and told him that I had firmly determined and was intent upon spending the rest of my life in continual devotion and silence, advising him at the same time, in case he should be able, to follow my example and to keep me company. He replied: `I swear by the great dignity of Allah and by our old friendship that I shall not draw breath, nor budge one step, unless he converses with me as formerly, and in his usual way; because it is foolish to insult friends and easy to expiate an oath. It is against propriety, and contrary to the opinions of wise men that the Zulfiqar of A'li should remain in the scabbard and the tongue of Sa`di in his palate.'

O intelligent man what is the tongue in the mouth? It is the key to the treasure-door of a virtuous man. When the door is closed how can one know Whether he is a seller of jewels or a hawker? Although intelligent men consider silence civil, It is better for thee to speak at the proper time. Two things betoken levity of intellect: to remain mute When it is proper to speak and to talk when silence is required.

In short, I had not the firmness to restrain my tongue from speaking to him, and did not consider it polite to turn away my face from his conversation, he being a congenial friend and sincerely affectionate.

When thou fightest with anyone, consider Whether thou wilt have to flee from him or he from thee.

I was under the necessity of speaking and then went out by way of diversion in the vernal season, when the traces of severe cold had disappeared and the time of the dominion of roses had arrived:

Green garments were upon the trees Like holiday robes on contented persons. On the first of the month Ardibihesht Jellali The bulbuls were singing on the pulpits of branches. Upon the roses pearls of dew had fallen, Resembling perspiration on an angry sweetheart's cheek.

I happened to spend the night in a garden with one of my friends and we found it to be a pleasant cheerful place with heart-ravishing entangled trees; its ground seemed to be paved with small glass beads whilst, from its vines, bunches like the Pleiads were suspended.

A garden the water of whose river was limpid A grove the melody of whose birds was harmonious.

The former full of bright-coloured tulips, The latter full of fruits of various kinds; The wind had in the shade of its trees Spread out a bed of all kinds of flowers.

The next morning when the intention of returning had prevailed over the opinion of tarrying, I saw that my friend had in his skirt collected roses, sweet basil, hyacinths and fragrant herbs with the determination to carry them to town; whereon

I said: `Thou knowest that the roses of the garden are perishable and the season passes away', and philosophers have said: `Whatever is not of long duration is not to be cherished.' He asked: `Then what is to be done?' I replied: `I may compose for the amusement of those who look and for the instruction of those who are present a book of a Rose Garden, a Gulistan, whose leaves cannot be touched by the tyranny of autumnal blasts and the delight of whose spring the vicissitudes of time will be unable to change into the inconstancy of autumn.

Of what use will be a dish of roses to thee? Take a leaf from my rose-garden. A flower endures but five or six days But this rose-garden is always delightful.

After I had uttered these words he threw away the flowers from his skirts, and attached himself to mine, saying: `When a generous fellow makes a promise he keeps it.'

On the same day I happened to write two chapters, namely on polite society and the rules of conversation, in a style acceptable to orators and instructive to letter-writers. In short, some roses of the garden still remained when the book of the Rose-garden was finished but it will in reality be completed only after approbation in the court of the Shah, who is the refuge of the world, the shadow of God, the ray of his grace, the treasury of the age, the asylum of the Faith, strengthened by heaven, aided against enemies, the arm of the victorious government, the lamp of the resplendent religion, the beauty of mankind, the boast of Islam, Sa'd son of Atabek the great, the majestic Shahanshah, owner of the necks of nations, lord of the kings of Arabia and Persia, the sultan of the land and the sea, the heir of the kingdom of Solomon, Muzaffaruddin Ibu Bekr, son of Sa'd Zanki, may Allah the most high perpetuate the prosperity of them both and direct their inclinations to every good thing.

Perused with a kind glance, Adorned with approbation by the sovereign, It will be a Chinese picture-gallery or design of the Arzank, Hopes are entertained that he will not be wearied By these contents because a Pose-garden is not a place of displeasure. The more so as its august preface is dedicated To Sa'd Abu Bekr Sa'd the son of Zanki.

RECORD OF THE GREAT AMIR FAKHRUDDIN BEN ABU BEKR, SON OF ABU NASSAR

Again, the bride of imagination can for want of beauty not lift up her head nor raise her eyes from the feet of bashfulness to appear in the assembly of persons endowed with pulchritude, unless adorned with the ornaments of approbation from the great Amir, who is learned, just, aided by heaven, victorious, supporter of the throne of the Sultanate and councillor in deliberations of the realm, refuge of the poor, asylum of strangers, patron of learned men, lover of the pious, glory of the dynasty of Pares, right hand of the kingdom, chief of the nobles, boast of the monarchy and of the religion, succour of Islam and of the Musalmans, buttress of kings and sultans, Abu Bekr, son of Abu Nassar, may Allah prolong his life, augment his dignity, enlighten his breast and increase his reward twofold, because he enjoys the praise of all great men and is the embodiment of every laudable quality.

Whoever reposes in the shadow of his favour, His sin is transmuted to obedience and his foe into a friend.

Every attendant and follower has an appointed duty and if, in the performance thereof, he gives way to remissness and indolence, he is certainly called to account and becomes subject to reproaches, except the tribe of dervishes, from whom thanks are due for the benefits they receive from great men as well as praises and prayers, all of which duties are more suitably performed in their absence than in their presence, because in the latter they look like ostentation and in the former they are free from ceremony.

The back of the bent sky became flat with joy, When dame nature brought forth a child like thee.

It is an instance of wisdom if the Creator Causes a servant to make the general welfare his special duty. He has found eternal happiness who lived a good life, Because, after his end, good repute will keep his name alive. No matter whether virtuous men praise you or not A lovely maid stands in no need of a tire woman.

EXCUSE FOR REMISSNESS IN SERVICE AND CAUSE FOR PREFERRING SOLITUDE

My negligence and backwardness in diligent attendance at the royal court resemble the case of Barzachumihr, whose merits the sages of India were discussing but could at last not reproach him with anything except slowness of speech because he delayed long and his hearers were obliged to wait till he delivered himself of what he had to say. When Barzachumihr heard of this he said: `It is better for me to consider what to speak than to repent of what I have spoken.'

A trained orator, old, aged, First meditates and then speaks. Do not speak without consideration. Speak well and if slow what matters it? Deliberate and then begin to talk. Say thyself enough before others say enough. By speech a man is better than a brute But a beast is better unless thou speakest properly.

How then could I venture to appear in the sight of the grandees of my lord, may his victory be glorious, who are an assembly of pious men and the centre of profound scholars? If I were to be led in the ardour of conversation to speak petulantly, I could produce only a trifling stock-in-trade in the noble presence but glass beads are not worth a barleycorn in the bazar of jewellers, a lamp does not shine in the presence of the sun, and a minaret looks low at the foot of Mount Alvend.

Who lifts up his neck with pretentions, Foes hasten to him from every side. Sa`di has fallen to be a hermit. No one came to attack a fallen man. First deliberation, then speech; The foundation was laid first, then the wall.

I know bouquet-binding but not in the garden. I sell a sweetheart but not in Canaan. Loqman the philosopher, being asked from whom he had learnt wisdom, replied: `From the blind, who do not take a step before trying the place.' First move about, then stir out.

Try thy virility first,, then marry. Though a cock may be brave in war He strikes his claws in vain on a brazen falcon. A cat is a lion in catching mice But a mouse in combat with a tiger. But, trusting in the liberal sentiments of the great, who shut their eyes to the faults of their inferiors and abstain from divulging the crimes of humble men, we have in this book recorded, by way of abridgment, some rare events, stories, poetry and accounts about ancient kings, spending a portion of our precious life in the task. This was the reason for composing the book Gulistan; and help is from Allah.

This well-arranged composition will remain for years, When every atom of our dust is dispersed. The intention of this design was that it should survive Because I perceive no stability in my existence, Unless one day a pious man compassionately Utters a prayer for the works of dervishes.

The author, having deliberated upon the arrangement of the book, and the adornment of the chapters, deemed it suitable to curtail the diction of this beautiful garden and luxuriant grove and to make it resemble paradise, which also has eight entrances. The abridgment was made to avoid tediousness.

I The Manners of Kings II On the Morals of Dervishes III On the Excellence of Content IV On the Advantages of Silence V On Love and Youth VI On Weakness and Old Age VII On the Effects of Education VIII On Rules for Conduct in Life

At a period when our time was pleasant The Hejret was six hundred and fifty-six. Our intention was advice and we gave it. We recommended thee to God and departed.

CHAPTER I: { THE MANNERS OF KINGS}

Story 1

I heard a padshah giving orders to kill a prisoner. The helpless fellow began to insult the king on that occasion of despair, with the tongue he had, and to use foul expressions according to the saying:

Who washes his hands of life Says whatever he has in his heart.

When a man is in despair his tongue becomes long and he is like a vanquished cat assailing a dog.

In time of need, when flight is no more possible, The hand grasps the point of the sharp sword.

When the king asked what he was saying, a good-natured vezier replied: `My lord, he says: Those who bridle their anger and forgive men; for Allah loveth the beneficent.' The king, moved with pity, forbore taking his life but another vezier, the antagonist of the former, said: `Men of our rank ought to speak nothing but the truth in the presence of padshahs. This fellow has insulted the king and spoken unbecomingly.' The king, being displeased with these words, said: `That lie was more acceptable to me than this truth thou hast uttered because the former proceeded from a conciliatory disposition and the latter from malignity; and wise men have said: ``A falsehood resulting in conciliation is better than a truth producing trouble."'

He whom the shah follows in what he says, It is a pity if he speaks anything but what is good.

The following inscription was upon the portico of the hall of Feridun:

O brother, the world remains with no one. Bind the heart to the Creator, it is enough. Rely not upon possessions and this world Because it has cherished many like thee and slain them. When the pure soul is about to depart, What boots it if one dies on a throne or on the ground?

Story 2

One of the kings of Khorasan had a vision in a dream of Sultan Mahmud, one hundred years after his death. His whole person appeared to have been dissolved and turned to dust, except his eyes, which were revolving in their orbits and looking about. All the sages were unable to give an interpretation, except a dervish who made his salutation and said: `He is still looking amazed how his kingdom belongs to others.'

Many famous men have been buried under ground Of whose existence on earth not a trace has remained And that old corpse which had been surrendered to the earth Was so consumed by the soil that not a bone remains. The glorious name of Nushirvan survives in good repute Although much time elapsed since he passed away. Do good, O man, and consider life as a good fortune, The more so, as when a shout is raised, a man exists no more.

Story 3

I have heard that a royal prince of short stature and mean presence, whose brothers were tall and good-looking, once saw his father glancing on him with aversion and contempt but he had the shrewdness and penetration to guess the meaning and said: `O father, a puny intelligent fellow is better than a tall ignorant man, neither is everything bigger in stature higher in price. A sheep is nice to eat and an elephant is carrion.'

The smallest mountain on earth is Jur; nevertheless It is great with Allah in dignity and station.

Hast thou not heard that a lean scholar One day said to a fat fool: `Although an Arab horse may be weak It is thus more worth than a stable full of asses.'

The father laughed at this sally, the pillars of the state approved of it, but the brothers felt much aggrieved.

While a man says not a word His fault and virtue are concealed. Think not that every desert is empty. Possibly it may contain a sleeping tiger.

I heard that on the said occasion the king was menaced by a powerful enemy and that when the two armies were about to encounter each other, the first who entered the battlefield was the little fellow who said:

`I am not he whose back thou wilt see on the day of battle But he whom thou shalt behold in dust and blood. Who himself fights, stakes his own life In battle but he who flees, the blood of his army.'

After uttering these words he rushed among the troops of the enemy, slew several warriors and, returning to his father, made humble obeisance and said:

`O thou, to whom my person appeared contemptible, Didst not believe in the impetuosity of my valour. A horse with slender girth is of use On the day of battle, not a fattened ox.'

It is related that the troops of the enemy were numerous, and that the king's, being few, were about to flee, but that the puny youth raised a shout, saying: `O men, take care not to put on the garments of women.' These words augmented the rage of the troopers so that they made a unanimous attack and I heard that they gained the victory on the said occasion. The king kissed the head and eyes of his son, took him in his arms and daily augmented his affection till he appointed him to succeed him on the throne. His brothers became envious and placed poison in his food but were perceived by his sister from her apartment, whereon she closed the window violently and the youth, shrewdly guessing the significance of the act, restrained his hands from touching the food, and said: `It is impossible that men of honour should die, and those who possess none should take their place.'

No one goes under the shadow of an owl Even if the homa should disappear from the world.

This state of affairs having been brought to the notice of the father, he severely reproved the brothers and assigned to each of them a different, but pleasant, district as a place of exile till the confusion was quelled and the quarrel appeased; and it has been said that ten dervishes may sleep under the same blanket but that one country cannot hold two padshahs.

When a pious man eats half a loaf of bread He bestows the other half upon dervishes. If a padshah were to conquer the seven climates He would still in the same way covet another.

Story 4

A band of Arab brigands having taken up their position on the top of a mountain and closed the passage of caravans, the inhabitants of the country were distressed by their stratagems and the troops of the sultan foiled because the robbers, having obtained an inaccessible spot on the summit of the mountain, thus had a refuge which they made their habitation. The chiefs of that region held a consultation about getting rid of the calamity because it would be impossible to offer resistance to the robbers if they were allowed to remain.

A tree which has just taken root May be moved from the place by the strength of a man But, if thou leavest it thus for a long time, Thou canst not uproot it with a windlass. The source of a fountain may be stopped with a bodkin But, when it is full, it cannot be crossed on an elephant. The conclusion was arrived at to send one man as a spy and to wait for the opportunity till the brigands departed to attack some people and leave the place empty. Then several experienced men, who had fought in battles, were despatched to keep themselves in ambush in a hollow of the mountain. In the evening the brigands returned from their excursion with their booty, divested themselves of their arms, put away their plunder and the first enemy who attacked them was sleep, till about a watch of the night had elapsed:

The disk of the sun went into darkness. Jonah went into the mouth of the fish.

The warriors leapt forth from the ambush, tied the hands of every one of the robbers to his shoulders and brought them in the morning to the court of the king, who ordered all of them to be slain. There happened to be a youth among them, the fruit of whose vigour was just ripening and the verdure on the rose-garden of whose cheek had begun to sprout. One of the veziers, having kissed the foot of the king's throne and placed the face of intercession upon the ground, said: `This boy has not yet eaten any fruit from the garden of life and has not yet enjoyed the pleasures of youth. I hope your majesty will generously and kindly confer an obligation upon your slave by sparing his life.' The king, being displeased with this request, answered:

`He whose foundation is bad will not take instruction from the good, To educate unworthy persons is like throwing nuts on a cupola.

`It is preferable to extirpate the race and offspring of these people and better to dig up their roots and foundations, because it is not the part of wise men to extinguish fire and to leave burning coals or to kill a viper and leave its young ones.

If a cloud should rain the water of life Never sip it from the branch of a willow-tree. Associate not with a base fellow Because thou canst not eat sugar from a mat-reed.'

The vezier heard these sentiments, approved of them nolens volens, praised the opinion of the king and said: `What my lord has uttered is the very truth itself because if the boy had been brought up in the company of those wicked men, he would have become one of themselves. But your slave hopes that he will, in the society of pious men, profit by education and will acquire the disposition of wise persons. Being yet a child the rebellious and perverse temper of that band has not yet taken hold of his nature and there is a tradition of the prophet that every infant is born with an inclination for Islam but his parents make him a Jew, a Christian or a Majusi.'

The spouse of Lot became a friend of wicked persons. His race of prophets became extinct. The dog of the companions of the cave for some days Associated with good people and became a man.

When the vezier had said these words and some of the king's court\-iers had added their intercession to his, the king no longer desired to shed the blood of the youth and said: `I grant the request although I disapprove of it.'

Knowest thou not what Zal said to the hero Rastam: `An enemy cannot be held despicable or helpless. I have seen many a water from a paltry spring Becoming great and carrying off a camel with its load.'

In short, the vezier brought up the boy delicately, with every comfort, and kept masters to educate him, till they had taught him to address persons in elegant language as well as to reply and he had acquired every accomplishment. One day the vezier hinted at his talents in the presence of the king, asserting that the instructions of wise men had taken effect upon the boy and had expelled his previous ignorance from his nature. The king smiled at these words and said:

`At last a wolf's whelp will be a wolf Although he may grow up with a man.'

After two years had elapsed a band of robbers in the locality joined him, tied the knot of friendship and, when the opportunity presented itself, he killed the vezier with his son, took away untold wealth and succeeded to the position of his own father in the robber-cave where he established himself. The king, informed of the event, took the finger of amazement between his teeth and said:

`How can a man fabricate a good sword of bad iron? O sage, who is nobody becomes not somebody by education. The rain, in the beneficence of whose nature there is no flaw, Will cause tulips to grow in a garden and weeds in bad soil. Saline earth will not produce hyacinths. Throw not away thy seeds or work thereon. To do good to wicked persons is like Doing evil to good men.'

Story 5

I saw at the palace-gate of Oglimish the son of a military officer who was endued with marvellous intellect, sagacity, perception and shrewdness; also the signs of future greatness manifested themselves on his forehead whilst yet a small boy.

From his head intelligence caused The star of greatness to shine. In short, he pleased the sultan because he had a beautiful countenance and a perfect understanding; and philosophers have said: 'Power consists in accomplishments, not in wealth and greatness in intellect, not in years.' His companions, being envious, made an attempt upon his life and desired to kill him but their endeavours remained fruitless.

What can a foe do when the friend is kind?

The king asked: `What is the cause of their enmity to thee?' He replied: `Under the shadow of the monarchy of my lord I have satisfied my contemporaries except the envious, who will not be contented but by the decline of my prosperity, and may the monarchy and good fortune of my lord be perpetual.'

I may so act as not to hurt the feelings of anyone But what can I do to an envious man dissatisfied with himself? Die, O envious man, for this is a malady, Deliverance from which can be obtained only by death. Unfortunate men sometimes ardently desire The decline of prosperous men in wealth and dignity. If in daytime, bat-eyed persons do not see Is it the fault of the fountain of light, the sun? Thou justly wishest that a thousand such eyes Should be blind rather than the sun dark.

Story 6

It is narrated that one of the kings of Persia had stretched forth his tyrannical hand to the possessions of his subjects and had begun to oppress them so violently that in consequence of his fraudulent extortions they dispersed in the world and chose exile on account of the affliction entailed by his violence. When the population had diminished, the prosperity of the country suffered, the treasury remained empty and on every side enemies committed violence.

Who desires succour in the day of calamity, Say to him: `Be generous in times of prosperity.' The slave with a ring in his ear, if not cherished will depart. Be kind because then a stranger will become thy slave.

One day the Shahnamah was read in his assembly, the subject being the ruin of the dominion of Zohak and the reign of Feridun. The vezier asked the king how it came to pass that Feridun, who possessed neither treasure nor land nor a retinue, established himself upon the throne. He replied: `As thou hast heard, the population enthusiastically gathered around him and supported him so that he attained royalty.' The vezier said: `As the gathering around of the population is the cause of royalty, then why dispersest thou the population? Perhaps thou hast no desire for royalty?'

It is best to cherish the army as thy life Because a sultan reigns by means of his troops.

The king asked: `What is the reason for the gathering around of the troops and the population?' He replied: `A padshah must practise justice that they may gather around him and clemency that they may dwell in safety under the shadow of his government; but thou possessest neither of these qualities.'

A tyrannic man cannot be a sultan As a wolf cannot be a shepherd. A padshah who establishes oppression Destroys the basis of the wall of his own reign.

The king, displeased with the advice of his censorious vezier, sent him to prison. Shortly afterwards the sons of the king's uncle rose in rebellion, desirous of recovering the kingdom of their father. The population, which had been reduced to the last extremity by the king's oppression and scattered, now assembled around them and supported them, till he lost control of the government and they took possession of it.

A padshah who allows his subjects to be oppressed Will in his day of calamity become a violent foe. Be at peace with subjects and sit safe from attacks of foes Because his subjects are the army of a just shahanshah.

Story 7

A padshah was in the same boat with a Persian slave who had never before been at sea and experienced the inconvenience of a vessel. He began to cry and to tremble to such a degree that he could not be pacified by kindness, so that at last the king became displeased as the matter could not be remedied. In that boat there happened to be a philosopher, who said: `With thy permission I shall quiet him.' The padshah replied: `It will be a great favour.' The philosopher ordered the slave to be thrown into the water so that he swallowed some of it, whereon be was caught and pulled by his hair to the boat, to the stern of which he clung with both his hands. Then he sat down in a corner and became quiet. This appeared strange to the king who knew not what wisdom there was in the proceeding and asked for it. The philosopher replied: `Before he had tasted the calamity of being drowned, he knew not the safety of the boat; thus also a man does not appreciate the value of immunity from a misfortune until it has befallen him.'

O thou full man, barley-bread pleases thee not. She is my sweetheart who appears ugly to thee. To the huris of paradise purgatory seems hell. Ask the denizens of hell. To them purgatory is paradise.

There is a difference between him whose friend is in his arms And him whose eyes of expectation are upon the door.

Story 8

Hormuzd, being asked what fault the veziers of his father had committed that he imprisoned them, replied: `I discovered no fault. I saw that boundless awe of me had taken root in their hearts but that they had no full confidence in my promises, wherefore I apprehended that they, fearing calamities would befall them, might attempt my life and I acted according to the maxim of sages who have said:

`Dread him who dreads thee, O sage, Although thou couldst cope with a hundred like him. Seest thou not when the cat becomes desperate How he plucks out with his claws the eyes of a tiger? The viper stings the shepherd's foot Because it fears he will strike his head with a stone.'

Story 9

An Arab king was sick in his state of decrepitude so that all hopes of life were cut off. A trooper entered the gate with the good news that a certain fort had been conquered by the good luck of the king, that the enemies had been captured and that the whole population of the district had been reduced to obedience. The king heaved a deep sigh and replied: `This message is not for me but for my enemies, namely the heirs of the kingdom.'

I spent my precious life in hopes, alas! That every desire of my heart will be fulfilled. My wishes were realized, but to what profit? Since There is no hope that my past life will return. The hand of fate has struck the drum of departure. O my two eyes, bid farewell to the head. O palm, forearm, and arm of my hand, All take leave from each other. Death, the foe of my desires, has fallen on me For the last time, O friends. Pass near me. My life has elapsed in ignorance. I have done nothing, be on your guard.

Story 10

I was constantly engaged in prayer, at the head of the prophet Yahia's tomb in the cathedral mosque of Damascus, when one of the Arab kings, notorious for his injustice, happened to arrive on a pilgrimage to it, who offered his supplications and asked for compliance with his needs.

The dervish and the plutocrat are slaves on the floor of this threshold And those who are the wealthiest are the most needy.

Then he said to me: `Dervishes being zealous and veracious in their dealings, unite thy mind to mine, for I am apprehensive of a powerful enemy.' I replied: `Have mercy upon thy feeble subjects that thou mayest not be injured by a strong foe.'

With a powerful arm and the strength of the wrist To break the five fingers of a poor man is sin. Let him be afraid who spares not the fallen Because if he falls no one will take hold of his hand. Whoever sows bad seed and expects good fruit Has cudgelled his brains for nought and begotten vain imaginations. Extract the cotton from thy ears and administer justice to thy people And if thou failest to do so, there is a day of retribution.

The sons of Adam are limbs of each other Having been created of one essence.

When the calamity of time afflicts one limb The other limbs cannot remain at rest. If thou hast no sympathy for the troubles of others Thou art unworthy to be called by the name of a man.

Story 11

A dervish, whose prayers met with answers, made his appearance, and Hejaj Yusuf, calling him, said: `Utter a good prayer for me', whereon the dervish exclaimed: `O God, take his life.' He replied: 'For God's sake, what prayer is this?' The dervish rejoined: `It is a good prayer for thee and for all Musalmans.'

O tyrant, who oppressest thy subjects, How long wilt thou persevere in this? Of what use is authority to thee? To die is better for thee than to oppress men.

Story 12

An unjust king asked a devotee what kind of worship is best? He replied: `For thee the best is to sleep one half of the day so as not to injure the people for a while.' I saw a tyrant sleeping half the day. I said: `This confusion, if sleep removes it, so much the better; But he whose sleep is better than his wakefulness Is better dead than leading such a bad life.'

Story 13

I heard a king, who had changed might into day by pleasures, saying in his drunkenness:

`We have in the world no moment more delightful than this, Because I care neither for good nor for bad nor for anyone.'

A naked dervish, who was sleeping outside in the cold, then said:

`O thou like whom in happiness there is no one in the world, I take it if thou carest not, we also do not care.'

The king, being pleased with these words of unconcern, held out a bag of a thousand dinars from the window and said: `Dervish, spread out thy skirt.' He replied: `Whence can I, who have no robe, bring a skirt?' The padshah took pity on his helpless condition, added a robe to his gift and sent it out to him but the dervish squandered the money in a short time and returned.

Property cannot abide in the hands of the free, Neither patience in the heart of a lover nor water in a sieve.

The case of the dervish having been brought to the notice of the king when he was not in good humour, he became angry and turned his face away. Therefore it has been said that intelligent and experienced men ought to be on their guard against the violence and despotism of kings because their thoughts are generally occupied with important affairs of state so that they cannot bear to be importuned by the crowd of vulgar persons.

He will be excluded from the beneficence of the padshah Who cannot watch for the proper opportunity. Before thou seest the occasion for speaking at hand Destroy not thy power by heedless talk.

The king said: `Drive away this impudent and prodigal mendicant who has in so short a time thrown away so much money. He does not know that the Beit-ulmal is intended to offer a morsel to the needy and not to feed the brothers of devils.'

The fool who burns by day a camphor-light Will soon not have an oil-lamp for the night.

One of councillor-veziers said: `My lord, it would seem proper to grant to such persons a sufficient allowance to be drawn from time to time so that they may not squander it. But anger and repulsion, as manifested by thee, are unworthy of a generous disposition as also to encourage a man by kindness and then again to distress him by disappointing his expectation.'

The door ought not to be opened to applicants so That, when it is ajar, it may not be shut again. Nobody sees the thirsty pilgrims to Hejaz Crowding at the bank of briny water. Wherever a sweet spring happens to be Men, birds and insects flock around it.

Story 14

One of the ancient kings neglected the government of his realm and kept the army in distress. Accordingly the whole of it ran away when a powerful enemy appeared.

If he refrains from giving treasure to the troops They refrain from putting their hands to the sword. What bravery will they display in battle array When their hands are empty and affairs deplorable? I was on terms of friendship with one of those who had acted treacherously and reproached him, telling him that it was base, ungrateful, despicable and undutiful to abandon an old master when his affairs have changed a little and to disregard the obligations incurred for benefits received during many years. He replied: `If I inform thee, perhaps thou wilt excuse me for my horse had no barley and my saddle-cloth was pawned. A sultan who grudges money to his troops, they cannot bravely risk their lives for him.'

Give gold to the soldier that he may serve thee. If thou witholdest gold, he will serve elsewhere.

When a warrior is full, he will be brave infight but if his belly be empty, he will be brave in flight.

Story 15

A vezier, who had been removed from his post, entered the circle of dervishes and the blessing of their society took such effect upon him that he became contented in his mind. When the king was again favourably disposed towards him and ordered him to resume his office, he refused and said: `Retirement is better than occupation.'

Those who have sat down in the corner of safety Have bound the teeth of dogs and tongues of men. They tore the paper up and broke the pen And are saved from the hands and tongues of slanderers.

The king said: `Verily we stand in need of a man of sufficient intelligence who is able to carry on the administration of the government.' He replied: `It is a sign of sufficient intelligence not to engage in such matters.'

The homa excels all other birds in nobility Because it feeds on bones and injures no living thing.

A donkey, having been asked for what salary he had elected to attend upon the lion, replied: `That I may consume the remnants of his prey and live in safety from my enemies by taking refuge under his bravery.' Being again asked that, as he had entered into the shadow of the lion's protection and gratefully acknowledged his beneficence, why he had not joined the circle of intimacy so as to be accounted one of his favourite servants, he replied: `I am in the same way also not safe of his bravery.' Should a Guebre kindle fire a hundred years If he falls one moment into it he will be burnt.

It may happen that a companion of his majesty the sultan receives gold and it is possible that he loses his head. Philosophers have said that it is necessary to be on guard of the fickle temper of padshahs because sometimes they are displeased with politeness and at others they bestow robes of honour for rudeness. It is also said that much jocularity is an accomplishment in courtiers but a fault in sages.

Abide thou by thy dignity and gravity. Leave sport and jocularity to courtiers.

Story 16

One of my friends complained of the unpropitious times, telling me that he had a slender income, a large family, without strength to bear the load of poverty and had often entertained the idea to emigrate to another country so that no matter how he made a living no one might become aware of his good or ill luck.

Many a man slept hungry and no one knew who he was. Many a man was at the point of death and no one wept for him.

He was also apprehensive of the malevolence of enemies who would laugh behind his back and would attribute the struggle he underwent for the benefit of his family to his want of manly independence and that they will say:

`Behold that dishonourable fellow who will never See the face of prosperity, Will choose bodily comfort for himself, Abandoning his wife and children to misery.'

He also told me that as I knew he possessed some knowledge of arithmetic, I might, through my influence, get him appointed to a post which would become the means of putting his mind at ease and place him under obligations to me, which he could not requite by gratitude during the rest of his life. I replied: `Dear friend! Employment by a padshah consists of two parts, namely, the hope for bread and the danger of life, but it is against the opinion of intelligent men to incur this danger for that hope.' No one comes to the house of a dervish To levy a tax on land and garden. Either consent to bear thy anxiety or grief Or carry thy beloved children to the crows.

He replied: `Thou hast not uttered these words in conformity with my case nor answered my question. Hast thou not heard the saying? "Whoever commits treachery let his hand tremble at the account."'

Straightness is the means of acceptance with God. I saw no one lost on the straight road.

Sages have said: `Four persons are for life in dread of four persons: a robber of the sultan, a thief of the watchman, an adulterer of an informer, and a harlot of the muhtasib. But what has he to fear whose account of the conscience is clear?'

Be not extravagant when in office, if thou desirest On thy removal to see thy foes embarrassed for imputations against thee. Be thou pure, O brother, and in fear of no one. Washermen beat only impure garments against stones.

I said: `The story of that fox resembles thy case, who was by some persons seen fleeing with much trouble and asked for the cause of his fear replied: `I have heard that camels are being forced into the service.' They said: `O fool, what connection hast thou with a camel and what resemblance does the latter bear to thee?' The fox rejoined: `Hush. If the envious malevolently say that I am a camel and I am caught, who will care to release me or investigate my case? Till the antidote is brought from Eraq the snake-bitten person dies.' Thou art a very excellent and honest man but enemies sit in ambush and competitors in every corner. If they describe thy character in a contrary manner, thou wouldst be called upon to give explanations to the padshah and incur reproof. Who would on that occasion venture to say anything? Accordingly I am of opinion that thou shouldst retire to the domain of contentment and abandon aspirations to dominion. Wise men have said:

`In the sea there are countless gains, But if thou desirest safety, it will be on the shore.'

My friend, having heard these words, became angry, made a wry face and began to reproach me, saying: `What sufficiency of wisdom and maturity of intellect is this? The saying of philosophers has come true, that friends are useful in prison because at table all enemies appear as friends.'

Account him not a friend who knocks at the door of prosperity, Boasts of amity and calls himself thy adopted brother. I consider him a friend who takes a friend's hand When he is in a distressed state and in poverty.

Seeing that he had thus changed and ascribed my advice to an interested motive, I paid a visit to the President of the State Council and, trusting in my old acquaintance with him, explained the case of my friend whom he then appointed to a small post. In a short time my friend's affable behaviour and good management elicited approbation so that he was promoted to a higher office. In this manner the star of his good luck ascended till he reached the zenith of his aspirations, became a courtier of his majesty the sultan, generally esteemed and trusted. I was delighted with his safe position and said:

`Be not apprehensive of tangled affairs and keep not a broken heart Because the spring of life is in darkness.'

Do not grieve, O brother in misery, Because the Ill-merciful has hidden favours.

Sit not morose on account of the turns of time; for patience, Although bitter, nevertheless possesses a sweet fruit.

At that time I happened to go with a company of friends on a journey to Mekkah and on my return he met me at a distance of two stages. I perceived his outward appearance to be distressed, his costume being that of dervishes. I asked: `What is the matter?' He replied: 'As thou hast predicted, some persons envied me and brought against me an accusation of treason. The king ordered no inquiry on its truthfulness and my old well-wishers with my kind friends who failed to speak the word of truth forgot our old intimacy.

`Seest thou not in front of the possessor of dignity They place the hands on their heads, praising him; But, if fortune's turn causes his fall, All desire to Place their foot on his head.

`In short, I was till this week undergoing various persecutions, when the news of the pilgrims' approach from Mekkah arrived, whereon I was released from my heavy bonds and my hereditary property confiscated.' I replied: `Thou hast not paid attention to my remarks when I said that the service of padshahs is like a sea voyage, profitable and dangerous, so that thou wilt either gain a treasure or perish in the waves.'

The khajah either takes gold with both hands to the shore Or the waves throw him one day dead upon the shore.

Not thinking it suitable to scratch the wound of the dervish more than I had already done and so sprinkle salt thereon, I contented myself with reciting the following two distichs:

Knewest thou not that thou wilt see thy feet in bonds If the advice of people cannot penetrate into thy ear?

Again, if thou canst not bear the pain of the sting Put not thy finger into the hole of a scorpion.

Story 17

Several men were in my company whose external appearance displayed the adornment of piety. A great man who had conceived a very good opinion of these persons had assigned them a fixed allowance but, after one of them had done something unbecoming the profession of dervishes, his opinion changed and they fell into disgrace. I desired in some way to save the allowance of my friends and intended to wait upon the great man but the doorkeeper would not allow me to enter and was rude. I pardoned him, because it has been said:

The door of an amir, vezier or sultan Is not to be approached without an introduction. When a dog or a doorkeeper sees a stranger The former takes hold of his skirt, the latter of his collar. When those who could at any time approach the presence of the said great man became aware of my case, they took me in with compliments and desired to assign me a high seat but I humbly took a lower one and said:

`Allow me who am the smallest slave To sit in the line of slaves.'

He said: `Allah, Allah, what need is there for such words?'

If thou sittest on my head and eyes I shall be polite, for thou art polite.

In short, I took a seat and we conversed on a variety of topics till the affair of the error of my companions turned up and I said:

`What crime has my lord seen, who was bountiful, To make the slave despicable in his sight? To God that magnanimity and bounty is surrendered Which beholds the crime but nevertheless bestows the bread.'

The governor, being pleased with these words, ordered the support of my friends to be attended to as before and the arrears to be made good. I expressed my gratitude, kissed the ground of obedience, apologized for my boldness, and said:

`Since the Ka'bah has become the Qiblah of wants from distant lands The people go to visit it from many farsangs. Thou must suffer the importunity of such as we are Because no one throws stones on a tree without fruit.'

Story 18

A royal prince, having inherited abundant treasures from his father, opened the hand of liberality and satisfied his impulse of generosity by lavishing without stint benefits upon the army and the population.

A tray of lignum aloes will emit no odour. Place it on fire, it will smell like ambergris. If thou wishest to be accounted great, be liberal Because grain will not grow unless it be sown.

One of his courtiers began heedlessly to admonish him, saying: 'Former kings have by their exertions accumulated this wealth and deposited it for a useful purpose. Cease this movement because calamities may arise in front and enemies in the rear. It is not meet for thee to be helpless at a time of necessity.'

If thou distributest a treasure to the multitude Each householder will receive a grain of rice. Why takest thou not from each a barley-corn of silver That thou mayest accumulate every day a treasure?

The royal prince turned away his face at these words and said: 'God the most high has made me the possessor of this country, to enjoy and to bestow, not to guard and to retain.'

Qarun, who possessed forty treasure houses, perished. Nushirvan has not died because he obtained a good reputation.

Story 19

It is related that, whilst some game was being roasted for Nushirvan the just during a hunting party, no salt could be found. Accordingly a boy was sent to an adjoining village to bring some. Nushirvan said: `Pay for the salt lest it should become a custom and the village be ruined.' Having been asked what harm could arise from such a trifling demand, Nushirvan replied: `The foundation of oppression was small in the world but whoever came augmented it so that it reached its present magnitude.'

If the king eats one apple from the garden of a subject His slaves will pull him up the tree from the roots.

For five eggs which the sultan allows to be taken by force The people belonging to his army will put a thousand fowls on the spit.

A tyrant does not remain in the world But the curse on him abides for ever.

Story 20

I heard that an oppressor ruined the habitations of the subjects to fill the treasury of the sultan, unmindful of the maxim of philosophers, who have said: 'Who offends God the most high to gain the heart of a created being, God will use that very being to bring on his destruction in the world.'

Fire burning with wild rue will not Cause a smoke like that of afflicted hearts.

The prince of all animals is the lion and the meanest of beasts the ass. Nevertheless sages agree that an ass who carries loads is better than a lion who destroys men.

The poor donkey though void of discernment Is nevertheless esteemed when he carries a burden. Oxen and asses who carry loads Are superior to men oppressing mankind.

When the king had obtained information of some of the oppressor's misdeeds and bad conduct, he had him put on the rack and slain by various tortures.

Thou wilt not obtain the approbation of the sultan Unless thou seekest the goodwill of his subjects. If thou desirest God to condone thy transgressions, Do good to the people whom God has created.

One of the oppressed who passed near him said:

'Not everyone who possesses strength of arm and office In the sultanate may with impunity plunder the people. A hard bone may be made to pass down the throat But it will tear the belly when it sticks in the navel.'

Story 21

It is narrated that an oppressor of the people, a soldier, hit the head of a pious man with a stone and that the dervish, having no means of taking vengeance, preserved the stone till the time arrived when the king became angry with that soldier, and imprisoned him in a well. Then the dervish made his appearance and dropped the stone upon his head. He asked:

`Who art thou, and why hast thou hit my head with this stone?' The man replied: `I am the same person whom thou hast struck on the head with this stone on such and such a day.' The soldier continued: `Where hast thou been all this time?' The dervish replied: `I was afraid of thy dignity but now when I beheld thee in the well I made use of the opportunity.'

When thou seest an unworthy man in good luck Intelligent men have chosen submission. If thou hast not a tearing sharp nail It will be better not to contend with the wicked. Who grasps with his fist one who has an arm of steel Injures only his own powerless wrist. Wait till inconstant fortune ties his hand. Then, to please thy friends, pick out his brains.

Story 22

A king was subject to a terrible disease, the mention of which is not sanctioned by custom. The tribe of Yunani physicians agreed that this pain cannot be allayed except by means of the bile of a person endued with certain qualities. Orders having been issued to search for an individual of this kind, the son of a landholder was discovered to possess the qualities mentioned by the doctors. The king summoned the father and mother of the boy whose consent he obtained by giving them immense wealth. The qazi issued a judicial decree that it is permissible to shed the blood of one subject for the safety of the king and the executioner was ready to slay the boy who then looked heavenwards and smiled. The king asked: `What occasion for laughter is there in such a position?' The youth replied: `A son looks to the affection of his father and mother to bring his case before the qazi and to ask justice from the padshah. In the present instance, however, the father and mother have for the trash of this world surrendered my blood, the qazi has issued a decree to kill me, the sultan thinks he will recover his health only through my destruction and I see no other refuge besides God the most high.'

To whom shall I complain against thy hand If I am to seek justice also from thy hand?

The sultan became troubled at these words, tears rushed to his eyes and he said: `It is better for me to perish than to shed innocent blood.' He kissed the head and eyes of the youth, presented him with boundless wealth and it is said that the king also recovered his health during that week.

I also remember the distich recited By the elephant-driver on the bank of the Nile: `If thou knewest the state of the ant under thy foot It is like thy own condition under the foot of an elephant.'

Story 23

One of the servants of Umrulais had fled but some men, having been sent in pursuit, brought him back. The vezier who bore a grudge towards him desired him to be killed that the other servants may not imitate his example. He placed his head on the ground before Umrulais and said:

`Whatever befalls my head is lawful with thy approbation. What plea can the slave advance? The sentence is the master's.'

`But, having been nourished by the bounty of this dynasty, I am loth that on the day of resurrection thou shouldst be punished for having shed my blood; but, if thou desirest to kill me, do so according to the provisions of the law.' He asked: `How am I to interpret it?' The slave continued: `Allow me to kill the vezier and then take my life in retaliation so that I may be killed justly.' The king smiled and asked the vezier what he thought of the matter. He replied: `My lord, give freedom to this bastard as an oblation to the tomb of thy father for fear he would bring trouble on me likewise. It is my fault for not having taken account of the maxim of philosophers who have said:

When thou fightest with a thrower of clods Thou ignorantly breakest thy own head. When thou shootest an arrow at the face of a foe Be on thy guard for thou art sitting as a target for him.'

Story 24

King Zuzan had a khajah of noble sentiments and of good aspect who served his companions when they were present and spoke well of them when they were absent. He happened to do something whereby he incurred the displeasure of the king who inflicted a fine on him and also otherwise punished him. The officials of the king, mindful of the benefits they had formerly received from him and being by them pledged to gratitude, treated him kindly whilst in their custody and allowed no one to insult him.

If thou desirest peace from the foe, whenever he Finds fault behind thy back praise him to his face. A vicious fellow's mouth must utter words. If thou desirest not bitter words, sweeten his mouth.

He was absolved of some accusations brought by the king against him but retained in prison for some. Another king in those regions secretly dispatched a message to him, to the purport that the sovereigns of that country, not knowing his excellent qualities, had dishonoured him, but that if his precious mind (may Allah prosper the end of his affairs) were to look in this direction, the utmost efforts would be made to please him, because the nobles of this realm would consider it an honour to see him and are waiting for a reply to this letter. The khajah, who had received this information, being apprehensive of danger, forthwith wrote a brief and suitable answer on the back of the sheet of paper and sent it back. One, however, of the king's courtiers, who noticed what had taken place, reported to him that the imprisoned khajah was in correspondence with the princes of the adjacent country. The king became angry and desired this affair to be investigated. The courier was overtaken and deprived of the letter, the contents of which were found on perusal to be as follows: `The good opinion of high personages is more than their servant's merit deserves, who is unable to comply with the honour of reception which they have offered him, because having been nourished by the bounty of this dynasty, he cannot become unthankful towards his benefactor in consequence of a slight change of sentiments of the latter, since it is said:

He who bestows every moment favours upon thee Is to be pardoned by thee if once in his life he injures thee.'

The king approved of his gratitude, bestowed upon him a robe of honour, gave him presents and asked his pardon, saying:

`I committed a mistake.' He replied: `My lord, it was the decree of God the most high that a misfortune should befall this servant but it was best that it should come from thy hands which had formerly bestowed favours upon him and placed him under obligations.' If people injure thee grieve not Because neither rest nor grief come from the people. Be aware that the contrasts of friend and foe are from God Because the hearts of both are in his keeping. Although the arrow is shot from the bow Wise men look at the archer.

Story 25

One of the Arab kings ordered his officials to double the allowance of a certain attendant because he was always at the palace expecting orders while the other servants were engaged in amusements and sports, neglecting their duties. A pious man who heard this remarked that high degrees at the court of heaven are similarly bestowed upon servants:

If a man comes two mornings to serve the shah He will on the third certainly look benevolently on him. Sincere worshippers entertain the hope That they will not be disappointed at the threshold of God. Superiority consists in attending to commands. The neglect of commands leads to exclusion. Who possesses the criterion of righteousness Places the head upon the threshold.

Story 26

It is narrated that a tyrant who purchased wood from dervishes forcibly gave it away to rich people gratuitously. A pious man passing near said:

`Thou art a snake, stingest whom thou beholdest, Or an owl; wherever thou sittest thou destroyest.

Although thy oppression may pass among us It cannot pass with the Lord who knows all secrets.

Oppress not the denizens of the earth That their supplications may not pass to heaven.'

The tyrant, being displeased with these words, got angry and took no notice of him until one night, when fire from the kitchen fell into the store of his wood and burnt all he possessed -- transferring him from his soft bed to a hot mound of ashes -- the same pious man happened again to pass and to hear him saying to his friends: `I do not know whence this fire has fallen into my house.' replied: `From the smoke of the hearts of dervishes.'

Beware of the smoke of internal wounds Because at last an internal wound will break out. Forbear to uproot one heart as long as thou canst Because one sigh may uproot a world.

Upon the diadem of Kaikhosru the following piece was inscribed:

For how many years and long lives Will the people walk over my head on the ground? As from hand to hand the kingdom came to us So it will also go to other hands.

Story 27

A man had attained great excellence in the art of wrestling, who knew three hundred and sixty exquisite tricks and daily exhibited something new. He had a particular affection for the beauty of one of his pupils whom he taught three hundred and fifty-nine tricks, refraining to impart to him only one.

At last the youth had attained such power and skill that no one was able to contend with him and he went so far as to say to the sultan: `I allow superiority to my teacher on account of his age and from gratitude for his instruction but my strength is not less than his and my skill equal.' The king, who was not pleased with this want of good manners, ordered them to wrestle with each other and a spacious locality having been fixed upon, the pillars of state and courtiers of his majesty made their appearance.

The youth made an onslaught like a mad elephant with an impulse which might have uprooted a mountain of brass from its place but the master, who knew that he was in strength superior to himself, attacked him with the rare trick he had reserved to himself and which the youth was unable to elude; whereon the master, lifting him up with his hands from the ground, raised him above his head and then threw him down. Shouts were raised by the spectators and the king ordered a robe of honour with other presents to be given to the teacher but reproached and blamed the youth for having attempted to cope with his instructor and succumbed.

He replied: `My lord, he has not vanquished me by his strength but there was a slender part in the art of wrestling which he had withheld from me and had today thereby got the upper hand of me.'

The master said: `I had reserved it for such an occasion because wise men have said: ``Do not give so much strength to thy friend that, if he becomes thy foe, he may injure thee." Hast thou not heard what the man said who suffered molestation from one whom he had educated?

Either fidelity itself does not exist in this world Or nobody practices it in our time. No one had learnt archery from me Without at last making a target of me.'

Story 28

A solitary dervish was sitting in a corner of the desert when a padshah happened to pass by but, ease having made him independent, he took no notice. The sultan, in conformity with his royal dignity, became angry and said: `This tribe of rag-wearers resembles beasts.'

The vezier said: `The padshah of the surface of the earth has passed near thee. Why hast thou not paid homage and shown good manners?' He replied: `Tell the king to look for homage from a man who expects benefits from him and also that kings exist for protecting subjects and subjects not for obeying kings.'

The padshah is the guardian of the dervish Although wealth is in the glory of his reign. The sheep is not for the shepherd But the shepherd for the service of it.

Today thou beholdest one man prosperous And another whose heart is wounded by struggling. Wait a few days till the earth consumes The brain in the head of the visionary. Distinction between king and slave has ceased When the decree of fate overtakes them. If a man were to open the tombs of the dead He would not distinguish a rich from a poor man.

The king, who was pleased with the sentiments of the dervish, asked him to make a request but he answered that the only one he had to make was to be left alone. The king then asked for advice and the dervish said:

`Understand now while wealth is in thy hand That fortune and kingdom will leave thy hand.'

Story 29

A vezier paid a visit to Zulnun Misri and asked for his favour, saying: `I am day and night engaged in the service of the sultan and hoping to be rewarded but nevertheless dread to be punished by him.' Zulnun wept and said: `Had I feared God, the great and glorious, as thou fearest the sultan, I would be one of the number of the righteous.'

If there were no hope of rest and trouble The foot of the dervish would be upon the sphere And if the vezier feared God Like the king he would be king.

Story 30

A padshah having issued orders to kill an innocent man, the latter said: `O king, seek not thine own injury on account of the anger thou bearest towards me.' He asked: `How?' The man replied: `This punishment will abide with me one moment but the sin of it for ever with thee.'

The period of life has passed away like the desert wind. Bitter and sweet, ugliness and beauty have passed away. The tyrant fanded he had done injury to us. It remained on his neck and passed away from us. This admonition having taken effect, the king spared his blood.

Story 31

The veziers of Nushirvan happened to discuss an important affair of state, each giving his opinion according to his knowledge. The king likewise gave his opinion and Barzachumihr concurred with it. Afterwards the veziers secretly asked him: `What superiority hast thou discovered in the opinion of the king above so many other reflections of wise men?' The philosopher replied: `Since the termination of the affair is unknown and it depends upon the will of God whether the opinion of the others will turn out right or wrong, it was better to agree with the opinion of the king so that, if it should turn out to have been wrong, we may, on account of having followed it, remain free from blame.' To proffer an opinion contrary to the king's Means to wash the hands in one's own blood. Should he in plain day say it is night, It is meet to shout: `Lo, the moon and the pleiads!'

Story 32

An impostor arranged his hair in a peculiar fashion, pretended to be a descendant of A'li and entered the town with a caravan from the Hejaz, saying that he had just arrived from a pilgrimage. He also presented an elegy to the king, alleging that he had himself composed it.

One of the king's courtiers, who had that year returned from a journey, said: `I have seen him at Bosrah on the Azhah festival, then how can he be a Haji?' Another said: `His father was a Christian at Melitah. How can he be a descendant of A'li? And his poetry has been found in the Divan of Anvari.' The king ordered him to be beaten and expelled the country for his great mendacity. The man said: `O lord of the surface of the earth, I shall say something more and, if it is not true, I shall deserve any punishment which thou mayest decree.'

He asked: `What is it?'

When a stranger brings before thee buttermilk Two measures of it will be water and a spoonful sour milk. If thou hast heard heedless talk from thy slave, be not offended. A man who has seen the world utters much falsehood.

The king laughed, told him that all his life he had not uttered more true words than these and ordered the present which the fellow hoped for to be got ready.

Story 33

One of the veziers of a king treated his subordinates with kindness and sought the goodwill of his colleagues. Once he happened to be called to account by the king for something he had done whereon his colleagues endeavoured to effect his liberation. Those who guarded him treated him leniently and the great men expatiated upon his good character to the padshah till he renounced all further inquiry. A pious man who took cognizance of this affair said:

`In order to gain the hearts of friends Sell even the garden of thy father. In order to boil the pot of well-wishers Burn even all the furniture of the house. Do good even to a malevolent fellow. Tie up the mouth of the dog with a sop.'

Story 34

One of the sons of Harun-ur-Rashid went to his father and angrily informed him that the son of an official had used insulting expressions towards him whereon Harun asked his courtiers what requital he deserved. One of them proposed capital punishment, another the amputation of the tongue whilst a third recommended fine and imprisonment. Then Harun said: `Oh my son, it would be generous to pardon him but, if thou art unable to do so, use likewise insulting expressions concerning his mother; not however to such a degree as to exceed the bounds of vengeance because in that case the wrong will be on thy side.'

He is not reputed a man by the wise Who contends with a furious elephant But he is a man in reality Who when angry speaks not idle words.

An ill-humoured fellow insulted a man Who patiently bore it saying: `O hopeful youth, I am worse than thou speakest of me For I am more conscious of my faults than thou.'

Story 35

I was sitting in a vessel with a company of great men when a boat which contained two brothers happened to sink near us. One of the great men promised a hundred dinars to a sailor if he could save them both. Whilst however the sailor was pulling out one, the other perished. I said: `He had no longer to live and therefore delay took place in rescuing him.' The sailor smiled and replied: `What thou hast said is certain. Moreover, I preferred to save this one because, when I once-happened to lag behind in the desert, he seated me on his camel, whereas I had received a whipping by the hands of the other. When I was a boy I recited: He, who doth right, doth it to his own soul and he, who doth evil, doth it against the same.'

As long as thou canst, scratch the interior of no one Because there are thorns on this road. Be helpful in the affairs of a dervish Because thou also hast affairs.

Story 36

There were two brothers: one of them in the service of the sultan and the other gaining his livelihood by the effort of his arm. The wealthy man once asked his destitute brother why he did not serve the sultan in order to be delivered from the hardship of labouring. He replied: `Why labourest thou not to be delivered from the baseness of service because philosophers have said that it is better to eat barley bread and to sit than to gird oneself with a golden belt and to stand in service?'

To leaven mortar of quicklime with the hand Is better than to hold them on the breast before the amir.

My precious life was spent in considering What I am to eat in summer and wear in winter. O ignoble belly, be satisfied with one bread Rather than to bend the back in service.

Story 37

Someone had brought information to Nushirvan the just that an enemy of his had been removed from this world by God the most high. He asked: `Hast thou heard anything about his intending to spare me?'

There is no occasion for our rejoicing at a foe's death Because our own life will also not last for ever.

Story 38

A company of philosophers were discussing a subject in the palace of Kesra and Barzachumihr, having remained silent, they asked him why he took no share in the debate. He replied: `Veziers are like physicians and the latter give medicine to the sick only but, as I perceive that your opinions are in conformity with propriety, I have nothing to say about them.'

When an affair succeeds without my idle talk It is not meet for me to speak thereon. But if I see a blind man near a well It is a crime for me to remain silent.

Story 39

Harun-ur-Rashid said when the country of Egypt was surrendered to him: 'In contrast to the rebel who had in his arrogance of being sovereign of Egypt pretended to be God, I shall bestow this country upon the meanest of my slaves.' He had a stupid negro, Khosaib by name, whom he made governor of Egypt but his intellect and discrimination were so limited that when the tribe of Egyptian agriculturists complained and stated that they had sown cotton along the banks of the Nile and that an untimely rain had destroyed it he replied: 'You ought to have sown wool.' A pious man heard this, and said:

'If livelihood were increased by knowledge None would be more needy than the ignorant. Nevertheless the ignorant receive a livelihood At which the learned stand aghast. The luck of wealth consists not in skill But only in the aid of heaven. It happens in the world that many Silly men are honoured and sages despised. If an alchemist has died in grief and misery, A fool discovered a treasure amidst ruins.'

Story 40

A Chinese slave-girl having been brought to a king, he desired to have connection with her whilst in a state of intoxication but, as she repelled him, he became angry and presented her to one of his negro-slaves whose upper lip was higher than his nostrils whilst the lower one hung down to his neck. His stature was such that the demon Sakhrah would have been put to flight and a fountain of pitch emitted stench from his armpits.

Thou wouldst say that, till the resurrection, ugliness Is his stamp as that of Joseph was beauty. His person was of so wretched an aspect That his ugliness surpassed all description And from his armpits we take refuge with Allah, They were like a corpse in the month of Merdad. At that time the desire of the negro was libidinous, his lust overcame him, his love leapt up and he took off the seal of her virginity. In the morning the king sought the girl but could not find her and, having obtained information of what had taken place, he became angry, ordered the negro and the girl to be firmly tied together by their hands and feet and to be thrown from the lofty building into a ditch. One of the veziers, placing the face of intercession upon the ground, pleaded that there was no guilt in the negro since all the servants of his majesty usually receive presents and benefits as he had received the girl. The king rejoined: `What would it have mattered if he had for one night delayed his enjoyment?' He said: `My lord, hast thou not heard that it was said:

When a man with a burning thirst reaches a limpid spring, Think not that he will care for a mad elephant. When a hungry infidel is in an empty house at table Reason will not believe that he cares for the Ramazan.'

The king, being pleased with this sally, exclaimed: `I make thee a present of the negro. What am I to do with the girl?' He replied: 'Give the girl to the negro because that half is also due to a dog of which he has consumed the other half.'

The thirsty heart does not wish for limpid water Half of which was consumed by a fetid mouth.

How can the king's hand again touch An orange after it has fallen into dung?

Story 41

Iskandur Rumi, having been asked how he had conquered the east and the west, considering that the treasures, territories, reigns and armies of former kings exceeded his own and they had not gained such a victory, replied: `Whatever country I conquered by the aid of God the most high, I abstained from distressing its population and spoke nothing but good of the king.'

The intelligent will not call him great Who speaks ill of the great. All this is nothing as it passes away: Throne and luck, command and prohibition, taking and giving. Injure not the name of those who have passed away In order that thy own name may subsist.

THE MORALS OF DERVISHES

Story 1

One of the great devotees having been asked about his opinion concerning a hermit whom others had censured in their conversation, he replied: `I do not see any external blemishes on him and do not know of internal ones.'

Whomsoever thou seest in a religious habit Consider him to be a religious and good man And, if thou knowest not his internal condition, What business has the muhtasib inside the house?

Story 2

I saw a dervish who placed his head upon the threshold of the Ka'bah, groaned, and said: `O forgiving, 0 merciful one, thou knowest what an unrighteous, ignorant man can offer to thee.'

I have craved pardon for the deficiency of my service Because I can implore no reward for my obedience. Sinners repent of their transgressions. Arifs ask forgiveness for their imperfect worship.

Devotees desire a reward for their obedience and merchants the price of their wares but I, who am a worshipper, have brought hope and not obedience. I have come to beg and not to trade. Deal with me as thou deemest fit.

Whether thou killest me or forgivest my crime, my face and head are on thy threshold. A slave has nothing to command; whatever thou commandest I obey.

I saw a mendicant at the door of the Ka'bah Who said this and wept abundantly: `I ask not for the acceptance of my service But for drawing the pen of pardon over my sins.'

Story 3

I saw A'bd-u-Qader Gaillani in the sanctuary of the Ka'bah with his face on the pebbles and saying: `O lord, pardon my sins and, if I deserve punishment, cause me to arise blind on the day of resurrection that I may not be ashamed in the sight of the righteous.'

With my face on the earth of helplessness I say Every morning as soon as I become conscious: O thou whom I shall never forget Wilt thou at all remember thy slave?

Story 4

A thief paid a visit to the house of a pious man but, although he sought a great deal, found nothing and was much grieved. The pious man, who knew this, threw the blanket upon which he had been sleeping into the way of the thief that he might not go away disappointed.

I heard that men of the way of God Have not distressed the hearts of enemies. How canst thou attain that dignity Who quarrelest and wagest war against friends?

The friendship of pure men, whether in thy presence or absence, is not such as Will find fault behind thy back and is ready to die for thee before thy face.

In thy presence gentle like a lamb, In thy absence like a man-devouring wolf. Who brings the faults of another to thee and enumerates them Will undoubtedly carry thy faults to others.

Story 5

Several travellers were on a journey together and equally sharing each other's troubles and comforts. I desired to accompany them but they would not agree. Then I said: `It is foreign to the manners of great men to turn away the face from the company of the poor and so deprive themselves of the advantage they might derive therefrom because I for one consider myself sufficiently strong and energetic to be of service to men and not an encumbrance. Although I am not riding on a beast, I shall aid you in carrying blankets.' One of them said: `Do not be grieved at the words thou hast heard because some days ago a thief in the guise of a dervish arrived and joined our company.'

How can people know who is in the dress? The writer is aware what the book contains.

As the state of dervishes is safe, they entertained no suspicion about him and received him as a friend.

The outward state of Arifs is the patched dress. It suffices as a display to the face of the people.

Strive by thy acts to be good and wear anything thou listest. Place a crown on thy head and a flag on thy back. The abandoning of the world, of lust, and of desire Is sanctity, not the abandonment of the robe only. It is necessary to show manhood in the fight. Of what profit are weapons of war to an hermaphrodite? We travelled one day till the night set in during which we slept near a fort and the graceless thief, taking up the water-pot of a companion, pretending to go for an ablution, departed for plunder.

A pretended saint who wears the dervish garb Has made of the Ka'bah's robes the covering of an ass.

After disappearing from the sight of the dervishes, he went to a tower from which he stole a casket and, when the day dawned, the dark-hearted wretch had already progressed a considerable distance. In the morning the guiltless sleeping companions were all taken to the fort and thrown into prison. From that date we renounced companionship and took the road of solitude, according to the maxim: Safety is in solitude.

When one of a tribe has done a foolish thing No honour is left either to the low or the high. Seest thou not how one ox of the pasturage Defiles all oxen of the village?

I replied: `Thanks be to the God of majesty and glory, I have not been excluded from the advantages enjoyed by dervishes, although I have separated myself from their society. I have profited by what thou hast narrated to me and this admonition will be of use through life to persons like me.'

For one rude fellow in the assembly The heart of intelligent men is much grieved. If a tank be filled with rose-water A dog falling into it pollutes the whole.

Story 6

A hermit, being the guest of a padshah, ate less than he wished when sitting at dinner and when he rose for prayers he prolonged them more than was his wont in order to enhance the opinion entertained by the padshah of his piety. O Arab of the desert, I fear thou wilt not reach the Ka'bah Because the road on which thou travellest leads to Turkestan.

When he returned to his own house, he desired the table to be laid out for eating. He had an intelligent son who said: `Father, hast thou not eaten anything at the repast of the sultan?' He replied: 'I have not eaten anything to serve a purpose.' The boy said: `Then likewise say thy prayers again as thou hast not done anything to serve that purpose.'

O thou who showest virtues on the palms of the hand But concealest thy errors under the armpit What wilt thou purchase, O vain-glorious fool, On the day of distress with counterfeit silver?

Story 7

I remember, being in my childhood pious, rising in the night, addicted to devotion and abstinence. One night I was sitting with my father, remaining awake and holding the beloved Quran in my lap, whilst the people around us were asleep. I said: `Not one of these persons lifts up his head or makes a genuflection. They are as fast asleep as if they were dead.' He replied: `Darling of thy father, would that thou wert also asleep rather than disparaging people.'

The pretender sees no one but himself Because he has the veil of conceit in front. If he were endowed with a God-discerning eye He would see that no one is weaker than himself.

Story 8

A great man was praised in an assembly and, his good qualities being extolled, he raised his head and said: `I am such as I know myself to be.'

O thou who reckonest my virtues, refrainest from giving me pain, These are my open, and thou knowest not my hidden, qualities.

My person is, to the eyes of the world, of good aspect But my internal wickedness makes me droop my head with shame. The peacock is for his beauteous colours by the people Praised whilst he is ashamed of his ugly feet.

Story 9

One of the devotees of Mount Lebanon, whose piety was famed in the Arab country and his miracles well known, entered the cathedral mosque of Damascus and was performing his purificatory ablution on the edge of a tank when his feet slipped and he fell into the reservoir but saved himself with great trouble. After the congregation had finished their prayers, one of his companions said: `I have a difficulty.' He asked: `What is it?' He continued: 'I remember that the sheikh walked on the surface of the African sea without his feet getting wetted and today he nearly perished in this paltry water which is not deeper than a man's stature. What reason is there in this?' The sheikh drooped his head into the bosom of meditation and said after a long pause: `Hast thou not heard that the prince of the world, Muhammad the chosen, upon whom be the benediction of Allah and peace, has said: I have time with Allah during which no cherubim nor inspired prophet is equal to me?' But he did not say that such was always the case. The time alluded to was when Gabriel or Michael inspired him whilst on other occasions he was satisfied with the society of Hafsah and Zainab. The visions of the righteous one are between brilliancy and obscurity.

Thou showest thy countenance and then hidest it Enhancing thy value and augmenting our desire.

I behold whom I love without an intervention. Then a trance befalls me; I lose the road; It kindles fire, then quenches it with a sprinkling shower. Wherefore thou seest me burning and drowning.

Story 10

One asked the man who had lost his son:

`O noble and intelligent old man! As thou hast smelt the odour of his garment from Egypt Why hast thou not seen him in the well of Canaan?'

He replied: `My state is that of leaping lightning. One moment it appears and at another vanishes. I am sometimes sitting in high heaven. Sometimes I cannot see the back of my foot. Were a dervish always to remain in that state He would not care for the two worlds.'

Story 11

I spoke in the cathedral mosque of Damascus a few words by way of a sermon but to a congregation whose hearts were withered and dead, not having travelled from the road of the world of form, the physical, to the world of meaning, the moral world. I perceived that my words took no effect and that burning fire does not kindle moist wood. I was sorry for instructing brutes and holding forth a mirror in a locality of blind people. I had, however, opened the door of meaning and was giving a long explanation of the verse We are nearer unto Him than the jugular vein till I said:

`The Friend is nearer to me than my self, But it is more strange that I am far from him. What am I to do? To whom can it be said that he Is in my arms, but I am exiled from him.'

I had intoxicated myself with the wine of these sentiments, holding the remnant of the cup of the sermon in my hand when a traveller happened to pass near the edge of the assembly, and the last turn of the circulating cup made such an impression upon him that he shouted and the others joined him who began to roar, whilst the raw portion of the congregation became turbulent. Whereon I said: 'Praise be to Allah! Those who are far away but intelligent are in the presence of Allah, and those who are near but blind are distant.'

When the hearer understands not the meaning of words Do not look for the effect of the orator's force But raise an extensive field of desire That the eloquent man may strike the ball of effect.

Story 12

One night I had in the desert of Mekkah become so weak from want of sleep that I was unable to walk and, laying myself down, told the camel driver to let me alone.

How far can the foot of a wretched pedestrian go When a dromedary gets distressed by its load? Whilst the body of a fat man becomes lean A weak man will be dead of exhaustion.

He replied: `O brother, the sanctuary is in front of us and brigands in the rear. If thou goest thou wilt prosper. If thou sleepest thou wilt die.' It is pleasant to sleep under an acacia on the desert road But alas! thou must bid farewell to life on the night of departure.

Story 13

I saw a holy man on the seashore who had been wounded by a tiger. No medicine could relieve his pain; he suffered much but he nevertheless constantly thanked God the most high, saying: `Praise be to Allah that I have fallen into a calamity and not into sin.' If that beloved Friend decrees me to be slain I shall not say that moment that I grieve for life Or say: What fault has thy slave committed? My grief will be for having offended thee.

Story 14

A dervish who had fallen into want stole a blanket from the house of a friend. The judge ordered his hand to be amputated but the owner of the blanket interceded, saying that he had condoned the fault. The judge rejoined: `Thy intercession cannot persuade me to neglect the provision of the law.' The man continued: `Thou hast spoken the truth but amputation is not applicable to a person who steals some property dedicated to pious uses. More over a beggar possesses nothing and whatever belongs to a dervish is dedicated to the use of the needy.' Thereon the judge released the culprit, saying: `The world must indeed have become too narrow for thee that thou hast committed no theft except from the house of such a friend.' He replied: `Hast thou not heard the saying: Sweep out the house of friends and do not knock at the door of foes.' If thou sinkest in a calamity be not helpless. Strip thy foes of their skins and thy friends of their fur-coats.

Story 15

A padshah, meeting a holy man, asked him whether he did not sometimes remember him for the purpose of getting presents. He replied: `Yes, I do, whenever I forget God.' Whom He drives from his door, runs everywhere. Whom He calls, runs to no one's door.

Story 16

A pious man saw in a dream a padshah in paradise and a devotee in hell whereon he asked for the reason of the former's exaltation and the latter's degradation, saying that he had imagined the contrary ought to be the case. He received the following answer: `The padshah had, for the love he bore to dervishes, been rewarded with paradise and the devotee had, for associating with padshahs, been punished in hell.'

Of what use is thy frock, rosary and patched dress? Keep thyself free from despicable practices. Then thou wilt have no need of a cap of leaves. Have the qualities of a dervish and wear a Tatar cap.

Story 17

A bareheaded and barefooted pedestrian who had arrived from Kufah with the Hejaz-caravan of pilgrims joined us, strutted about and recited:

`I am neither riding a camel nor under a load like a camel. I am neither a lord of subjects nor the slave of a potentate. Grief for the present, or distress for the past, does not trouble me. I draw my breath in comfort and thus spend my life.'

A camel-rider shouted to him: `O dervish, where art thou going? Return, for thou wilt expire from hardships.' He paid no attention but entered the desert and marched. When we reached the station at the palm-grove of Mahmud, the rich man was on the point of death and the dervish, approaching his pillow, said: `We have not expired from hardship but thou hast died on a dromedary.'

A man wept all night near the head of a patient. When the day dawned he died and the patient revived.

Many a fleet charger had fallen dead While a lame ass reached the station alive. Often healthy persons were in the soil Buried and the wounded did not die.

Story 18

A hermit, having been invited by a padshah, concluded that if he were to take some medicine to make himself weak he might perhaps enhance the opinion of the padshah regarding his merits. But it is related that the medicine was lethal so that when he partook of it he died.

Who appeared to thee all marrow like a pistachio Was but skin upon skin like an onion. Devotees with their face towards the world Say their prayers with their back to the Qiblah. When a worshipper calls upon his God, He must know no one besides God.

Story 19

A caravan having been plundered in the Yunan country and deprived of boundless wealth, the merchants wept and lamented, beseeching God and the prophet to intercede for them with the robbers, but ineffectually.

When a dark-minded robber is victorious What cares he for the weeping of the caravan?

Loqman the philosopher being among the people of the caravan, one of them asked him to speak a few words of wisdom and advice to the robbers so that they might perhaps return some of the property they had plundered because the loss of so much wealth would be lamentable. Loqman replied: `It would be lamentable to utter one word of wisdom to them.'

The rust which has eaten into iron Cannot be removed by polishing. Of what use is preaching to a black heart? An iron nail cannot be driven into a rock.

Help the distressed in the day of prosperity Because comforting the poor averts evil from thyself. When a mendicant implores thee for a thing, Give it or else an oppressor may take it by force.

Story 20

Despite the abundant admonitions of the most illustrious Sheikh Abulfaraj Ben Juzi to shun musical entertainments and to prefer solitude and retirement, the budding of my youth overcame me, my sensual desires were excited so that, unable to resist them, I walked some steps contrary to the opinion of my tutor, enjoying myself in musical amusements and convivial meetings. When the advice of my sheikh occurred to my mind,

I said: 'If the qazi were sitting with us, he would clap his hands. If the muhtasib were bibbing wine, he would excuse a drunkard.'

Thus I lived till I paid one night a visit to an assembly of people in which I saw a musician.

Thou wouldst have said he is tearing up the vital artery with his fiddle-bow. His voice was more unpleasant than the wailing of one who lost his father.

The audience now stopped their ears with their fingers, and now put them on their lips to silence him. We became ecstatic by the sounds of pleasing songs but thou art such a singer that when thou art silent we are pleased.

No one feels pleased by thy performance Except at the time of departure when thou pleasest.

When that harper began to sing I said to the host: 'For God's sake Put mercury in my ear that I may not hear Or open the door that I may go away.'

In short, I tried to please my friends and succeeded after a considerable struggle in spending the whole night there.

The muezzin shouted the call to prayers out of time, Not knowing how much of the night had elapsed. Ask the length of the night from my eyelids For sleep did not enter my eyes one moment.

In the morning I took my turban from my head, with one dinar from my belt by way of gratification, and placed them before the musician whom I embraced and thanked. My friends who saw that my appreciation of his merits was unusual attributed it to the levity of my intellect and laughed secretly. One of them, however, lengthened out his tongue of objection and began to reproach me, saying that I had committed an act repugnant to intelligent men by bestowing a portion of my professional dress upon a musician who had all his life not a dirhem laid upon the palm of his hand nor filings of silver or of gold placed on his drum.

A musician! Far be he from this happy abode. No one ever saw him twice in the same place. As soon as the shout rose from his mouth The hair on the bodies of the people stood on end.

The fowls of the house, terrified by him, flew away Whilst he distracted our senses and tore his throat. I said: `It will be proper to shorten the tongue of objection because his talent has become evident to me.' He then asked me to explain the quality of it in order to inform the company so that all might apologize for the jokes they had cracked about me. I replied: 'Although my sheikh had often told me to abandon musical entertainments and had given me abundant advice, I did not mind it. This night my propitious horoscope and my august luck have guided me to this place where I have, on hearing the performance of this musician, repented and vowed never again to attend at singing and convivial parties.'

A pleasant voice, from a sweet palate, mouth and lips, Whether employed in singing or not, enchants the heart But the melodies of lovers of Isfahan or of the Hejaz From the windpipe of a bad singer are not nice.

Story 21

Loqman, being asked from whom he had learnt civility, replied: `From those who had no civility because what appeared to me unbecoming in them I refrained from doing.'

Not a word is said even in sport Without an intelligent man taking advice thereby. But if a hundred chapters of wisdom are read to a fool All strike his ear merely as sport.

Story 22

It is related that a hermit consumed during one night ten mann of food and perused the whole Quran till morning. A pious fellow who had heard of this said: `It would have been more excellent if he had eaten half a loaf and slept till the morning.'

Keep thy interior empty of food That thou mayest behold therein the light of marifet. Thou art empty of wisdom for the reason That thou art replete with food up to the nose.

Story 23

A man had by his sins forfeited the divine favour but the lamp of grace nevertheless so shone upon his path that it guided him into the circle of religious men and, by the blessing of his association with dervishes, as well as by the example of their righteousness, the depravities of his character were transmuted into virtues and he refrained from lust and passion.

But the tongues of the malevolent were lengthened with reference to his character, alleging that it was the same as it had ever been and that his abstinence and piety were spurious.

By apology and penitence one may be saved from the wrath of God But cannot be saved from the tongues of men.

He could no longer bear the reviling tongues and complained to the pir of the Tariqat. The sheikh wept and said: `How wilt thou be able to be sufficiently grateful for this divine favour that thou art better than the people imagine?'

How long wilt thou say: `The malevolent and envious Are searching out the defects of my humble self. Sometimes they arise to shed my blood. Sometimes they sit down to curse me.' To be good and to be in spoken of by the people Is better than to be bad and considered good by them.

Look at me whom the good opinion of our contemporaries deems to be perfect whereas I am imperfection itself.

If I were doing what I speak I would be of good conduct and a devotee.

Verily I am veiled from the eyes of my neighbours But Allah knows my secret and my overt concerns.

The door is locked to the access of people That they may not spread out my faults. What profiteth a closed door? The Omniscient Knows what I conceal or reveal.

Story 24

I complained to one of the sheikhs that a certain man had falsely accused me of lasciviousness. He replied: `Put him to shame by thy good conduct.'

Be thou well behaved that a maligner May not find occasion to speak of thy faults. When the harp is in proper tune How can the hand of the musician correct it?

Story 25

One of the sheikhs of Syria, being asked on the true state of the Sufis, replied: `In former times they were a tribe in the world, apparently distressed, but in reality contented whereas today they are people outwardly satisfied but inwardly discontented.'

If my heart roams away from thee every hour, Thou wilt find no tranquillity in solitude But if thou possessest property, dignity, fields and wares, If thy heart be with God, thou wilt be a recluse.

Story 26

I remember having once walked all night with a caravan and then slept on the edge of the desert. A distracted man who had accompanied us on that journey raised a shout, ran towards the desert and took not a moment's rest. When it was daylight, I asked him what state of his that was. He replied: `I saw bulbuls commencing to lament on the trees, the partridges on the mountains, the frogs in the water and the beasts in the desert so I bethought myself that it would not be becoming for me to sleep in carelessness while they all were praising God.'

Yesterday at dawn a bird lamented, Depriving me of sense, patience, strength and consciousness. One of my intimate friends who Had perhaps heard my distressed voice Said: `I could not believe that thou Wouldst be so dazed by a bird's cry.' I replied: `It is not becoming to humanity That I should be silent when birds chant praises.'

Story 27

It once happened that on a journey to the Hejaz a company of young and pious men, whose sentiments harmonized with mine, were my fellow-travellers. They occasionally sung and recited spiritual verses but we had with us also an a'bid, who entertained a bad opinion of the behaviour of the dervishes and was ignorant of their sufferings. When we reached the palm-grove of the Beni Hallal, a black boy of the encampment, falling into a state of excitement, broke out in a strain which brought down the birds from the sky. I saw, however, the camel of the a'bid, which began to prance, throwing him and running into the desert.

Knowest thou what that matutinal bulbul said to me? What man art thou to be ignorant of love? The Arabic verses threw a camel into ecstasy and joy. If thou hast no taste thou art an ill-natured brute. When a camel's head is turned by the frenzy of joy And a man does not feel it, he must be an ass.

When the winds blow over the plain The branches of the ban-tree bend, not hard rocks.

Whatever thou beholdest chants his praises. He knows this who has the true perception. Not only the bulbul on the rosebush sings praises But every bramble is a tongue, extolling him.

Story 28

The life of a king was drawing to a close and he had no successor. He ordered in his last testament that the next morning after his death the first person entering the gate of the city be presented with the royal crown and be entrusted with the government of the realm. It so happened that the first person who entered was a mendicant who had all his life subsisted on the morsels he collected and had sewn patch after patch upon his clothes.

The pillars of the state and grandees of the court executed the injunction of the king and bestowed upon him the government and the treasures; whereon the dervish reigned for a while until some amirs of the monarchy withdrew their necks from his obedience and kings from every side began to rise for hostilities and to prepare their armies for war. At last his own troops and subjects also rebelled and deprived him of a portion of his dominions. This event afflicted the mind of the dervish until one of his old friends, who had been his companion when he was yet himself a dervish, returned from a journey and, seeing him in such an exalted position, said: 'Thanks be to God the most high and glorious that thy rose has thus come forth from the thorn and thy thorn was extracted from thy foot. Thy high luck has aided thee and prosperity with fortune has guided thee till thou hast attained this position. Verily hardship is followed by comfort.'

A flower is sometimes blooming and sometimes withering. A tree is at times nude and at times clothed.

He replied: `Brother, condole with me because there is no occasion for congratulation. When thou sawest me last, I was distressed for bread and now a world of distress has overwhelmed me.'

If I have no wealth I grieve. If I have some the love of it captivates me. There is no greater calamity than worldly goods. Both their possession and their want are griefs.

If thou wishest for power, covet nothing Except contentment which is sufficient happiness. If a rich man pours gold into thy lap Care not a moment for thanking him. Because often I heard great men say The patience of a dervish is better than the gift of a rich man.

Story 29

A man had a friend, who held the office of devan to the padshah, but whom he had not seen for a long time; and, a man having asked him for the reason, he replied: `I do not want to see him.' A dependent however of the devan, who also happened to be present, queried: 'What fault has he committed that thou art unwilling to meet him?' He replied: `There is no fault in the matter but a friend who is a devan may be seen when he is removed from office.'

Whilst in greatness and in the turmoil of busines They do not like to be troubled by neighbours But when they are depressed and removed from office They will lay open their heart's grief to friends.

Story 30

Abu Harirah, may the approbation of Allah be upon him, was in the habit of daily waiting upon the Mustafa, peace on him, who said: 'Abu Harira, visit me on alternate days that our love may increase.' A man said to a devotee: `Beautiful as the sun is, I never heard that anybody took it for a friend or fell in love with it', and he replied: `This is because it may be seen daily, except in winter when it is veiled and beloved.'

There is no harm in visiting people But not till they say: `It is enough!' If thou findest fault with thyself Thou wilt not hear others reproaching thee.

Story 31

A man, being tormented story by a contrary wind in his belly and not having the power to retain it, unwittingly allowed it to escape. He said: `Friends, I had no option in what I did, the fault of it is not to be ascribed to me and peace has resulted to my internal parts. Kindly excuse me.'

The belly is a prison of wind, O wise man. No sage retains wind in captivity. If wind twists thy belly let it out Because wind in the belly is a burden to the heart.

Story 32

Having become tired of my friends in Damascus, I went into the desert of Jerusalem and associated with animals till the time when I became a prisoner of the Franks, who put me to work with infidels in digging the earth of a moat in Tarapolis, when one of the chiefs of Aleppo, with whom I had formerly been acquainted, recognized me and said: `What state is this?' I recited: `I fled from men to mountain and desert Wishing to attend upon no one but God. Imagine what my state at present is When I must be satisfied in a stable of wretches.

The feet in chains with friends Is better than to be with strangers in a garden.'

He took pity on my state and ransomed me for ten dinars from the captivity of the Franks, taking me to Aleppo where he had a daughter and married me to her with a dowry of one hundred dinars. After some time had elapsed, she turned out to be ill-humoured, quarrelsome, disobedient, abusive in her tongue and embittering my life:

A bad wife in a good man's house Is his hell in this world already. Alas for a bad consort, alas! Preserve us, O Lord from the punishment of fire.

Once she lengthened her tongue of reproach and said: `Art thou not the man whom my father purchased from the Franks for ten dinars?' I replied: `Yes, he bought me for ten dinars and sold me into thy hands for one hundred dinars.'

I heard that a sheep had by a great man Been rescued from the jaws and the power of a wolf. In the evening he stroked her throat with a knife Whereon the soul of the sheep complained thus: Thou hast snatched me away from the claws of a wolf, But at last I see thou art thyself a wolf.'

Story 33

A padshah asked a hermit: `How spendest thou thy precious time?' He replied: `I am all night engaged in prayer, during the morning in supplications and the rest of the day in restricting my expenses.' Then the king ordered a sufficient allowance to be allotted to him so as to relieve him of the cares of his family.

O thou who art encumbered with a family, Think no more of ever enjoying freedom. Cares for children, raiment and food Restrain thee from the heavenly kingdom. Every day I renew my determination To wait upon God until the night. In the night, while tying the knot of prayer, I think what my children will eat on the morrow.

Story 34

A man, professing to be a hermit in the desert of Syria, attended for years to his devotions and subsisted on the leaves of trees. A padshah, who had gone in that direction by way of pilgrimage, approached him and said: `If thou thinkest proper, we shall prepare a place for thee in the town where thou wilt enjoy leisure for thy devotions and others may profit by thy spiritual advice as well as imitate thy good works.' The hermit refused compliance but the pillars of the State were of opinion that, in order to please the king, he ought to spend a few days in town to ascertain the state of the place; so that if he feared that the purity of his precious time might become turbid by association with strangers, he would still have the option to refuse compliance. It is related that the hermit entered the town where a private garden-house of the king, which was a heart-expanding and soul refreshing locality, had been prepared to receive him.

Its red roses were like the cheeks of belles, Its hyacinths like the ringlets of mistresses Protected from the inclemency of mid-winter Like sucklings who have not yet tasted the nurse's milk.

And branches with pomegranates upon them: Fire suspended from the green-trees.

The king immediately sent him a beautiful slave-girl: After beholding this hermit-deceiving crescent-moon Of the form of an angel and the beauty of a peacock, After seeing her it would be impossible To an anchorite's nature to remain patient.

After her he sent likewise a slave-boy of wonderful beauty and graceful placidity: People around him are dying with thirst And he, who looks like a cupbearer, gives no drink.

The sight cannot be satisfied by seeing him Like the dropsical man near the Euphrates.

The hermit began to eat delicious food, to wear nice clothes, to enjoy fruit and perfumed confectionery as well as to contemplate the beauty of the slave-boy and girl in conformity with the maxim of wise men, who have said that the curls of belles are fetters to the feet of the intellect and a snare to a sagacious bird.

In thy service I lost my heart and religion with all my learning, I am indeed the sagacious bird and thou the snare.

In short, the happiness of his former time of contentedness had come to an end, as the saying is: Any faqih, pir and murid Or pure minded orator, Descending into the base world, Sticks in the honey like a fly.

Once the king desired to visit him but saw the hermit changed from his former state, as he had become red, white and corpulent. When the king entered, he beheld him reclining on a couch of gold brocade whilst the boy and the fairy stood near his head with a fan of peacocks' feathers. He expressed pleasure to behold the hermit in so comfortable a position, conversed with him on many topics and said at the conclusion of the visit: `I am afraid of these two classes of men in the world: scholars and hermits.' The vezier, who was a philosopher and experienced in the affairs of the world, being present, said: `O king, the conditions of friendship require thee to do good to both classes. Bestow gold upon scholars that they may read more but give nothing to hermits that they may remain hérmits.'

A hermit requires neither dirhems nor dinars. If lie takes any, find another hermit.

Who has a good behaviour and a secret with God Is an anchorite without the waqfbread or begged morsel.

With a handsome figure and heart-ravishing ear-tip A girl is a belle without turquoise-ring or pendants.

A dervish of good behaviour and of happy disposition Requires not the bread of the rebat nor the begged morsel. A lady endowed with a beauteous form and chaste face Requires no paint, adornment or turquoise-ring.

When I have and covet more It will not be proper to call me an anchorite.

Story 35

In conformity with the above sentiments an affair of importance emerged to a padshah, who thereon vowed that, if it terminated according to his wishes, he would present devotees with a certain sum of money. His wish having been fulfilled, it became necessary to keep his promise. Accordingly he gave a purse of dirhems to one of his confidential servants to distribute it among recluses. It is related that the slave was intelligent and shrewd. He walked about all day and returning at nightfall, kissed the dirhems and deposited them before the king with the remark that he had not found any devotees. The king rejoined: `What nonsense is this? As far as I know there are four hundred devotees in this town. He said: `Lord of the world, who is a devotee does not accept money and who accepts it is not a devotee.' The king smiled and said to his courtiers: `Despite of my wishing to do good to this class of worshippers of God, this rogue bears them emnity and thwarts my wish but truth is on his side.'

If a devotee has taken dirhems and dinars Find another who is more a devotee than he.

Story 36

One of the ulemma of solid learning, having been asked for his opinion about waqfbread, answered: `If it be accepted to insure tranquillity of mind from cares for food and to obtain leisure for devotion, it is lawful but if it be taken for maintenance it is forbidden.'

Bread is taken for the corner of devotion By pious men and not the corner of devotion for bread.

Story 37

A dervish arrived in a place, the owner of which was of a noble disposition, and had surrounded himself with a company of distinguished and eloquent men, each of whom uttered something elegant or jocular, according to the fashion of wits. The dervish who had travelled through the desert and was fatigued had eaten nothing. One of the company asked him by way of encouragement likewise to say something. The dervish replied: `I do not possess distinction and eloquence like you and have read nothing so you must be satisfied with one distich of mine.' The company having agreed with pleasure he recited: `I am hungry and opposite to a table of food Like a bachelor at the door of a bath of females.'

The company, having thus been apprised of his famished condition, produced a table with bread but as he began to eat greedily the host said: `Friend, at any rate stop a while till my servants roast some minced meat'; whereon the dervish lifted his head and recited: `Do not order pounded meat for my table. To a pounded man simple bread is pounded meat.'

Story 38

A murid said to his pir: `What am I to do? I am troubled by the people, many of whom pay me visits. By their coming and going they encroach upon my precious time.' He replied: `Lend something to every one of them who is poor and ask something from every one who is rich and they will come round thee no more.'

If a mendicant were the leader of the army of Islam, The infidels would for fear of his importunity run as far as China.

Story 39

The son of a faqih said to his father: 'These heart-ravishing words of moralists make no impression upon me because I do not see that their actions are in conformity with their speeches.'

They teach people to abandon the world But themselves accumulate silver and corn. A scholar who only preaches and nothing more Will not impress anyone when he speaks. He is a scholar who commits no evil, Not he who speaks to men but acts not himself. Will you enjoin virtue to mankind and forget your own souls? A scholar who follows his lusts and panders to his body Is himself lost although he may show the way.

The father replied: 'My son, it is not proper merely on account of this vain fancy to turn away the face from the instruction of advisers, to travel on the road of vanity, to accuse the ullemma of aberration, and whilst searching for an immaculate scholar, to remain excluded from the benefits of knowledge, like a blind man who one night fell into the mud and shouted: "O Musalmans, hold a lamp on my path." Whereon a courtesan who heard him asked: "As thou canst not see the lamp, what wilt thou see with the lamp?" In the same way the preaching assembly is like the shop of a dealer in linen because if thou bringest no money thou canst obtain no wares and if thou bringest no inclination to the assembly thou wilt not get any felicity.'

He said: 'Listen with thy soul's ear to a scholar Although his actions may not be like his doctrines.' In vain does the gainsayer ask: 'How can a sleeper awaken a sleeper? A man must receive into his ears The advice although it be written on a wall.' A pious man came to the door of a college from a monastery. He broke the covenant of the company of those of the Tariq. I asked him what the difference between a scholar and a monk amounts to? He replied: 'The former saves his blanket from the waves Whilst the latter strives to save the drowning man.'

Story 40

A man was sleeping dead-drunk on the highway and the bridle of spontaneity had slipped from his hands. A hermit passed near him and considered the disgraceful condition he was in. The youth raised his head and recited: When they passed near something contemptible, they passed it kindly. When thou beholdest a sinner be concealing and meek.

Turn not thy face from a sinner, O anchorite. Look upon him with benignity. If I am ignoble in my actions Pass me by like a noble fellow.

Story 41

A company of vagabonds met a dervish, spoke insulting words to him, struck him and otherwise molested him; whereon he complained to his superior and explained the case. The pir replied: `My son, the patched frock of dervishes is the garment of resignation and who, wearing it, cannot bear injuries is a pretender not entitled to the frock.'

A large river will not become turbid from stones. The Arif who feels aggrieved is shallow water yet.

If he injures thee, bear it Because pardon will purify thee from sin. O brother, as the end is dust, be dust before thou art turned into dust.

Story 42

Listen to this story how in Baghdad A flag and a curtain fell into dispute. Travel stained, dusty and fatigued, the flag Said to the curtain by way of reproach: `I and thou, we are both fellow servants, Slaves of the sultan's palace. Not a moment had I rest from service In season and out of season I travelled about. Thou hast suffered neither toil nor siege, Not from the desert, wind, nor dust and dirt. My step in the march is more advancing. Then why is thy honour exceeding mine? Thou art upon moon-faced servants Or jessamine scented slave girls. I have fallen into prentice hands. I travel with foot in fetters and head fluttering.' The curtain said: `My head is on the threshold Not like thine in the heavens. Who carelessly lifts up his neck Throws himself upon his neck.'

Story 43

A pious man saw an acrobat in great dudgeon, full of wrath and foaming at the mouth. He asked: `What is the matter with this fellow?' A bystander said: `Someone has insulted him.' He remarked: 'This base wretch is able to lift a thousand mann of stones and has not the power to bear one word.'

Abandon thy claim to strength and manliness. Thou art weak-minded and base, whether thou be a man or woman. If thou art able, make a sweet mouth. It is not manliness to strike the fist on a mouth.

Although able to tear up an elephant's front He is not a man who possessed no humanity. A man's nature is of earth. If he is not humble he is not a man.

Story 44

I asked a good man concerning the qualities of the brethren of purity. He replied: `The least of them is that they prefer to please their friends rather than themselves; and philosophers have said that a brother who is fettered by affairs relating to himself is neither a brother nor a relative.'

If thy fellow traveller hastens, he is not thy fellow. Tie not thy heart to one whose heart is not tied to thine. When a kinsman possesses no virtue and piety Then severing connection is better than love of kinship.

I remember that an opponent objected to the last two lines, saying: `God the most high and glorious has in his noble book prohibited the severing of connection with relatives and has commanded us to love them. What thou hast alleged is contrary to it.' I replied: `Thou art mistaken because according to the Quran, Allah the most high has said: If they both father and mother, strive to induce thee to associate with me that concerning which thou hast no knowledge, obey them not.

A thousand kinsmen who are strangers to God Are the sacrifice for one stranger who knows him.

Story 45

A kind old man in Baghdad Gave his daughter to a cobbler. The cruel little man so bit her That blood flowed from the daughter's lips. Next morning the father saw her thus And going to the bridegroom asked him: `O mean wretch, what teeth are these? Chewest thou thus her lips? They are not leather. I do not say these words in jest, Leave joking off and enjoy her seriously. If ill humour becomes fixed in a nature It will not leave it till the time of death.'

Story 46

A faqih had a very ugly daughter and when she attained puberty no one was inclined to marry her in spite of her dowry and wealth.

Bad is the brocade and damask cloth Which is upon an ugly bride. At last it became necessary to marry her to a blind man and it is related that on the said occasion a physician arrived from Serandip who was able to restore sight to the blind. The faqih, being asked why he had not put his son-in-law under treatment, replied: `I fear that if he is able to see he will divorce my daughter.' It is better if the husband of an ugly woman is blind.

Story 47

A padshah was casting a glanced of contempt upon a company of dervishes and one of them, understanding by his sagacity the meaning of it, said: `O king, in this world we are inferior to thee in dignity but more happy in life. In death we are equal and in the resurrection superior to thee.'

Though the master of a country may have enjoyment And the dervish may be in need of bread In that hour when both of them will die They will take from the world not more than a shroud. When thou takest thy departure from the realm It will be better to be a mendicant than a padshah.

Externally the dervish shows a patched robe and a shaved head but in reality his heart is living and his lust dead.

He does not sit at the door of pretence away from people To fight against them if they oppose him Because when a millstone rolls from a mountain He is not an A'rif who gets out of the way of the stone.

The way of dervishes is praying, gratitude, service, obedience, almsgiving, contentment, professing the unity of God, trust, submission and patience. Whoever possesses these qualities is really a dervish, although he may wear an elegant robe, whereas a prattler who neglects his orisons, is luxurious, sensual, turns day into night in the bondage of lust, and night into day in the sleep of carelessness, eats whatever he gets, and speaks whatever comes upon his tongue, is a profligate, although he may wear the habit of a dervish. O thou whose interior is denuded of piety But wearest outwardly the garb of hypocrisy Do not display a curtain of seven colours. Thou hast reed mats inside thy house.

Story 48

I saw bouquets of fresh roses Tied upon a cupola of grass. I asked: `What is despicable grass To sit also in the line of the roses?' The grass wept and said: `Hush! Companionship does not obliterate nobility. Although I have no beauty, colour and perfume, Am I not after all the grass of his garden? I am the slave of a bountiful lord, Cherished from old by his liberality. Whether I possess virtue or not I hope for grace from the Lord Although I possess no property No capital to offer as obedience. He knows the remedy for the slave To whom no support remains. It is customary that the owner gives a writ Of emancipation to an old slave. O God, who hast adorned the universe, Be bountiful to thy old slave.' Sa`di, take the road to the Ka'bah of submission. O man of God, follow the way of God. Unlucky is he who turns his head Away from this door for he will find no other door.

Story 49

A sage having been asked whether liberality or bravery is better replied: `He who possesses liberality needs no bravery.' It is written on the tomb of Behram Gur: `A liberal hand is better than a strong arm.' Hatim Tai has passed away but for ever His high name will remain celebrated for beneficence. Set aside the zekat from thy property because the exuberant vines When pruned by the vintner will yield more grapes.

ON THE EXCELLENCE OF CONTENTMENT

Story 1

A Maghrabi supplicant said in Aleppo in the row of linen-drapers: 'Lords of wealth, if you were just and we contented, the trade of begging would vanish from the world.' O contentment, make me rich For besides thee no other wealth exists. Loqman selected the corner of patience. Who has no patience has no wisdom.

Story 2

Two sons of amirs were in Egypt, the one acquiring science, the other accumulating wealth, till the former became the ullemma of the period and the other the prince of Egypt; whereon the rich man looked with contempt upon the faqih and said: `I have reached the sultanate whilst thou hast remained in poverty as before.'

He replied: `O brother, I am bound to be grateful to the most high Creator for having obtained the inheritance of prophets whilst thou hast attained the inheritance of Pharaoh and of Haman, namely the kingdom of Egypt.'

I am that ant which is trodden under foot Not that wasp, the pain of whose sting causes lament. How shall I give due thanks for the blessing That I do not possess the strength of injuring mankind?

Story 3

I heard that a dervish, burning in the fire of poverty and sewing patch upon patch, said to comfort his mind: `We are contented with dry bread and a patched robe For it is easier to bear the load of one's own trouble than that of thanks to others.'

Someone said to him: `Why sittest thou? A certain man in this town possesses a benevolent nature, is liberal to all, has girded his loins to serve the pious and is ready to comfort every heart. If he becomes aware of thy case, he will consider it an obligation to comfort the mind of a worthy person.' He replied: `Hush! It is better to die of inanition than to plead for one's necessities before any man.'

It is better to patch clothes and sit in the corner of patience Than to write petitions for robes to gentlemen. Verily it is equal to the punishment of hell To go to paradise as a flunkey to one's neighbour.

Story 4

One of the kings of Persia had sent an able physician to wait upon the Mustafa, the benediction of Allah and peace be on him; and he remained for some years in the Arab country without anyone coming to him to make a trial of his ability or desiring to be treated by him. He went to the Prophet, salutation to him, and complained that although he had been sent to treat the companions, none of them had up to this time taken notice of him or required the services incumbent upon him. The Apostle, salutation to him, replied: `It is a law with these people not to eat until appetite overpowers them and when some of it yet remains they withdraw their hands from food.' The doctor said: `This is the cause of health', and kissing the earth of service departed.

The sage begins to speak Or points his fingers to the dish When silence would be dangerous Or abstinance would bring on death. No doubt his wisdom is in speaking And his eating bears the fruit of health.

Story 5

A man often made vows of repentance but broke them again till one of the sheikhs said to him: `I think thou art in the habit of eating a great deal and that thy power of restraining appetite is more slender than a hair, whilst an appetite such as thou nourishest would rupture a chain and a day may come when it will tear thee up.'

A man brought up a wolf's whelp. When it was brought up it tore him up.

Story 6

It is narrated in the life of Ardeshir Babekan that he asked an Arab physician how much food he must consume daily. He replied: `The weight of one hundred dirhems will be enough.' The king queried: 'What strength will this quantity give me?' He replied: `This quantity will carry thee, and whatever is more than that, thou wilt be the carrier of it.'

Eating is for living and praying. Thou thinkest living is for eating.

Story 7

Two Khorasani dervishes travelled together. One of them, being weak, broke his fast every second night whilst the other who was strong consumed every day three meals. It happened that they were captured at the gate of a town on suspicion of being spies; whereon each of them was confined in a closet and the aperture of it walled up with mud bricks. After two weeks it became known that they were guiltless. Accordingly the doors were opened and the strong man was found to be dead whilst the weak fellow had remained alive. The people were astonished but a sage averred that the contrary would have been astonishing because one of them having been voracious possessed no strength to suffer hunger and perished whilst the other who was abstemious merely persevered in his habit and remained safe.

When eating little has become the nature of a man He takes it easy when a calamity befalls him But when the body becomes strong in affluence He will die when a hardship overtakes him.

Story 8

One of the philosophers forbade his son to eat much because repletion keeps people ailing. The boy replied: `O father, it is hunger that kills. Hast thou not heard of the maxim of the ingenious that it is better to die satiated than to bear hunger?' He rejoined: `Be moderate. Eat and drink but not to excess.'

Eat not so much that it comes up to thy mouth Nor so little that from weakness thy soul comes up.

Although maintenance of life depends upon food Victuals bring on disease when eaten to excess. If thou eatest rose-confectionery without appetite it injures thee But eating dry bread after a long fast is like rose-preserve.

Story 9

A sick man having been asked what his heart desired replied: `That it may not desire anything.'

When the bowels are full and the belly pains There is no use in all other things being right.

Story 10

A grain dealer to whom Sufis were owing some money asked them for it every day in the town of Waset and used harsh language towards them. The companions had become weary of his reproaches but had no other remedy than to bear them; and one of them who was a pious man remarked: `It is more easy to pacify a hungry stomach with promises of food than a grain dealer with promises of money.'

It is preferable to be without the bounty of a gentleman Than to bear the insults of the gate-keepers. It is better to die wishing for meat Than to endure the expostulations of butchers.

Story 11

A brave warrior who had received a dreadful wound in the Tatar war was informed that a certain merchant possessed a medicine which he would probably not refuse to give if asked for; but it is related that the said merchant was also well known for his avarice.

If instead of bread he had the sun in his table-cloth No one could see daylight till the day of resurrection.

The warrior replied: `If I ask for the medicine he will either give it or refuse it and if he gives it maybe it will profit me, and maybe not. At any rate the inconvenience of asking it from him is a lethal poison.'

Whatever thou obtainest by entreaties from base men Will profit thy body but injure thy soul.

And philosophers have said: `If for instance the water of life were to be exchanged for a good reputation, no wise man would purchase it because it is preferable to die with honour than to live in disgrace.'

To eat coloquinth from the hand of a sweet-tempered man Is better than confectionery from the hand of an ill-humoured fellow.

Story 12

One of the ullemma had many eaters to provide for and only a slender income. This fact he communicated to a great man of whose character he entertained a very favourable opinion but his expectations were disappointed because the man made a wry face and averred that according to his opinion applications from respectable persons for aid are unbecoming.

With a face made sad by misfortune, to a dear friend Do not go because thou wilt embitter his life also. For the needful for which thou appliest, go with a fresh and smiling face. The man of joyful countenance will not be unsuccessful in his affairs.

It is related that the great man augmented his stipend a little but considerably diminished his familiarity towards him and when he perceived after some days that it was not as usual, he recited:

`Evil is the food which the time of degradation acquires. The kettle is indeed placed but the dignity is lowered.'

He increased my bread but diminished my honour. Poverty is better than the degradation of asking.

Story 13

A dervish wanted something and a man told him that a certain individual possessed untold wealth who, if he were made aware of his want, would not consider it proper to fail in supplying it forthwith. The dervish answering that he had no acquaintance with him, the man proposed to show him the house and when the dervish entered he caught sight of a person with hanging lips and sitting morosely. He returned immediately and being asked what he had done replied: `I excused him from making me a present when I saw his face.' Carry not thy necessity to a sour-faced fellow Because his ill-humour will crush thy hopes. If thou confidest thy heart's grief, tell it to one Whose face will comfort thee like ready cash.

Story 14

A year of dearth set in at Alexandria so that even a dervish lost the reins of patience from his hands, the pearls of heaven were withheld from the earth and the lamentations of mankind ascended to the firmament.

There was no wild beast, fowl, fish or ant Whose wailings prompted by distress had not reached the sky. For a wonder the heart-smoke of the people did not condense To form clouds and the torrents of their tears rain.

In such a year there was an hermaphrodite. I owe it to my friends not to describe him because it would be an abandonment of good manners, especially in the presence of great men. On the other hand, it would likewise be improper and in the way of negligence not to mention anything about him because certain people would impute it to the ignorance of the narrator. Accordingly I shall briefly describe him in the following two distichs because a little indicates much and a handful is a sample of a donkey load.

If a Tatar slays that hermaphrodite The Tatar must not be slain in return.

How long will he be like the bridge of Baghdad With water flowing beneath and men on the back?

Such a man, a portion of whose eulogy thou hast now heard, possessed in that year boundless wealth, bestowed silver and gold upon the needy and laid out tables for travellers. A company of dervishes who were by the presence of distress on the point of starvation were inclined to accept of his hospitality and consulted me on the subject but I struck my head back from assenting and replied:

A lion does not eat the half of which a dog consumed Although he may die of hunger in his lair. Though getting rich in wealth and property like Feridun A worthless man is to be considered of no account.

Story 15

Hatim Tai, having been asked whether he had seen in the world anyone of more exalted sentiments than himself, replied: 'Yes, one day I slaughtered forty camels to entertain Arab amirs. I had occasion to go out on some business into a corner of the desert, where I noticed a gatherer of briars, who had accumulated a hillock of thistles, and I asked him why he had not become a guest of Hatim since many people had come round to his banquet but he replied: "Who eats bread by the work of his own hand Will not bear to be obliged to Hatim Tai."

Then I saw that his sentiments were more exalted than mine.'

Story 16

Moses, to whom be salutation, beheld a dervish who had on account of his nudity concealed himself in the sand exclaiming: `O Moses, utter a supplication to God the most high to give me an allowance because I am, on account of my distress, on the point of starvation.' Moses accordingly prayed and departed but returning a few days afterwards he saw that the dervish was a prisoner and surrounded by a crowd of people. On asking for the reason he was informed that the dervish had drunk wine, quarrelled, slain a man and was to be executed in retaliation. If the humble cat possessed wings He would rob the world of every sparrow-egg. It may happen that when a weak man obtains power He arises and twists the hands of the weak.

And if Allah were to bestow abundance upon his servants, they would certainly rebel upon earth.

What has made thee wade into danger, O fool, Till thou hast perished. Would that the ant had not been able to fly!

When a base fellow obtains dignity, silver and gold, His head necessarily demands to be knocked. Was not after all this maxim uttered by a sage? `That ant is the best which possesses no wings.'

The heavenly father has plenty of honey but the son has a hot disease.

He who does not make thee rich Knows better what is good for thee than thyself.

Story 17

I noticed an Arab of the desert sitting in a company jewellers at Bosrah and narrating stories to them. He said: `I had once lost my road in the desert and consumed all my provisions. I considered that I must perish when I suddenly caught sight of a bag full of pearls and I shall never forget the joy and ecstasy I felt on thinking they might be parched grain nor the bitterness and despair when I discovered them to be pearls.'

In a dry desert and among moving sand It is the same to a thirsty man whether he has pearls or shells in his mouth. When a man has no provisions and his strength is exhausted It matters not whether his girdle is adorned with pearls or potsherds.

Story 18

An Arab suffering in the desert from extreme thirst recited:

`Would that before my death I could one day enjoy my wish That a river's waves might strike my knee And I might fill my water-bag.'

In the same manner another traveller lost himself in an extensive region having neither any strength nor food left but he possessed some money and roamed about and the road leading him nowhere he perished from exhaustion. Some people afterwards discovered his corpse with the money in front of it and the following written on the ground:

If possessed of all the Ja'feri gold, It will avail nothing to a hungry man. To a poor man burnt in the desert Boiled turnips are more valuable than pure silver.

Story 19

I never lamented about the vicissitudes of time or complained of the turns of fortune except on the occasion when I was barefooted and unable to procure slippers. But when I entered the great mosque of Kufah with a sore heart and beheld a man without feet I offered thanks to the bounty of God, consoled myself for my want of shoes and recited:

`A roast fowl is to the sight of a satiated man Less valuable than a blade of fresh grass on the table And to him who has no means nor power A burnt turnip is a roasted fowl.'

Story 20

A king with some of his courtiers had during a hunting party and in the winter season strayed far from inhabited places but when the night set in he perceived the house of a dehqan and said: `We shall spend the night there to avoid the injury of the cold.' One of the veziers, however, objected alleging that it was unworthy of the high dignity of a padshah to take refuge in the house of a dehqan and that it would be best to pitch tents and to light fires on the spot. The dehqan who had become aware of what was taking place prepared some food he had ready in his house, offered it, kissed the ground of service and said: `The high dignity of the sultan would not have been so much lowered, but the courtiers did not wish the dignity of the dehqan to become high.' The king who was pleased with these words moved for the night into the man's house and bestowed a dress of honour upon him the next morning. When he accompanied the king a few paces at the departure he was heard to say:

`Nothing was lost of the sultan's power and pomp By accepting the hospitality of a dehqan, But the corner of the dehqan's cap reached the sun When a sultan such as thou overshadowed his head.'

Story 21

It is related that a sultan thus addressed a miserly beggar who had accumulated great riches: `It is evident that thou possessest boundless wealth and we have an affair on hand in which thou canst aid us by way of a loan. When the finances of the country are in a flourishing condition it will be repaid.' The miser replied: `It is not befitting the power and dignity of a padshah to soil the hands of his noble aspirations with the property of an individual like myself who has collected it grain by grain.' The king replied: `It does not matter because the money will be spent upon infidels: The wicked women should be joined to the wicked men."

If the water of a Christian's well is impure What matters it if thou washest a dead Jew therein?

They said: `The lime-mortar is not clean.' We replied: `We shall plug therewith the privy holes."

I heard that he refused to comply with the behest of the king, began to argue and to look insolently; whereon the king ordered the sum in question to be released from his grasp by force and with a reprimand.

If an affair cannot be accomplished with gentleness He forsooth turns his head to impudence. Who has no regard for himself It is proper that no one should pay him any.

Story 22

I met a trader who possessed one hundred and fifty camel loads of merchandise with forty slaves and servants. One evening in the oasis of Kish he took me into his apartment and taking all night no rest kept up an incoherent gabble, saying: `I have such and such a warehouse in Turkestan, such and such goods in Hindostan; this is the title-deed of such and such an estate and in this affair such and such a man is security.' He said: `I intend to go to Alexandria because it has a good climate', and correcting himself continued: 'No, because the African sea is boisterous. O Sa`di, I have one journey more to undertake and after performing it I shall during the rest of my life sit in a corner and enjoy contentment.' I asked: `What journey is that?' He replied: `I shall carry Persian brimstone to China because I heard that it fetched a high price. I shall also carry Chinese porcelain to Rum and Rumi brocade to India and Indian steel to Aleppo, convey glass-ware of Aleppo to Yemen, striped cloth of Yemen to Pares. After that I shall abandon trading and shall sit down in a shop.' He had talked so much of this nonsenses that no more strength remained in him so he said: `O Sa`di, do thou also tell me something of what thou hast seen and heard.' I recited:

`Thou mayest have heard that in the plain of Ghur Once a leader fell down from his beast of burden, Saying: ``The narrow eye of a wealthy man Will be filled either by content or by the earth of the tomb."'

Story 23

I heard about a wealthy man who was as well known for his avarice as Hatim Tai for his liberality. Outwardly he displayed the appearance of wealth but inwardly his sordid nature was so dominant that he would not for his life give a morsel of bread to anyone or bestow a scrap upon the kitten of Abu Harirah or throw a bone to the dog of the companions of the cave. In short, no one had seen the door of his house open or his table-doth spread. The dervish got nothing of his food except the smell. The fowl picked up the crumbs after his bread-dinner.

I heard that he was sailing in the Mediterranean with the pride of Pharaoh in his head -- according to the words of the most high, Until drowning overtook him -- when all of a sudden a contrary wind befell the ship, as it is said: What can thy heart do to thy distressed nature for the wind is not fair? It is not at all times suitable for a ship.

He uplifted the hands of supplication and began to lament in vain but Allah the most high has commanded: When they sail in a ship they call upon Allah, sincerely exhibiting unto him their religion.

Of what use is the hand of supplication to a needy worshipper Which is uplifted to God in the time of prayer but in the armpit in the time of bounty? Bestow comfort with gold and with silver And thereby also profit thyself. As this house of thine will remain, Build it with a silver and a gold brick.

It is narrated that he had poor relations in Egypt who became rich by the remainder of his wealth, tearing up their old cloths and cutting new ones of silk and of Damiari. During the same week I also beheld one of them riding a fleet horse with a fairy-faced slave boy at his heels. I said: `Wah! If the dead man were to return Among his kinsfolk and connections The refunding of the inheritance would be more painful To the heirs than the death of their relative.'

On account of the acquaintance which had formerly subsisted between us, I pulled his sleeve, and said: `Eat thou, O virtuous and good man, What that mean fellow gathered and did not eat.'

Story 24

A weak fisherman caught a strong fish in his net and not being able to retain it the fish overcame him and pulled the net from his hand.

A boy went to bring water from the torrent. The torrent came and took the boy away. The net brought every time a fish.

This time the fish went and carried off the net. The other fishermen were sorry and blamed him for not being able to retain such a fish which had fallen into his net. He replied: `O brothers, what can be done? My day was not lucky but the fish had yet one remaining. `Moral: A fisherman cannot catch a fish in the Tigris without a day of luck and a fish cannot die on dry ground without the decree of fate.

Story 25

A man whose hands and feet had been amputated killed a millipede and a pious passer-by exclaimed: `Praised be Allah! In spite of the thousand feet he possessed he could not escape from a man without hands and feet when his fate had overtaken him.' When the life-taking foe comes in the rear Fate ties the legs of a running man. At the moment when the enemy has slowly arrived It is useless to draw the Kayanian bow.

Story 26

I have seen a fat fool, dressed in a costly robe, with a turban of Egyptian linen on his head, riding on an Arab horse. Someone said: 'Sa`di, what thinkest thou of this famous brocade upon this ignorant animal?' I replied: `It is like ugly characters scrawled with gold-water.'

Verily he is like an ass among men, A calf, a body which is bleating.

This animal cannot be said to resemble a man Except in his cloak, turban and outward adornment. Examine all his property and belongings of his estate Thou wilt find nothing lawful to take except his blood. If a noble man becomes impoverished imagine not That his high worth will also decrease. But if into a silver threshold golden nails are driven By a Jew, think not that he will thereby become noble.

Story 27

A thief said to a mendicant: `Art thou not ashamed to stretch out thy hand for a grain of silver to every sordid fellow?' He replied: `To hold out the hand for a grain of silver Is better than to get it cut off for one dane and a half.'

Story 28

It is related that an athlete had been reduced to the greatest distress by adverse fortune. His throat being capacious and his hands unable to fill it, he complained to his father and asked him for permission to travel as he hoped to be hoped to be able to gain a livelihood by the strength of his arm.

Excellence and skill are lost unless exhibited. Lignum aloes is placed on fire and musk rubbed.

The father replied: `My son, get rid of this vain ideá and place the feet of contentment under the skirt of safety because great men have said that happiness does not consist in exertion and that the remedy against want is in the moderation of desires.

No one can grasp the skirt of luck by force. It is useless to put vasmah on a bald man's brow.

If thou hast two hundred accomplishments for each hair of thy head They will be of no use if fortune is unpropitious.

What can an athlete do with adverse luck? The arm of luck is better than the arm of strength.

The son rejoined: `Father, the advantages of travel are many, such as recreation of the mind entailing profit, seeing of wonderful and hearing of strange things, recreation in cities, associating with friends, acquisition of dignity, rank, property, the power of discriminating among acquaintances and gaining experience of the world, as the travellers in the Tariqat have said:

As long as thou walkest about the shop or the house Thou wilt never become a man, 0 raw fellow. Go and travel in the world Before that day when thou goest from the world.'

The father replied: `My son, the advantages of travel such as thou hast enumerated them are countless but they regard especially five classes of men: firstly, a merchant who possesses in consequence of his wealth and power graceful male and female slaves and quick-handed assistants, alights every day in another town and every night in another place, has recreation every moment and sometimes enjoys the delights of the world.'

A rich man is not a stranger in mountain, desert or solitude. Wherever he goes he pitches a tent and makes a sleeping place; Whilst he who is destitute of the goods of this world Must be in his own country a stranger and unknown.

Secondly, a scholar, who is for the pleasantness of his speech, the power of his eloquence and the fund of his instruction, waited upon and honoured wherever he goes.

The presence of a learned man is like pure gold Whose power and price is known wherever he goes. An ignorant fellow of noble descent resembles Shahrua, Which nobody accepts in a foreign country.

Thirdly, handsome fellows with whom the souls of pious men are inclined to commingle because it has been said that a little beauty is better than much wealth. An attractive face is also said to be a slave to despondent hearts and the key to locked doors, wherefore the society of such a person is everywhere known to be very acceptable: A beautiful person meets with honour and respect everywhere Although perhaps driven away in anger by father and mother. I have seen a peacock feather in the leaves of the Quran. I said: `I see thy position is higher than thy deserts.' It said: `Hush, whoever is endowed with beauty, Wherever he places his foot, hands are held out to receive it.'

When a boy is symmetrical and heart-robbing It matters not if his father disowns him. He is a jewel which must not remain in a shell. A precious pearl everyone desires to buy.

Fourthly, one with a sweet voice, who retains, with a David-like throat, water from flowing and birds from soaring. By means of this talent he holds the hearts of people captive and religious men are delighted to associate with him.

My audition is intent on the beautiful melody. Who is that performing on the double chord?

How pleasant is the gentle and melancholy lay To the ear of the boon companions who quaff the morning draught! Better than a handsome face is a pleasant voice. The former is joy to the senses, the latter food for the soul.

Fifthly, the artisan, who gains a sufficient livelihood by the strength of his arm, so that his reputation is not lost in struggling for bread; as wise men have said:

If he goes abroad from his own town The patcher of clothes meets with no bardship or trouble But if the government falls into ruin The king of Nimruz will go to bed hungry.

The qualities which I have explained, 0 my son, are in a journey the occasion of satisfaction to the mind, stimulants to a happy life but he, who possesses none of them, goes with idle fancies into the world and no one will ever hear anything about his name and fame.

He whom the turning world is to afflict Will be guided by the times against his aim. A pigeon destined not to see its nest again Will be carried by fate towards the grain and net.

The son asked: `O father, how can I act contrary to the injunctions of the wise, who have said, that although food is distributed by predestination the acquisition of it depends upon exertion and that, although a calamity may be decreed by fate, it is incumbent on men to show the gates by which it may enter?

`Although daily food may come unawares It is reasonable to seek it out of doors And though no one dies without the decree of fate Thou must not rush into the jaws of a dragon.

`As I am at present able to cope with a mad elephant and to wrestle with a furious lion, it is proper, O father, that I should travel abroad because I have no longer the endurance to suffer misery.

`When a man has fallen from his place and station Why should he eat more grief? All the horizons are his place. At night every rich man goes to an inn. The dervish has his inn where the night overtakes him.'

After saying this, he asked for the good wishes of his father, took leave of him, departed and said to himself:

`A skilful man, when his luck does not favour him, Goes to a place where people know not his name.'

He reached the banks of a water, the force of which was such that it knocked stones against each other and its roaring was heard to a farsang's distance.

A dreadful water, in which even aquatic birds were not safe, The smallest wave would whirl off a millstone from its bank.

He beheld a crowd of people, every person sitting with a coin of money at the crossing-place, intent on a passage. The youth's hands of payment being tied, he opened the tongue of laudation and although he supplicated the people greatly, they paid no attention and said:

`No violence can be done to anyone without money But if thou hast money thou hast no need of force.'

An unkind boatman laughed at him and said: `If thou hast no money thou canst not cross the river by force. What boots the strength of ten men? Bring the money for one.'

The young man's heart was irritated by the insult of the boatman and longed to take vengeance upon him. The boat had, however, started; accordingly he shouted: `If thou wilt be satisfied with the robe I am wearing, I shall not grudge giving it to thee.' The boatman was greedy and turned the vessel back.

Desire sews up the vision of a shrewd man. Greediness brings fowl and fish into the snare.

As soon as the young man's hand could reach the beard and collar of the boatman, he immediately knocked him down and a comrade of the boatman, who came from the vessel to rescue him, experienced the same rough treatment and turned back. The rest of the people then thought proper to pacify the young man and to condone his passage money.

When thou seest a quarrel be forbearing Because gentlemen will shut the door of strife. Use kindness when thou seest contention. A sharp sword cannot cut soft silk. By a sweet tongue, grace, and kindliness, Thou wilt be able to lead an elephant by a hair.

Then the people fell at his feet, craving pardon for what had passed. They impressed some hypocritical kisses upon his head and his eyes, received him into the boat and started, progressing till they reached a pillar of Yunani workmanship, standing in the water. The boatman said: `The vessel is in danger. Let one of you, who is the strongest, go to the pillar and take the cable of the boat that we may save the vessel.' The young man, in the pride of bravery which he had in his head, did not think of the offended foe and did not mind the maxim of wise men who have said: `If thou hast given offence to one man and afterwards done him a hundred kindnesses, do not be confident that he will not avenge himself for that one offence, because although the head of a spear may come out, the memory of an offence will remain in the heart.'

`How well,' said Yaktash to Khiltash, `Hast thou scratched a foe? Do not think thou art safe.'

Be not unconcerned for thou wilt be afflicted If by thy hand a heart has been afflicted. Throw not a stone at the rampart of a fort Because possibly a stone may come from the fort.

As soon as he had taken the rope of the boat on his arm, he climbed to the top of the pillar, whereon the boatman snatched it from his grasp and pushed the boat off. The helpless man was amazed and spent two days in misery and distress. On the third, sleep took hold of his collar and threw him into the water. After one night and day he was cast on the bank, with some life still remaining in him. He began to eat leaves of trees and to pull out roots of grass so that when he had gained a little strength, he turned towards the desert and walked till thirst began to torment him. He at last reached a well and saw people drinking water for a pashizi but possessing none he asked for a coin and showed his destitute condition. The people had, however, no mercy with him, whereon he began to insult them but likewise ineffectually. Then he knocked down several men but was at last overpowered, struck and wounded:

A swarm of gnats will overpower an elephant Despite of all his virility and bravery. When the little ants combine together They tear the skin of a furious lion.

As a matter of necessity he lagged in the rear of the caravan, which reached in the evening a locality very dangerous on account of thieves. The people of the caravan trembled in all their limbs but he said: `Fear nothing because I alone am able to cope with fifty men and the other youths of the caravan will aid me.' These boastful words comforted the heart of the caravan-people, who became glad of his company and considered it incumbent upon themselves to supply him with food and water. The fire of the young man's stomach having blazed into flames and deprived his hands of the bridle of endurance, hunger made him partake of some morsels of food and take a few draughts of water, till the dev of his interior was set at rest and he fell asleep. An experienced old fellow, who was in the caravan, said: `O ye people, I am more afraid of this guard of yours than of the thieves because there is a story that a stranger had accumulated some dirhems but could not sleep in the house for fear of the Luris. Accordingly he invited one of his friends to dispel the terrors of solitude by his company. He spent several nights with him, till he became aware that he had money and took it, going on a journey after spending it. When the people saw the stranger naked and weeping the next morning, a man asked: ``What is the matter? Perhaps a thief has stolen those dirhems of mine?" He replied: ``No, by Allah. The guard has stolen them."'

I never sat secure from a serpent Till I learnt what his custom was. The wound from a foe's tooth is severe Who appears to be a friend in the eyes of men.

`How do you know whether this man is not one of the band of thieves and has followed us as a spy to inform his comrades on the proper occasion? According to my opinion we ought to depart and let him sleep.' The youths approved of the old man's advice and became suspicious of the athlete, took up their baggage and departed, leaving him asleep. He knew this when the sun shone upon his shoulders and perceived that the caravan had started. He roamed about a great deal without finding the way and thirsty as well as dismayed as he was, he sat down on the ground, with his heart ready to perish, saying:

Who will speak to me after the yellow camels have departed? A stranger has no companion except a stranger.

He uses harshness towards strangers Who has not himself been exiled enough.

The poor man was speaking thus whilst the son of a king who happened to be in a hunting party, strayed far from the troops, was standing over his head, listening. He looked at the figure of the athlete, saw that his outward appearance was respectable but his condition miserable. He then asked him whence he had come and how he had fallen into this place.

The athlete briefly informed him of what had taken place, whereon the royal prince, moved by pity, presented him with a robe of honour and a large sum of money and sent a confidential man to accompany him till he again reached his native town. His father was glad to see him and expressed gratitude at his safety. In the evening he narrated to his father what had befallen him with the boat, mentioned the violence of the boatman, the harshness of the rustics near the well and the treachery of the caravan people on the road. The father replied: `My son, have not I told thee at thy departure that the brave hands of empty-handed persons are like the broken paw of a lion?'

How well has that empty-handed fighter said: `A grain of gold is better than fifty mann of strength.'

The son replied: `O father, thou wilt certainly not obtain a treasure except by trouble, wilt not overcome thy foe unless thou hazardest thy life and wilt not gather a harvest unless thou scatterest seed. Perceivest thou not how much comfort I gained at the cost of the small amount of trouble I underwent and what a quantity of honey I have brought in return for the sting I have suffered.

Although not more can be acquired than fate has decreed Negligence in striving to acquire is not commendable.

If a diver fears the crocodile's throat He will never catch the pearl of great price. The nether millstone is immovable, and therefore must bear a heavy load.

What will a fierce lion devour at the bottom of his den? What food does a fallen hawk obtain? If thou desirest to catch game at home Thou must have hands and feet like a spider. The father said to his son: `On this occasion heaven has been propitious to thee and good luck helpful so that a royal person has met thee, has been bountiful to thee and has thereby healed thy broken condition. Such coincidences occur seldom and rare events cannot be reckoned upon.'

The hunter does not catch every time a jackal. It may happen that some day a tiger devours him.

Thus it happened that one of the kings of Pares, who possessed a ring with a costly b^azle, once went out by way of diversion with some intimate courtiers to the Masalla of Shiraz and ordered his ring to be placed on the dome of Asad, promising to bestow the seal-ring upon any person who could make an arrow pass through it. It happened that every one of the four hundred archers in his service missed the ring, except a little boy who was shooting arrows in sport at random and in every direction from the flat roof of a monastery. The morning breeze caused his arrow to pass through the ring, whereon he obtained not only the ring but also a robe of honour and a present of money. It is related that the boy burnt his bow and arrows and on being asked for the cause replied: `That the first splendour may be permanent.'

It sometimes happens that an enlightened sage Is not successful in his plans. Sometimes it happens that an ignorant child By mistake hits the target with his arrow.

Story 29

I heard that a dervish, sitting in a cave, had closed the doors upon the face of the world, so that no regard for kings and rich persons remained in the eyes of his desire.

Who opens to himself a door for begging Will till he dies remain a needy fellow. Abandon greediness and be a king Because a neck without desire is high.

One of the kings of that region sent him the information that, trusting in the good manners of the respected dervish, he hoped he would partake of bread and salt with him. The sheikh agreed because it is according to the sonna to accept an invitation. The next day the king paid him a visit, the a'bid. leapt up, embraced him, caressed him and praised him. After the monarch's departure the sheikh was asked by one of his companions why he had, against his custom, paid so many attentions to the padshah, the like of which he had never seen before. He replied: `Hast thou not heard that one of the pious said:

``In whose company thou hast been sitting To do him service thou must necessarily rise.

Possibly an ear may during a lifetime Not hear the sound of drum, lute or fife. The eye may be without the sight of a garden. The brain may be without the rose or nasrin. If no feather pillow be at hand Sleep may be had with a stone under the head And if there be no sweetheart to sleep with The hand may be placed on one's own bosom, But this disreputable twisting belly Cannot bear to exist without anything."'

ON THE ADVANTAGES OF SILENCE

Story 1

I said to a friend that I have chosen rather to be silent than to speak because on most occasions good and bad words are scattered concurrently but enemies perceive only the latter. He replied: `That enemy is the greatest who does not see any good.'

The brother of enmity passes not near a good man Except to consider him as a most wicked liar.

Virtue is to the eyes of enmity the greatest fault. Sa`di is a rose but to the eye of enemies a thorn.

The world illumining sun and fountain of light Look ugly to the eye of the mole.

Story 2

A merchant, having suffered loss of a thousand dinars, enjoined his son not to reveal it to anyone. The boy said: `It is thy order and I shall not tell it but thou must inform me of the utility of this proceeding and of the propriety of concealment.' He replied: 'For fear the misfortune would be double; namely, the loss of the money and, secondly, the joy of neighbours at our loss.' Reveal not thy grief to enemies Because they will say `La haul' but rejoice.

Story 3

An intelligent youth possessed an abundant share of accomplishments and discreet behaviour so that he was allowed to sit in assemblies of learned men but he refrained from conversing with them. His father once asked him why he did not likewise speak on subjects he was acquainted with. He replied: `I fear I may be asked what I do not know and be put to shame.'

Hast thou heard how a Sufi drove A few nails under his sandals And an officer taking him by the sleeve Said to him: `Come and shoe my horse.'

For what thou hast not said no one will trouble thee But when thou hast spoken bring the proof.

Story 4

A scholar of note had a controversy with an unbeliever but, being unable to cope with him in argument, shook his head and retired. Someone asked him how it came to pass that, with all his eloquence and learning, he had been unable vanquish an irreligious man. He replied: `My learning is in the Quran, in tradition and in the sayings of sheikhs, which he neither believes in nor listens to. Then of what use is it to me to hear him blaspheming?'

To him of whom thou canst not rid thyself by the Quran and tradition The best reply is if thou dost not reply anything.

Story 5

Galenus saw a fool hanging on with his hands to the collar of a learned man and insulting him, whereon he said: `If he were learned he would not have come to this pass with an ignorant man.' Two wise men do not contend and quarrel Nor does a scholar fight with a contemptible fellow. If an ignorant man in his rudeness speaks harshly An intelligent man tenderly reconciles his heart. Two pious men keep a hair between them untorn And so does a mild with a headstrong man. If however both sides are fools If there be a chain they will snap it. An ill-humoured man insulted someone. He bore it and replied: `O man of happy issue, I am worse than thou canst say that I am Because I know thou art not aware of my faults as I am.

Story 6

Subhan Vail is considered to have had no equal in rhetorics because he had addressed an assembly during a year and had not repeated the same word but, when the same meaning happened to occur, he expressed it in another manner and this is one of the accomplishments of courtiers and princes.

A word if heart-binding and sweet Is worthy of belief and of approbation. When thou hast once said it do not utter it again Because sweets, once partaken of, suffice.

Story 7

I heard a philosopher say that no one has ever made a confession of his own folly except he who begins speaking, whilst another has not yet finished his talk.

Words have a head, O shrewd man, and a tail. Do not insert thy words between words of others. The possessor of deliberation, intelligence and shrewdness Does not say a word till he sees silence.

Story 8

Several officials of Sultan Mahmud asked Hasan Muimandi one day what the sultan had told him about a certain affair. He replied: `You must yourselves have heard it.' They rejoined: `What he says to thee he does not think proper to communicate to the like of us.' He answered: `Because he trusts that I shall not reveal it. Then why do you ask me to do so?'

A knowing man will not utter every word which occurs to him. It is not proper to endanger one's head for the king's secret.

Story 9

I was hesitating in the conclusion of a bargain for the purchase of a house when a Jew said: `Buy it for I am one of the landholders of this ward. Ask me for a description of the house as it is and it has no defect.' I replied: `Except that thou art the neighbour of it.'

A house which has a neighbour like thee Is worth ten dirhems of a deficient standard But the hope must be entertained That after thy death it will be worth a thousand.

Story 10

A poet went to an amir of robbers and recited a panegyric but he ordered him to be divested of his robe. As the poor man was departing naked in the world, he was attacked from behind by dogs, whereon he intended to snatch up a stone but it was frozen to the ground and, being unable to do so, he exclaimed: `What whore-sons of men are these? They have let loose the dogs and have tied down the stones.' The amir of the robbers who heard these words from his room laughed and said: `O philosopher, ask something from me.' He replied: `I ask for my robe if thou wilt make me a present of it.'

We are satisfied of thy gift by departure.

A man was hoping for the gifts of people. I hope no gift from thee. Do me no evil.

The robber chief took pity upon him, ordered his robe to be restored to him and added to it a sheepskin jacket with some dirhems.

Story 11

An astrologer, having entered his own house, saw a stranger and, getting angry, began to insult him, whereon both fell upon each other and fought so that turmoil and confusion ensued. A pious man who had the scene exclaimed:

`How knowest thou what is in the zenith of the sky If thou art not aware who is in thy house?'

Story 12

A preacher imagined his miserable voice to be pleasing and raised useless shouts, thou wouldst have said that the crow of separation had become the tune of his song; and the verse - for the most detestable of voices is surely the voice of asses - appears to have been applicable to him. This distich also concerns him: When the preacher Abu-l-Fares brays At his voice Istakhar-Fares quakes.

On account of the position he occupied the inhabitants of the locality submitted to the hardship and did not think proper to molest him. In course of time, however, another preacher of that region, who bore secret enmity towards him, arrived on a visit and said to him: `I have dreamt about thee, may it end well!' `What hast thou dreamt?' `I dreamt that thy voice had become pleasant and that the people were comfortable during thy sermons.'

The preacher meditated a while on these words and then said: `Thou hast dreamt a blessed dream because thou hast made me aware of my defect. It has become known to me that I have a disagreeable voice and that the people are displeased with my loud reading. Accordingly I have determined henceforth not to address them except in a subdued voice':

I am displeased with the company of friends To whom my bad qualities appear to be good. They fancy my faults are virtues and perfection. My thorns they believe to be rose and jessamine. Say. Where is the bold and quick enemy To make me aware of my defects?

He whose faults are not told him Ignorantly thinks his defects are virtues.

Story 13

A man used to shout superfluous calls to prayers in the mosque of Sinjar and in a voice which displeased all who heard it. The owner of the mosque, who was a just and virtuous amir, not desirous to give him pain, said: `My good fellow, in this mosque there are old muezzins' to each of whom I pay five dinars monthly but to thee I shall give ten, if thou wilt go to another place.' The man agreed and went away. Some time afterwards however, he returned to the amir and said: `My lord, thou hast injured me by turning me away for ten dinars from this place because where I next went they offered me twenty dinars to go to another locality but I refused.' The amir smiled and said: `By no means accept them because will give thee even fifty dinars.' No one can scrape the mud from gravel with an axe As thy discordant shouting scrapes the heart.

Story 14

A fellow with a disagreeable voice happened to be reading the Quran, when a pious man passed near, and asked him what his monthly salary was. He replied: `Nothing.' He further inquired: `Then why takest thou this trouble?' He replied: `I am reading for God's sake.' He replied: `For God's sake do not read.'

If thou readest the Quran thus Thou wilt deprive the religion of splendour.

ON LOVE AND YOUTH

Story 1

Hasan Maimundi was asked that, as the Sultan Mahmud possesses so many beautiful slaves, each of whom is a marvel in the world, how it happens that he manifests towards none of them so much inclination and love as to Iyaz, although he is not more handsome than the others. He replied: `Whatever descends into the heart appears good to the eye.'

He whose murid' the sultan is If he does everything bad, it will be good. But he whom the padshah throws away Will not be cared for by anyone in the household.

If anyone looks with an unfavourable eye Even the figure of Joseph will indicate ugliness And if he looks with the eye of desire on a demon, He will appear an angel, a cherub in his sigh].

Story 2

It is said that a gentleman possessed a slave of exquisite beauty, whom he regarded with love and affection. He nevertheless said to a friend: `Would that this slave of mine, with all the beauty and good qualities he possesses, had not a long and uncivil tongue!' He replied: `Brother, do not expect service, after professing friendship; because when relations between lover and beloved come in, the relations between master and servant are superseded':

When a master with a fairy-faced slave Begins to play and to laugh What wonder if the latter coquets like the master And the gentleman bears it like a slave?

A slave is to draw water and make bricks. A pampered slave will strike with the fist.

Story 3

I saw a religious man, who had fallen in love with a fellow to such a degree that he had neither strength to remain patient nor to bear the talk of the people but would not relinquish his attachment, despite of the reproaches he suffered and the grief he bore, saying:

I shall not let go my hold of thy skirt Even if thou strike me with a sharp sword. After thee I have no refuge nor asylum. To thee alone I shall flee if I flee.

I once reproached him, asking him what had become of his exquisite intellect so that it had been overcome by his base proclivity. He meditated a while and then said:

'Wherever love has become sultan Piety's arm has no strength left. How can a helpless fellow live purely Who has sunk up to his neck in impurity?'

Story 4

One had lost his heart and bidden farewell to his life because the target which he aimed at was in a dangerous locality, portending destruction and no chance promising a morsel easily coming to the palate nor a bird falling into the trap.

When thy sweetheart's eye has no regard for gold Mud and gold are of equal value to thee.

I once advised him to abandon his aspiration to a fancy impossible of realization because many persons are enslaved by the same passion like himself, the feet of their hearts being in chains. He lamented and said:

'Tell my friends not to give me advice Because my eyes are fixed on her wishes. By the strength of fist and shoulders warriors Slay enemies but sweethearts a friend.'

It is against the requirements of love to renounce affection to our sweethearts for fear of losing our lives.

Thou who art a slave to thy selfishness Art mendacious in the game of love. If there be no way to reach the friend Friendship demands to die in pursuit of it.

I rise as no other source is left to me Though the foe may smite me with arrow and sword. If chance serves me I shall take hold of her sleeve. Or else I shall go and die on her threshold.

His friends, who considered his position, pitied his state, gave him advice and at last confined him but all to no purpose.

Alas, that the physician should prescribe patience, Whereas this greedy lust requires sugar.

Hast thou heard that the mistress secretly Told him who had lost his heart: `As long as thou possessest thy own dignity, What will mine amount to in thy eyes?'

It is related that the royal prince who was the object of his affection had been informed to the effect that a good-natured and sweet-spoken youth was constantly attending on the plain, uttering graceful words; and strange tales having been heard of him, it appeared that his heart is inflamed and that he has a touch of insanity in his head. The boy knew that his heart had become attached to him and that he had raised this dust of calamity. Accordingly he galloped towards him. When the youth perceived the prince approaching him, he we and said:

`He who has slain me has come back again. It seems his heart burns for him whom he has slain.'

Although he accosted the youth graciously, asking him whence he came and what his occupation was, he was so plunged in the depths of the ocean of love that he could not breathe: If thou recitest the seven portions of the lesson by heart, When thou art demented by love thou knowest not the A, B, C.

The prince said: `Why speakest thou not to me? I also belong to the circle of dervishes; nay I am even in their service.' In consequence of the force of the friendly advances of his beloved, he raised his head from the dashing waves of love and said: `It is a marvel that with thy existence mine remains That when thou speakest words to me remain.'

Saying these words he uttered a shout and surrendered his life.

It would not be strange if he had been slain at his tent door But it would be strange that if alive he should escape safe.

Story 5

A schoolboy was so perfectly beautiful and sweet-voiced that the teacher, in accordance with human nature, conceived such an affection towards him that' he often recited the following verses: I am not so little occupied with thee, O heavenly face, That remembrance of myself occurs to my mind. From thy sight I am unable to withdraw my eyes Although when I am opposite I may see that an arrow comes.

Once the boy said to him: `As thou strivest to direct my studies, direct also my behaviour. If thou perceivest anything reprovable in my conduct, although it may seem approvable to me, inform me thereof that I may endeavour to change it.' He replied: `O boy, make that request to someone else because the eyes with which I look upon thee behold nothing but virtues.'

The ill-wishing eye, be it torn out Sees only defects in his virtue. But if thou possessest one virtue and seventy faults A friend sees nothing except that virtue.

Story 6

I remember that one night a dear friend of mine entered when I jumped up in such a heedless way that the lamp was extinguished by my sleeve. A vision appeared in the night and by its appearance the darkness was illuminated.

I was amazed at my luck exclaiming whence this felicity?

He took a seat and began reproving me saying that when I beheld him I extinguished the lamp. I said: `I thought the sun had risen and wits have said:

When an ugly person comes before the lamp Arise to him and pull him into the assembly But if it be a sugar-smiled, sweet-lipped one Pull him by the sleeve and extinguish the lamp.'

Story 7

One who had for a considerable time not seen his friend asked him where he had been and said he had been longing. He replied: `To be longing is better than to be satisfied.'

Thou hast come late, O intoxicated idol, We shall not soon let go thy skirt from the hand. He who sees his sweetheart at long intervals Is after all better off than if he sees too much of her. When thou comest with friends to visit me Although thou comest in peace thou art attacking.

If my sweetheart associates one moment with strangers It wants but little and I die of jealousy. She said smiling: `I am the lamp of the assembly, O Sa`di, What is it to me if a moth kills itself?'

Story 8

I remember how in former times I and another friend kept company with each other like two almond kernels in one skin. Suddenly a separation took place but after a time, when my companion returned, he commenced to blame me for not having sent him a messenger during it. I replied: `I thought it would be a pity that the eyes of a messenger should be brightened by thy beauty and I deprived thereof.'

Tell my old friend not to give me advice with the tongue Because even a sword will not compel me to repent. I am jealous that anyone should see thee to satiety. Again I say that no one will be satiated.

Story 9

I knew a learned man who had fallen in love with someone but his secret having fallen from the veil of concealment into publicity, he endured abundant persecution and displayed boundless patience. I said once to him by way of consolation: `I know thou entertainest no worldly motive nor inclination for baseness. It is nevertheless unbecoming the dignity of a scholar to expose himself to suspicions and to bear the persecutions of mannerless persons.' He replied: `O friend, take off the hand of reproach from my skirt because I have often meditated on the opinion which thou entertainest but have found it easier to bear persecution for his sake than not to see him; and philosophers have said that it is easier to accustom the heart to strife, than to turn away the eye from seeing the beloved.

Who has his heart with a heart-ravisher Has his beard in another's hand. A gazelle with a halter on the neck Is not able to walk of its own accord. If he, without whom one cannot abide, Becomes insolent it must be endured. I one day told him to beware of his friend But I often asked pardon for that day. A friend does not abandon a friend. I submit my heart to what he wills. Whether he kindly calls me to himself Or drives me away in anger he knows best.

Story 10

In the exuberance of youth, as it usually happens and as thou knowest, I was on the closest terms of intimacy with a sweetheart who had a melodious voice and a form beautiful like the moon just rising.

He, the down of whose cheek drinks the water of immortality, Whoever looks at his sugar lips eats sweetmeats.

I happened to notice something in his behaviour which was contrary to nature and not approved of by me. Accordingly I gathered up my skirt from him and, picking up the pieces of the chess-game of friendship, recited: `Go and do as thou listest. Thou hast not our head; follow thine.'

I heard him saying when he went away: `If the bat desires not union with the sun The beauty of the sun will not decrease.'

Saying this, he departed and his distress took effect on me:

I lost the time of union and man is ignorant Of the value of delightful life before adversity. Return. Slay me. For to die in thy presence Is more sweet than to live after thee.

Thanks be to the bounty of God, he returned some time afterwards but his melodious voice had changed, his Joseph like beauty had faded, on the apple of his skin dust had settled as upcn a quince so that the splendour of his beauty had departed. He wanted me to embrace him. I complied and said: `On the day when thou hadst a beauteous incipient beard Thou drovest him, who desired the sight, from thy sight. Today thou camest to make peace with him But hast exhibited Fathah and Zammah.

His fresh spring is gone and he has become yellow. Bring not the kettle because our fire is extinguished. How long wilt thou strut about, showing arrogance, Imagining felicity which has elapsed? Go to him who will purchase thee. Coquet with him who asks for thee.

They said: ``Verdure in the garden is pleasing." He knows it who utters these words. Namely, heartfelt affection for that green line Fascinates the hearts of lovers more and more. Thy garden is a bed of leeks. The more thou weedest it the more they grow.

Whether thou pluckest out thy beard or not This happiness of youthful days must end. Had I the power of life as thou of the beard I would not let it end till resurrection-day.

I asked and said: What has befallen the beauty of thy face That ants are crawling round the moon? He replied, smiling: ``I know not what is the matter with my face. Perhaps it wears black as mourning for my beauty."'

Story 11

I asked one of the people of Baghdad what he thought of beardless youths. He replied: `There is no good in them for when one of them is yet delicate and wanted he is insolent; but when he becomes rough and is not wanted he is affable.'

When a beardless youth is beautiful and sweet His speech is bitter, his temper hasty. When his beard grows and he attains puberty He associates with men and seeks affection.

Story 12

One of the ullemma had been asked that, supposing one sits with a moon-faced beauty in a private apartment, the doors being closed, companions asleep, passion inflamed, and lust raging, as the Arab says, the date is ripe and its guardian not forbidding, whether he thought the power of abstinence would cause the man to remain in safety. He replied: `If he remains in safety from the moon-faced one, he will not remain safe from evil speakers.'

If a man escapes from his own bad lust He will not escape from the bad suspicions of accusers.

It is proper to sit down to one's own work But it is impossible to bind the tongues of men.

Story 13

A parrot, having been imprisoned in a cage with a crow, was vexed by the sight and said: `What a loathsome aspect is this! What an odious figure! What cursed object with rude habits! 0 crow of separation, would that the distance of the east from the west were between us.' Whoever beholds thee when he rises in the morning The morn of a day of safety becomes evening to him. An ill-omened one like thyself is fit to keep thee company But where in the world is one like thee?

More strange still, the crow was similarly distressed by the proximity of the parrot and, having become disgusted, was shouting `La haul', and lamenting the vicissitudes of time. He rubbed the claws of sorrow against each other and said: `What ill-luck is this? What base destiny and chameleonlike times? It was befitting my dignity to strut about on a garden-wall in the society of another crow.

`It is sufficient imprisonment for a devote To be in the same stable with profligates.

`What sin have I committed that I have already in this life, as a punishment for it, fallen into the bonds of this calamity in company with such a conceited, uncongenial and heedless fool?'

No one will approach the foot of the wall Upon which they paint thy portrait. If thy place were in paradise Others would select. hell.

I have added this parable to let thee know that no matter how much a learned man may hate an ignorant man the latter hates him equally.

A hermit was among profligates When one of them, a Balkhi beauty, said: `If thou art tired of us sit not sour For thou art thyself bitter in our midst.'

An assembly joined together like roses and tulips! Thou art withered wood, growing in its midst, Like a contrary wind and unpleasant frost, Like snow inert, like ice bound fast.

Story 14

I had a companion with whom I had travelled for years and eaten salt. Boundless intimacy subsisted between us till at last he suffered my mind to be grieved for the sake of some paltry gain and our friendship closed. Despite of an this, however, mutual attachment of heart still subsisted between us because I heard him one day reciting in an assembly the following two distichs of my composition: When my sweetheart enters sweetly smiling She adds more salt to my bleeding wound. How would it be if the tip of her curls fell into my hand Like the sleeve of the bountiful into the hands of dervishes?

Some friends bore witness not so much to the gracefulness of these verses as to the beauty of my conduct which they approved; and among the rest, the said friend likewise added his share of praise, regretting the loss of our former companionship and confessing his fault so that his affection became known. Accordingly I sent the following distichs and made peace: Was not there a covenant of friendship between us? Thou hast been cruel and not loving. I once tied my heart to thee, disregarding the world. Not knowing thou wouldst turn back so soon. If thou yet desirest conciliation, return Because thou wilt be more beloved than before.

Story 15

The beautiful wife of a man died but her mother, a decrepit old hag, remained in the house on account of the dowry. The man saw no means of escaping from contact with her until a company of friends paid him a visit of condolence and one of them asked him how he bore the loss of his beloved. He replied: `It is not as painful not to see my wife as to see the mother of my wife.' The rose has been destroyed and the thorn remained.

The treasure has been taken and the serpent left. It is better that one's eye be fixed on a spear-head Than that it should behold the face of an enemy. It is incumbent to sever connection with a thousand friends Rather than to behold a single foe.

Story 16

I remember having in the days of my youth passed through a street, intending to see a moon-faced beauty. It was in Temuz, whose heat dried up the saliva in the mouth and whose simum boiled the marrow in my bones. My weak human nature being unable to endure the scorching sun, I took refuge in the shadow of a wall, wishing someone might relieve me from the summer heat and quench my fire with some water; and lo, all of a sudden, from the darkness of the porch of a house a light shone forth, namely a beauty, the grace of which the tongue of eloquence is unable to describe. She came out like the rising dawn after an obscure night or the water of immortality gushing from a dark cavern, carrying in her hand a bowl of snow-water, into which sugar had been poured and essence of roses mixed. I knew not whether she had perfumed it with rose-water or whether a few drops from her rosy face had fallen into it. In short, I took the beverage from her beautiful hands, drank it and began to live again.

The thirst of my heart cannot be quenched By sipping limpid water even if I drink oceans of it.

Blessed is the man of happy destiny whose eye Alights every morning on such a countenance. One drunk of wine awakens at midnight, One drunk of the cupbearer on the morn of resurrection.

Story 17

In the year when Muhammad Khovarezm Shah concluded peace with the king of Khata to suit his own purpose, I entered the cathedral mosque of Kashgar and saw an extremely handsome, graceful boy as described in the simile:

Thy master has taught thee to coquet and to ravish hearts, Instructed thee to oppose, to dally, to blame and to be severe. A person of such figure, temper, stature and gait I have not seen; perhaps he learnt these tricks from a fairy. He was holding in his hand the introduction to Zamaksharni's Arabic syntax and reciting: Zaid struck Amru and was the injurer of Amru. I said: `Boy! Khovarezm and Khata have concluded peace, and the quarrel between Zaid and Amru still subsists!' He smiled and asked for my birthplace. I replied: `The soil of Shiraz.' He continued: `What rememberest thou of the compositions of Sa`di?' I recited: `I am tired by a nahvi who makes a furious attack Upon me, like Zaid in his opposition to Amru. When Zaid submits he does not raise his head And how can elevation subsist when submission is the regent?

He considered awhile and then said: `Most of his poetry current in this country is in the Persian language. If thou wilt recite some, it will be more easily understood.' Then I said:

`When thy nature has enticed thee with syntax It blotted out the form of intellect from our heart. Alas, the hearts of lovers are captive in thy snare. We are occupied with thee but thou with Amru and Zaid.'

The next morning, when I was about to depart, some people told him that I was Sa`di, whereon he came running to me and politely expressed his regret that I had not revealed my identity before so that he might have girded his loins to serve me in token of the gratitude due to the presence of a great man.

In spite of thy presence no voice came to say: I am he.

He also said: `What would it be if thou wert to spend in this country some days in repose that we might derive advantage by serving thee?' I replied: `I cannot on account of the following adventure which occurred to me: I beheld an illustrious man in a mountain region Who had contentedly retired from the world into a cave. Why, said I, comest thou not into the city For once to relax the bonds of thy heart? He replied: `Fairy-faced maidens are there. When clay is plentiful, elephants will stumble.'

This I said. Then we kissed each other's heads and faces and took leave of each other. What profits it to kiss a friend's face And at the same time to take leave of him? Thou wouldst say that he who parts from friends is an apple. One half of his face is red and the other yellow. If I die not of grief on the day of separation Reckon me not faithful in friendship.

Story 18

A man in patched garments' accompanied us in a caravan to the Hejaz and one of the Arab amirs presented him with a hundred dinars to spend upon his family but robbers of the Kufatcha tribe suddenly fell upon the caravan and robbed it clean of everything. The merchants began to wail and to cry, uttering vain shouts and lamentations.

Whether thou implorest or complainest The robber will not return the gold again.

The dervish alone had not lost his equanimity and showed no change. I asked: `Perhaps they have not taken thy money?' He replied: `Yes, they have but I was not so much accustomed to that money that separation therefrom could grieve my heart':

The heart must not be tied to any thing or person Because to take off the heart is a difficult affair.

I replied: `What thou hast said resembles my case because, when I was young, my intimacy with a young man and my friendship for him were such that his beauty was the Qiblah of my eye and the chief joy of my life union with him': Perhaps an angel in heaven but no mortal Can be on earth equal in beauty of form to him. I swear by the amity, after which companionship is illicit, No human sperm will ever become a man like him.

All of a sudden the foot of his life sank into the mire of non-existence. The smoke of separation arose from his family. I kept him company on his grave for many days and one of my compositions on his loss is as follows: Would that on the day when the thorn of fate entered thy foot The hand of heaven had struck a sword on my head; So that this day my eye could not see the world without thee. Here I am on thy grave, would that it were over my head.

He who could take neither rest nor sleep Before he had first scattered roses and narcissi. The turns of heaven have strewn the roses of his face. Thorns and brambles are growing on his tomb. After separation from him I resolved and firmly determined to fold up the carpet of pleasure during the rest of my life and to retire from mixing in society:

Last night I strutted about like a peacock in the garden of union But today, through separation from my friend, I twist my head like a snake. The profit of the sea would be good if there were no fear of waves. The company of the rose would be sweet if there were no pain from thorns.

Story 19

A king of the Arabs, having been informed of the relations subsisting between Laila and Mejnun, with an account of the latter's insanity, to the effect that he had in spite of his great accomplishments and eloquence, chosen to roam about in the desert and to let go the reins of self-control from his hands; he ordered him to be brought to his presence, and this having been done, he began to reprove him and to ask him what defect he had discovered in the nobility of the human soul that he adopted the habits of beasts and abandoned the society of mankind. Mejnun replied: `Many friends have blamed me for loving her. Will they not see her one day and understand my excuse?'

Would that those who are reproving me Could see thy face, O ravisher of hearts, That instead of a lemon in thy presence They might heedlessly cut their hands.

That the truth may bear witness to the assertion: This is he for whose sake ye blamed me.

The king expressed a wish to see the beauty of Laila in order to ascertain the cause of so much distress. Accordingly he ordered her to be searched for. The encampments of various Arab families having been visited, she was found, conveyed to the king and led into the courtyard of the palace. The king looked at her outward form for some time and she appeared despicable in his sight because the meanest handmaids of his harem excelled her in beauty and attractions. Mejnun, who shrewdly understood the thoughts of the king, said: `It would have been necessary to look from the window of Mejnun's eye at the beauty of Laila when the mystery of her aspect would have been revealed to thee.'

If the record of the glade which entered my ears Had been heard by the leaves of the glade they would have lamented with me. O company of friends, say to him who is unconcerned `Would that thou knewest what is in a pining heart. Who are healthy have no pain from wounds. I shall tell my grief to no one but a sympathizer. It is useless to speak of bees to one Who never in his life felt their sting. As long as thy state is not like mine My state will be but an idle tale to thee.

Story 20

It is related that the qazi of Hamdan, having conceived affection towards a farrier-boy and the horseshoe of his heart being on fire, he sought for some time to meet him, roaming about and seeking for opportunities, according to the saying of chroniclers: That straight tall cypress my eyes beheld It robbed me of my heart and threw me down. Those wanton eyes have taken my heart with a lasso. If thou desirest to preserve thy heart shut thy eyes.

I was informed that the boy, who had heard something of the qazi's passion, happening to meet him in a thoroughfare, manifested immense wrath, assailed the qazi with disrespectful and insulting words, snatched up a stone and left no injury untried. The qazi said to an ullemma of repute who happened to be of the same opinion with him: `Look at that sweetheart and his getting angry, And that bitter knot of his sweet eyebrow.'

The Arab says: `A slap from a lover is a raisin.

A blow from the hand on the mouth Is sweeter than eating bread with one's own hand.

In the same way the boy's impudence might be indicating kindness as padshahs utter hard words whilst they secretly wish for peace: Grapes yet unripe are sour. Wait two or three days, they will become sweet.

After saying these words he returned to his court of justice, where some respectable men connected with him kissed the ground of service and said: `With thy permission we shall, doing obeisance, speak some words to thee although they may be contrary to politeness because illustrious men have said:

It is not permissible to argue on every topic. To find fault with great men is wrong.

`But as in consequence of favours conferred by thy lordship in former times upon thy servants it would be a kind of treachery to withhold the opinion they entertain, they inform thee that the proper way is not to yield to thy inclinations concerning this boy but to fold up the carpet of lascivious desires because thy dignity as qazi is high and must not be polluted by a base crime. The companion thou hast seen is this, and our words thou hast heard are these: One who has done many disreputable things Cares nothing for the reputation of anyone. Many a good name of fifty years Was trodden under foot by one bad name."

The qazi approved of the unanimous advice of his friends and appreciated their good opinion as well as their steadfast fidelity, saying that the view taken by his beloved friends on the arrangement of his case was perfectly right and their arguments admitting of no contradiction. Nevertheless:

Although love ceases in consequence of reproval I heard that just men sometimes concoct falsehoods.

Blame me as much as thou listest Because blackness cannot be washed off from a negro.

Nothing can blot out my remembrance of thee. I am a snake with broken head and cannot turn.

These words he said and sent some persons to make inquiries about him, spending boundless money because it is said that whoever has gold in his hand possesses strength of arm and he who has no worldly goods has no friends in the whole world:

Whoever has seen gold droops his head, Although he may be hard to bend like iron-backed scales.

In short, one night he obtained privacy but during that night the police obtained information that the qazi is spending the whole of it with wine in his hand and a sweetheart on his bosom, enjoying himself, not sleeping, and singing: Has this cock perhaps not crowed at the proper time this night And have the lovers not had their fill of embrace, and kiss Whilst alas for only a moment the eye of confusion is asleep? Remain awake that life may not elapse in vain Till thou hearest the morning call from the Friday-mosque Or the noise of kettle-drums on Atabek's palace-gate. Lips against lips like the cock's eye Are not to part at the crowing of a silly cock.

Whilst the qazi was in this state one of his dependants entered and said: `Arise and run as far as thy feet will carry thee because the envious have not only obtained a handle for vexation but have spoken the truth. We may, whilst the fire of confusion is yet burning low, perchance extinguish it with the water of stratagem but when it blazes up high it may destroy a world.' The qazi, however, replied: `When the lion has his claws on the game What boots it if a jackal makes his appearance? Keep thy face on the face of the friend and leave The foe to chew the back of his own hand in rage.'

The same night information was also brought to the king that in his realm such a wickedness had been perpetrated and he was asked what he thought of it. He replied: `I know that he is one of the most learned men, and I account him to be the paragon of our age. As it is possible that enemies have devised a plot against him, I give no credit to this accusation unless I obtain ocular evidence because philosophers have said: He who grasps the sword in haste Will repenting carry the back of his hand to his teeth and bite it.'

I heard that at dawn the king with some of his courtiers arrived at the pillow of the qazi, saw a lamp standing, the sweetheart sitting, the wine spilled, the goblet broken and the qazi plunged in the sleep of drunkenness, unaware of the realm of existence. The king awakened him gently and said: `Get up for the sun has risen.' The qazi, who perceived the state of affairs, asked: `From what direction?' The sultan was astonished and replied: `From the east as usual.' The qazi exclaimed: `Praise be to Allah! The door of repentance is yet open because according to tradition the gate Of repentance will not be locked against worshippers till the sun rises in its setting place.'

These two things impelled me to sin: My ill-luck and my imperfect understanding. If thou givest me punishment I deserve it And if thou forgivest pardon is better than revenge.

The king replied: `As thou knowest that thou must suffer capital punishment, it is of no use to repent. But their faith availed them not after they had beholden our vengeance. `What is the use to promise to forego thieving When a lasso cannot be thrown up to the palace? Say to the tall man: ``Do not pluck the fruit", For he who is short cannot reach the branch.

`For thee, who hast committed such wickedness, there is no way of escape.' After the king had uttered these words, the men appointed for the execution took hold of him, whereon he said: `I have one word more to speak in the service of the sultan.' The king, who heard him, asked: `What is it?' And he recited: `Thou who shakest the sleeve of displeasure upon me Expect not that I shall withdraw my hand from thy skirt. If escape be impossible from this crime which I committed I trust to the clemency which thou possessest.'

The king replied: `Thou hast adduced this wonderful sally and hast enounced a strange maxim but it is impossible according to reason and contrary to usage that thy accomplishments and eloquence should this day save thee from the punishment which I have decreed; and I consider it proper to throw thee headlong from the castle that others may take an example.' He continued: `O lord of the world, I have been nourished by the bounty of this dynasty, and this crime was not committed only by me in the world. Throw another man headlong that I may take the example.' The king burst out laughing, pardoned his crime and said to his dependents who desired the qazi to be slain: `Everyone of you who are bearers of your own faults Ought not to blame others for their defects.'

Story 21

A virtuous and beauteous youth Was pledged to a chaste maiden. I read that in the great sea They fell into a vortex together. When a sailor came to take his hand, Lest he might die in that condition, He said in anguish from the waves: `Leave me. Take the hand of my love.' Whilst saying this, he despaired of life. In his agony he was heard to exclaim: `Learn not the tale of love from the wretch Who forgets his beloved in distress.' Thus the lives of the lovers terminated. Learn from what has occurred that thou mayest know Because Sa`di is of the ways and means of love affairs Well aware in the Arabian city of Baghdad. Tie thy heart to the heart-charmer thou possessest And shut thy eye to all the rest of the world. If Mejnun and Laila were to come to life again They might indite a tale of love on this occurrence.

ON WEAKNESS AND OLD AGE

Story 1

I was holding a disputation with a company of learned men in the cathedral mosque of Damascus when a youth stepped among us, asking whether anyone knew Persian, whereon most of them pointed to me. I asked him what the matter was and he said that an old man, aged one hundred and fifty years, was in the agony of death but saying something in Persian which nobody could understand and that if I were kindly to go and see him I might obtain the information whether he was perhaps desirous of making his last will. When I approached his pillow, he said: `A while ago I said I shall take some rest But alas, the way of my breath is choked. Alas, that from the variegated banquet of life We were eating a while and told it is enough.'

I interpreted these words in the Arabic language to the Damascenes and they were astonished that despite of his long life he regretted the termination of it so much. I asked him how he felt and he replied: 'What shall I say?'

Hast thou not seen what misery he feels, The teeth of whose mouth are being extracted? Consider what his state will be at the hour When life, so precious to him, abandons his body.

I told him not to worry his imagination with the idea of death and not to allow a hallucination to obtain dominion over his nature because Ionian philosophers have said that although the constitution may be good no reliance is to be placed on its permanence and although a malady may be perilous it does not imply a full indication of death. I asked: `If thou art willing, I shall call a physician to treat thee?' He lifted his eyes and said, smiling: `The skilled doctor strikes his hands together On beholding a rival prostrate like a potsherd. A gentleman is engaged in adorning his hall with paintings Whilst the very foundation of the house is ruined.

An aged man was lamenting in his last agony Whilst his old spouse was rubbing him with sandal. When the equilibrium of the constitution is destroyed Neither incantations nor medicines are of any avail.'

Story 2

It is related that an old man, having married a girl, was sitting with her privately in an apartment adorned with roses, fixing his eyes and heart upon her. He did not sleep during long nights but spent them in telling her jokes and witty stories, hoping to gain her affection and to conquer her shyness. One night, however, he informed her that luck had been friendly to her and the eye of fortune awake because she had become the companion of an old man who is ripe, educated, experienced in the world, of a quiet disposition, who had felt cold and warm, had tried good and bad, who knows the diities of companionship, is ready to fulfil the conditions of love, is benevolent, kind, good-natured and sweet-tongued.

As far as I am able I shall hold thy heart And if injured I shall not injure in return. Though sugar may be thy food as of a parrot I shall sacrifice sweet life to thy support.

Thou hast not fallen into the hands of a giddy youth, fun of whims, headstrong, fickle minded, running about every moment in search of another pleasure and entertaining another opinion, sleeping every night in another place and taking every day another friend.

Young men are joyous and of handsome countenance But inconstant in fidelity to anyone. Expect not faithfulness from nightingales Who sing every moment to another rose.

Contrary to aged men who spend their lives according to wisdom and propriety; not according to the impulses of folly and youth. Find one better than thyself and consider it fortunate Because with one like thyself thou wilt be disappointed.

The old man said: `I continued in this strain, thinking that I had captivated her heart and that it had become my prey.'

She drew, however, a deep sigh from her grief-filled heart and said: `All the words thou hast uttered, weighed in the scales of my understanding, are not equivalent to the maxim I once heard enounced in my tribe: An arrow in the side of a young woman is better than an old man.'

When she perceived in the hands of her husband Something pendant like the nether lip of a fasting man, She said: `This fellow has a corpse with him But incantations are for sleepers not for corpses.'

A woman who arises without satisfaction from a man Will raise many a quarrel and contention. An old man who is unable to rise from his place, Except by the aid of a stick, how can his own stick rise?

In short, there being no possibility of harmony, a separation at last took place. When the time of the lady's uddat had terminated, she was given in marriage to a young man who was violent, ill-humoured and empty-handed. She suffered much from his bad temper and tyrannical behaviour, and experienced the miseries of penury. She nevertheless said: `Praise be to Allah for having been delivered from that wretched torment, and attained this permanent blessing.'

Despite of all this violence and hasty nature I shall try to please thee because thou art beauteous. To be with thee in hell burning is for me Better than to be with the other in paradise. The smell of an onion from the mouth of a pretty face Is indeed better than a rose from an ugly hand. A nice face and a gown of gold brocade, Essence of roses, fragrant aloes, paint, perfume and lust: All these are ornaments of women. Take a man; and his testicles are a sufficient ornament.

Story 3

I was in Diarbekr, the guest of an old man, who possessed abundant wealth and a beautiful son. One night he narrated to me that he had all his life no other son but this boy, telling me that in the locality people resorted to a certain tree in a valley to offer petitions and that he had during many nights prayed at the foot of the said tree, till the Almighty granted him this son. I overheard the boy whispering to his companion:

`How good it would be if I knew where that tree is that I might pray for my father to die.' Moral: The gentleman is delighted that his son is intelligent and the boy complains that his father is a dotard. Years elapse without thy visiting The tomb of thy father. What good hast thou done to him To expect the same from thy son?

Story 4

One day, in the pride of youth, I had travelled hard and arrived perfectly exhausted in the evening at the foot of an acclivity. A weak old man, who had likewise been following the caravan, came and asked me why I was sleeping, this not being the place for it. I replied: `How am I to travel, having lost the use of my feet?' He said: `Hast thou not heard that it is better to walk gently and to halt now and then than to run and to become exhausted?' O thou who desirest to reach the station Take my advice and learn patience. An Arab horse gallops twice in a race. A camel ambles gently night and day.

Story 5

The active, graceful, smiling, sweet-tongued youth happened once to be in the circle of our assembly. His heart had been entered by no kind of grief and his lips were scarcely ever closed from laughter. After some time had elapsed, I accidentally met him again and I learned that he had married a wife and begotten children but I saw that the root of merriment had been cut and the roses of his countenance were withered. I asked him how he felt and what his circumstances were. He replied: `When I had obtained children I left off childishness.'

Where is youth when age has changed my ringlets? And the change of time is a sufficient monitor.

When thou art old abstain from puerility. Leave play and jokes to youths. Seek not a youth's hilarity in an old man For the water gone from the brook returns no more. When the harvest-time of a field arrives It will no longer wave in the breeze like a young crop.

The period of youth has departed. Alas, for those heart-enchanting times. The force of the lion's claws is gone. Now we are satisfied with cheese Eke a leopard. An old hag had dyed her hair black. I said to her: `O little mother of ancient days, Thou hast cunningly dyed thy hair but consider That thy bent back will never be straight.'

Story 6

In the folly of youth I one day shouted at my mother who then sat down with a grieved heart in a corner and said, weeping: `Hast thou forgotten thy infancy that thou art harsh towards me?'

How sweetly said the old woman to her son When she saw him overthrow a tiger, and elephant-bodied: `If thou hadst remembered the time of thy infancy How helpless thou wast in my arms Thou would'st this day not have been harsh For thou art a lion-like man, and I an old woman.'

Story 7

The son of a wealthy but avaricious old man, having fallen sick, his well-wishers advised him that it would be proper to get the whole Quran recited or else to offer a sacrifice. He meditated a while and then said: `It is preferable to read the Quran because the flock is at a distance.' A holy man, who had heard this, afterwards remarked: `He selected the reading of the Quran because it is at the tip of the tongue but the money at the bottom of the heart.' It is useful to bend the neck in prayers If they are to be accompanied by almsgiving. For one dinar he would remain sticking in mud like an ass, But if thou askest for Alhamdu he will recite it a hundred times.

Story 8

An old man, having been asked why he did not marry, replied that he could not be happy with an aged woman, and on being told that as he was a man of property, he might take a young one, he said: `I being an old man and unwilling to associate with an old woman, how could a young one conceive friendship for me who am aged?' Let not a man of seventy years make love. Thou art confessedly blind, kiss her and sleep. The lady wants strength, not gold. One passage is preferable to her than ten mann of flesh.

Story 9

I have heard that in these days a decrepit aged man Took the fancy in his old head to get a spouse. He married a beauteous little girl, Jewel by name, When he had concealed his casket of jewels from the eyes of men A spectacle took place as is customary in weddings. But in the first onslaught the organ of the sheikh fell asleep. He spanned the bow but hit not the target; it being impossible to sew A tight coarse robe except with a needle of steel. He complained to his friends and showed proofs That his furniture had been utterly destroyed by her impudence. Such fighting and contention arose between man and wife That the affair came before the qazi; and Sa`di said: `After all this reproach and villainy the fault is not the girl's. Thou whose hand trembles, how canst thou bore a Jewel?'

ON THE EFFECTS OF EDUCATION

Story 1

A vezier who had a stupid son gave him in charge of a scholar to instruct him and if possible to make him intelligent. Having been some time under instruction but ineffectually, the learned man sent one to his father with the words: `The boy is not becoming intelligent and has made a fool of me.'

When a nature is originally receptive Instruction will take effect thereon. No kind of polishing will improve iron Whose essence is originally bad. Wash a dog in the seven oceans, He will be only dirtier when he gets wet. If the ass of Jesus be taken to Mekkah He will on his return still be an ass.

Story 2

A sage, instructing boys, said to them: `O darlings of your fathers, learn a trade because property and riches of the world are not to be relied upon; also silver and gold are an occasion of danger because either a thief may steal them at once or the owner spend them gradually; but a profession is a living fountain and permanent wealth; and although a professional man may lose riches, it does not matter because a profession is itself wealth and wherever he goes he will enjoy respect and sit in high places, whereas he who has no trade will glean crumbs and see hardships: It is difficult to obey after losing dignity And to bear violence from men after being caressed.

Once confusion arose in Damascus. Everyone left his snug corner. Learned sons of peasants Became the veziers of padshahs. Imbecile sons of the veziers Went as mendicants to peasants.

If you wanted thy father's inheritance, acquire his knowledge Because this property of his may be spent in ten days.

Story 3

An illustrious scholar, who was the tutor of a royal prince, had the habit of striking him unceremoniously and treating him severely. The boy, who could no longer bear this violence, went to his father to complain and when he had taken off his coat, the father's heart was moved with pity. Accordingly he called for the tutor and said: `Thou dost not permit thyself to indulge in so much cruelty towards the children of my subjects as thou inflictest upon my son. What is the reason?' He replied: `It is incumbent upon all persons in general to converse in a sedate manner and to behave in a laudable way but more especially upon padshahs because whatever they say or do is commented on by everybody, the utterances or acts of common people being of no such consequence.

`If a hundred unworthy things are committed by a dervish His companions do not know one in a hundred. But if a padshah utters only one jest It is borne from country to country.

`It is the duty of a royal prince's tutor to train up the sons of his lord in refinement of morals -- and Allah caused her to grow up as a beautiful plant -- more diligently than the sons of common people.' He whom thou hast not punished when a child Will not prosper when he becomes a man. While a stick is green, thou canst bend it as thou listest. When it is dry, fire alone can make it straight.

The king, being pleased with the appropriate discipline of the tutor and with his explanatory reply, bestowed upon him a robe of honour with other gifts and raised him to a higher position.

Story 4

I saw a schoolmaster in the Maghrib country, who was sour-faced, of uncouth speech, ill-humoured, troublesome to the people, of a beggarly nature and without self-restraint, so that the very sight of him disgusted the Musalmans and when reading the Quran he distressed the hearts of the people. A number of innocent boys and little maidens suffered from the hand of his tyranny, venturing neither to laugh nor to speak because he would slap the silver-cheeks of some and put the crystal legs of others into the stocks. In short, I heard that when his behaviour had attained some notoriety, he was expelled from the school and another installed as corrector, who happened to be a religious, meek, good and wise man. He spoke only when necessary and found no occasion to deal harshly with anyone so that the children lost the fear they had entertained for their first master and, taking advantage of the angelic manners of the second, they acted like demons towards each other and, trusting in his gentleness, neglected their studies, spending most of their time in play, and breaking on the heads of each other the tablets' of their unfinished tasks.

If the schoolmaster happens to be lenient The children will play leapfrog in the bazar.

Two weeks afterwards I happened to pass near that same mosque where I again saw the first master whom the people had made glad by reconciliation and had reinstalled in his post. I was displeased, exclaimed `La haul', and asked why they had again made Iblis the teacher of angels. An old man, experienced in the world, who had heard me, smiled and said: `Hast thou not heard the maxim?

A padshah placed his son in a school, Putting in his lap a silver tablet With this inscription in golden letters: The severity of a teacher is better than the love of a father.'

Story 5

The son of a pious man inherited great wealth left him by some uncles, whereon he plunged into dissipation and profligacy, became a spendthrift and, in short, left no heinous transgression unperpetrated and no intoxicant untasted. I advised him and said: `My son, income is a flowing water and expense a turning mill; that is to say, only he who has a fixed revenue is entitled to indulge in abundant expenses.

`If thou hast no income, spend but frugally Because the sailors chant this song: ``If there be no rain in the mountains The bed of the Tigris will be dry in one year."

`Follow wisdom and propriety, abandon play and sport because thy wealth will be exhausted, whereon thou wilt fall into trouble and will repent.' The youth was prevented by the delights of the flute and of drink from accepting my admonition but found fault therewith, saying that it is contrary to the opinion of intelligent men to embitter present tranquillity by cares concerning the future: Why should possessors of enjoyment and luck Bear sorrow for fear of distress? Go, be merry, my heart-rejoicing friend. The pain of tomorrow must not be eaten today.

And how could I restrain myself, who am occupying the highest seat of liberality, have bound the knot of generosity and the fame of whose beneficence has become the topic of general conversation? Who has become known for his liberality and generosity Must not put a lock upon his dirhems. When the name of a good fellow has spread in a locality The door cannot be dosed against it.

When I perceived that he did not accept my advice and that my warm breath was not taking effect upon his cold iron, I left off admonishing him and turned away my face from his companionship, acting according to the words of philosophers, who said: Impart to them what thou hast and if they receive it not, it is not thy fault.

Although thou knowest thou wilt not be heard, say Whatever thou knowest of good wishes and advice. It may soon happen that thou wilt behold a silly fellow With both his feet fallen into captivity, Striking his hands together, and saying: `Alas, I have not listened to the advice of a scholar.'

After some time I saw the consequences of his dissolute behaviour -- which I apprehended -- realized. When I beheld him sewing patch upon patch and gathering crumb after crumb, my heart was moved with pity for his destitute condition, in which I did not consider it humane to scratch his internal wounds with reproaches or to sprinkle salt upon them. Accordingly, I said to myself:

A foolish fellow in the height of intoxication Cares not for the coming day of distress. The tree which sheds its foliage in spring Will certainly have no leaves remaining in winter.

Story 6

A padshah entrusted a tutor with the care of his son, saying: 'This is thy son. Educate him as if he were one of thy own children.' He kept the prince for some years and strove to instruct him but could effect nothing, whilst the sons of the tutor made the greatest progress in accomplishments and eloquence. The king reproved and threatened the learned man with punishment, telling him that he had acted contrary to his promise and had been unfaithful. He replied: `O king, the instruction is the same but the natures are different.'

Although both silver and gold come from stones All stones do not contain silver and gold. Canopus is shining upon the whole world But produces in some places sack-leather and in others adim.

Story 7

I heard a pir-instructor say to his murid: `The mind of man is so much occupied with thoughts about maintenance that he would surpass the position of angels if he were to devote as many of them to the giver of maintenance.'

Yazed has not forgotten thee at the time When thou wast sperm, buried, insensible. He gave thee a soul, nature, intellect and perception, Beauty, speech, opinion, meditation and acuteness. He arranged five fingers on thy fist. He fixed two arms to thy shoulders. O thou whose aspirations are base, thinkest he will now Forget to provide thee with a maintenance?

Story 8

I saw an Arab of the desert who said to his boy: `O son, on the day of resurrection thou wilt be asked what thou hast gained and not from whom thou art descended, that is to say, thou wilt be asked what thy merit is and not who thy father was.'

The covering of the Ka'bah which is kissed Has not been ennobled by the silkworm. It was some days in company with a venerable man Wherefore it became respected like himself.

Story 9

It is narrated in the compositions of philosophers that scorpions are not born in the same manner like other living beings but that they devour the bowels of their mother and, after gnawing through the belly, betake themselves to the desert. The skins which may be seen in the nests of scorpions are the evidence of this. I narrated this story to an illustrious man who then told me that his own heart bore witness to the truth of it for the case could not be otherwise inasmuch as they, having in their infancy dealt thus with their fathers and mothers, they were beloved and respected in the same manner when they grow old.

A father thus admonished his son: O noble fellow, remember this advice. 'Whoever is not faithful to his origin Will not become the companion of happiness.' A scorpion, having been asked why he did not go out in winter, replied: 'What honour do I enjoy in summer that I should come out also in winter?'

Story 10

The wife of a dervish had become enceinte and when the time of her confinement was at hand, the dervish who had no child during all his life said: 'If God the most high and glorious presents me with a son, I shall bestow everything I possess as alms upon dervishes, except this patched garment of mine which I am wearing.' It happened that the infant was a son. He rejoiced and gave a banquet to the dervishes, as he had promised. Some years afterwards when I returned from a journey to Syria, I passed near the locality of the dervish and asked about his circumstances but was told that he had been put in prison by the police. Asking for the cause, I was told that his son, having become drunk, quarrelled and having shed the blood of a man, had fled; whereon his father was instead of him loaded with a chain on his neck and heavy fetters on his legs. I replied: `He had himself asked God the most high and glorious for this calamity.' If pregnant women, O man of intellect, Bring forth serpents at the time of birth, It is better in the opinion of the wise Than to give birth to a wicked progeny.

Story 11

When I was a child I asked an illustrious man about puberty. He replied: `It is recorded in books that it has three signs. First, the age of fifteen years; secondly nocturnal pollutions; and thirdly, sprouting of hair on the pudenda; but in reality there is only one sign which is sufficient that thou shouldst seek the approbation of the most high and glorious rather than to be in the bondage of sensual pleasures; and whoever does not entertain this disposition is by erudite men considered not to have attained puberty.'

The form of man was attained by a drop of water Which remained forty days in the womb. If in forty years it has not attained sense and propriety It can in reality not be called a man. Virility consists in liberality and amiableness. Think not that it is only in the material figure. Virtue is necessary because the form may be painted In halls with vermilion or verdigris. If a man possesses not excellence and goodness What is the difference between him and a picture on the wall? It is no virtue to gain the whole world. Gain the heart of one person if thou canst.

Story 12

One year discord had arisen in a caravan among the walking portion and I also travelled on foot. To obtain justice we attacked each other's heads and faces, giving full vent to pugnacity and contention. I saw a man sitting in a camel litter and saying to his companion: 'How wonderful! A pawn of ivory travels across the chess-board and becomes a farzin, and the footmen of the Haj travelled across the whole desert only to become worse.'

Tell on my part to the man-biting Haji Who tears the skins of people with torments: Thou art not a Haji but a camel is one Because, poor brute, it feeds on thorns and bears loads.

Story 13

An Indian who was learning how to throw naphtha was thus reproved by a sage: `This is not a play for thee whose house is made of reeds.' Speak not unless thou knowest it is perfectly proper And ask not what thou knowest will not elicit a good reply.

Story 14

A little man with a pain in his eyes went to a farrier to be treated by him. The farrier applied to his eyes what he used to put in those of quadrupeds so that the man became blind and lodged a complaint with the judge who, however, refrained from punishing the farrier, saying: `Had this man not been an ass, he would not have gone to a farrier.' The moral of this story is to let thee know that whoever entrusts an inexperienced man with an important business and afterwards repents is by intelligent persons held to suffer from levity of intellect. A shrewd and enlightened man will not give Affairs of importance to a base fellow to transact. A mat-maker although employed in weaving Is not set to work in a silk-factory.

Story 15

An illustrious man had a worthy son who died. Being asked what he desired to be written upon the sarcophagus of the tomb, he replied: 'The verses of the glorious book' are deserving of more honour than to be written on such a spot, where they would be injured by the lapse of time, would be walked upon by persons passing by and urinated upon by dogs. If anything is necessarily to be written, let what follows suffice:

Wah! How-every time the plants in the garden Sprouted-glad became my heart. Pass by, O friend, that in the spring Thou mayest see plants sprouting from my loam.'

Story 16

A pious man happened to pass near a rich fellow who had a slave and was just chastising him after having tied his feet and hands. He said: `My son, God the most high and glorious has given a creature like thyself into thy power and has bestowed upon thee superiority over him. Give thanks to the Almighty and do not indulge in so much violence towards the man because it is not meet that in the morn of resurrection he should be better than thyself and put thee to shame.'

Be not much incensed against a slave. Oppress him not, grieve not his heart. Thou hast purchased him for ten dirhems And hast not after all created him by thy power. How long is this command, pride and power to last? There is a Master more exalted than thou. O thou owner of Arslan and of Aghosh, Do not forget him who is thy commander. There is a tradition that the prince of the world, upon whom be the benediction of Allah and peace, has said: 'It will occasion the greatest sorrow on the day of resurrection when a pious worshipper is conveyed to paradise and a lord of profligacy to hell.'

Upon the slave subject to thy service Vent not boundless anger but treat him gently Because on the day of reckoning it will be a shame To see the slave free and his owner in chains.

Story 17

One year I travelled from Balkh with Damascenes and the road being full of danger on account of robbers, a young man accompanied us as an escort. He was expert with the shield and the bow, handled every weapon and so strong that ten men were not able to span his bow-string. Moreover the athletes of the face of the earth could not bend his back down to the ground. He was, however, rich, brought up in the shade, without experience in the world, the drum-sounds of warriors never having reached his ears nor the lightning of the swords of horsemen dazzled his eyes.

He had not fallen prisoner into the hands of a foe. No shower of arrows had rained around him. I happened to be running together with this youth, who threw down by the force of his arm every wall that came in his way, and pulled up by the strength of his fist every big tree he saw, exclaiming, boastingly: Where is the elephant that he may see the shoulders of the heroes? Where is the lion that he may see the fists of men?

On that occasion two Indians showed their heads from behind a rock, desirous to attack us. One of them had a club in his hand whilst the other showed a sling under his arm. I asked our youth what he was waiting for.

Show what thou hast of bravery and strength For here is the foe, coming on his own feet to the grave. I saw the arrow and bow falling from the hands of the young man and his bones trembling: Not everyone who splits a hair with a cuirass-piercing arrow Can, on the day of attack by warriors, extricate his feet.

We saw no other remedy but to abandon our baggage, arms and clothes, whereby we saved our lives.

Employ an experienced man in important affairs Who is able to ensnare a fierce lion with his lasso. A youth, though he may have a strong arm and elephant-body, His joints will snap asunder for fear in contact with a foe. The issue of a battle is known by a tried man before the contest Like the solution of a legal question to a learned man.

Story 18

I noticed the son of a rich man, sitting on the grave of his father and quarreling with a dervish-boy, saying: `The sarcophagus of my father's tomb is of stone and its epitaph is elegant. The pavement is of marble, tesselated with turquois-like bricks. But what resembles thy father's grave? It consists of two contiguous bricks with two handfuls of mud thrown over it.' The dervish-boy listened to all this and then observed: `By the time thy father is able to shake off those heavy stones which cover him, mine will have reached paradise.'

An ass with a light burden No doubt walks easily.

A dervish who carries only the load of poverty Will also arrive lightly burdened at the gate of death Whilst he who lived in happiness, wealth and ease Will undoubtedly on all these accounts die hard. At all events, a prisoner who escapes from all his bonds Is to be considered more happy than an amir taken prisoner.

Story 19

I asked an illustrious man for the reason of the tradition: Account as an enemy the passion which is between thy two loins. He replied: `The reason is because whatever enemy thou propitiatest becomes thy friend, whereas the more thou indulgest in a passion, the more it will oppose thee.'

Man attains angelic nature by eating sparingly But if he be voracious like beasts he falls like a stone. He whose wishes thou fulfillest will obey thy command Contrary to passion, which will command, when obeyed.

Story 20

Contention of Sa`di with a Disputant concerning Wealth and Poverty

I saw a man in the form but not with the character of a dervish, sitting in an assembly, who had begun a quarrel; and, having opened the record of complaints, reviled wealthy men, alleging at last that the hand of power of dervishes to do good was tied and that the foot of the intention of wealthy men to do good was broken.

The liberal have no money. The wealthy have no liberality.

I, who had been cherished by the wealth of great men, considered these words offensive and said: `My good friend, the rich are the income of the destitute and the hoarded store of recluses, the objects of pilgrims, the refuge of travellers, the bearers of heavy loads for the relief of others. They give repasts and partake of them to feed their dependants and servants, the surplus of their liberalities being extended to widows, aged persons, relatives and neighbours.'

The rich must spend for pious uses, vows and hospitality, Tithes, offerings, manumissions, gifts and sacrifices. How canst thou attain their power of doing good who art able To perform only the prayer-flections and these with a hundred distractions?

If there be efficacy in the power to be liberal and in the ability of performing religious duties, the rich can attain it better because they possess money to give alms, their garments are pure, their reputation is guarded, their hearts are at leisure. Inasmuch as the power of obedience depends upon nice morsels and correct worship upon elegant clothes, it is evident that hungry bowels have but little strength, an empty hand can afford no liberality, shackled feet cannot walk, and no good can come from a hungry belly. He sleeps troubled in the night Who has no support for the morrow. The ant collects in summer a subsistence For spending the winter in ease.

Freedom from care and destitution are not joined together and comfort in poverty is an impossibility. A man who is rich is engaged in his evening devotions whilst another who is poor is looking for his evening meal. How can they resemble each other?

He who possesses means is engaged in worship. Whose means are scattered, his heart is distracted.

The worship of those who are comfortable is more likely to meet with acceptance, their minds being more attentive and not distracted or scattered. Having a secure income, they may attend to devotion. The Arab says: `I take refuge with Allah against base poverty and neighbours whom I do not love. There is also a tradition: Poverty is blackness of face in both worlds.' He retorted by asking me whether I had heard the Prophet's saying: Poverty is my glory. I replied: `Hush! The prince of the world alluded to the poverty of warriors in the battlefield of acquiescence and of submission to the arrow of destiny; not to those who don the patched garb of righteousness but sell the doles of food given them as alms.'

O drum of high sound and nothing within, What wilt thou do without means when the struggle comes? Turn away the face of greed from people if thou art a man. Trust not the rosary of one thousand beads in thy hand.

A dervish without divine knowledge rests not until his poverty, culminates in unbelief; for poverty is almost infidelity, because a nude person cannot be clothed without money nor a prisoner liberated. How can the like of us attain their high position and how does the bestowing resemble the receiving hand? Knowest thou not that God the most high and glorious mentions in his revealed word the Pleasures of paradise -- They shall have a certain provision in paradise -- to inform thee that those who are occupied with cares for a subsistence are excluded from the felicity of piety and that the realm of leisure is under the ring of the certain provision.

The thirsty look in their sleep On the whole world as a spring of water.

Wherever thou beholdest one who has experienced destitution and tasted bitterness, throwing himself wickedly into fearful adventures and not avoiding their consequences, he fears not the punishment of Yazed and does not discriminate between what is licit or illicit.

The dog whose head is touched by a clod of earth Leaps for joy, imagining it to be a bone. And when two men take a corpse on their shoulders, A greedy fellow supposes it to be a table with food.

But the possessor of wealth is regarded with a favourable eye by the Almighty for the lawful acts he has done and preserved from the unlawful acts he might commit. Although I have not fully explained this matter nor adduced arguments, I rely on thy sense of justice to tell me whether thou hast ever seen a mendicant with his hands tied up to his shoulders or a poor fellow sitting in prison or a veil of innocence rent or a guilty hand amputated, except in consequence of poverty? Lion-hearted men were on account of their necessities captured in mines which they had dug to rob houses and their heels were perforated. It is also possible that a dervish, impelled by the cravings of his lust and unable to restrain it, may commit sin because the stomach and the sexual organs are twins, that is to say, they are the two children of one belly and as long as one of these is contented, the other will likewise be satisfied.

I heard that a dervish had been seen committing a wicked act with a youth, and although he had been put to shame, he was also in danger of being stoned. He said: `O Musalmans, I have no power to marry a wife and no patience to restrain myself. What am I to do? There is no monasticism in Islam." Among the number of causes producing internal tranquility and comfort in wealthy people, the fact may be reckoned that they take every night a sweetheart in their arms and may every day contemplate a youth whose brightness excels that of the shining morn and causes the feet of walking cypresses to conceal themselves abashed.

Plunging the fist into the blood of beloved persons, Dying the finger-tips with the colour of the jujube-fruit.

It is impossible that with his beauteous stature he should prowl around prohibited things or entertain intentions of ruin to himself.

How could he who took as booty a Huri of paradise Take any notice of the benes of Yaghma?

Who has before him fresh dates which he loves Has no need to throw stones on clusters upon trees.

Mostly empty handed persons pollute the skirt of modesty by transgression, and those who are hungry steal bread.

When a ferocious dog has found meat He asks not whether it is of the camel of Saleh or the ass of Dujjal.

What a number of modest women have on account of poverty fallen into complete profligacy, throwing away their precious reputation to the wind of dishonour!

With hunger the power of abstinence cannot abide. Poverty snatches the reins from the hands of piety.

Whilst I was uttering these words, the dervish lost the bridle of patience from his hands, drew forth the sword of his tongue, caused the steed of eloquence to caper in the plain of reproach and said: 'Thou hast been so profuse in this panegyric of wealthy men and hast talked so much nonsense that they might be supposed to be the antidote to poverty or the key to the storehouse of provisions; whereas they are a handful of proud, arrogant, conceited and abominable fellows intent upon accumulating property and money and so thirsting for dignity and abundance, that they do not speak to poor people except with insolence, and look upon them with contempt. They consider scholars to be mendicants and insult poor men on account of the wealth which they themselves possess and the glory of dignity which they imagine is inherent in them. They sit in the highest places and believe they are better than anyone else. They never show kindness to anybody and are ignorant of the maxim of sages that he who is inferior to others in piety but superior in riches is outwardly powerful but in reality a destitute man. If a wretch on account of his wealth is proud to a sage Consider him to be the podex of an ass, though he may be a perfumed ox.'

I said: `Do not think it allowable to insult them for they are possessors of generosity.' He rejoined: `Thou art mistaken. They are slaves of money. Of what use is it that they are like bulky clouds and rain not, like the fountain of light, the sun, and shine upon no one? They are mounted on the steed of ability but do not use it; they would not stir a step for God's sake nor spend one dirhem without imposing obligation and insult. They accumulate property with difficulty, guard it with meanness and abandon it with reluctance, according to the saying of illustrious men that the silver of an avaricious man will come up from the ground when he goes into the ground.

One man gathers wealth with trouble and labour And if another comes, he takes it without either.'

I retorted: `Thou hast not become aware of the parsimony of wealthy men except by reason of mendicancy or else, to him who has laid aside covetousness, a liberal and an avaricious man would appear to be the same. The touchstone knows what gold is and the beggar knows him who is stingy.' He rejoined: `I am speaking from experience when I say that they station rude and insolent men at their gates to keep off worthy persons, to place violent hands upon men of piety and discretion, saying: ``Nobody is here", and verily they have spoken the truth.'

Of him who has no sense, intention, plan or opinion, The gatekeeper has beautifully said: `No one is in the house.'

I said this is excusable because they are teased out of their lives by people expecting favours and driven to lamentation by petitions of mendicants; it being according to common sense an impossibility to satisfy beggars even if the sand of the desert were to be transmuted into pearls.

The eye of greediness, the wealthy of the world Can no more fill than dew can replenish a well.

Hatim Tai dwelt in the desert; had he been in a town he would have been helpless against the assaults of beggars and they would have torn to pieces his upper garments as it is recorded in the Tayibat:

Look not at me that others may not conceive hopes Because there is no reward to be got from beggars.

He said: `No. I take pity on their state.' I replied: `No. Thou enviest them their wealth.' We were thus contending with each other, every pawn he put forward I endeavoured to repel, and every time he announced check to my king, I covered him with my queen until he had gambled away all his ready cash and had shot off all the arrows of his quiver in arguing.

Have a care; do not throw away the shield when attacked by an orator Who has nothing except borrowed eloquence to show, Practise thou religion and marifet because a Suja-speaking orator Displays weapons at the gate but no one is in the fort.

At last no arguments remained to him and, having been defeated, he commenced to speak nonsense as is the custom of ignorant men who, when they can no more address proofs against their opponent, shake the chain of enmity like the idol-carver Azer who being unable to overcome his son in argument began to quarrel with him saying if thou forbearest not I will surely stone thee. The man insulted me. I spoke harshly to him. He tore my collar and I caught hold of his chin-case.

He falling upon me and I on him, Crowds running after us and laughing, The finger of astonishment of a world On the teeth; from what was said and heard by us.

In short we carried our dispute to the qazi and agreed to abide by a just decision of the judge of Musalmans, who would investigate the affair and tell the difference between the rich and the poor. When the qazi had seen our state and heard our logic, he plunged his head into his collar and after meditating for a while spoke as follows: 'O thou, who hast lauded the wealthy and hast indulged in violent language towards dervishes, thou art to know that wherever a rose exists, there also thorns occur; that wine is followed by intoxication, that a treasure is guarded by a serpent, and that wherever royal pearls are found, men-devouring sharks must also be. The sting of death is the sequel of the delights of life and a cunning demon bars the enjoyment of paradise. `What will the violence of a foe do if it cannot touch the seeker of the Friend? Treasure, serpent; rose, thorn; grief and pleasure are all linked together.

`Perceivest thou not that in a garden there are musk-willows as well as withered sticks? And likewise in the crowd of the rich there are grateful and impious men, as also in the circle of dervishes some are forbearing and some are impatient.

`If every drop of dew were to become a pearl The bazar would be full of them as of ass-shells.

`Those near to the presence of the most high and glorious are rich men with the disposition of dervishes and dervishes with the inclination of the rich. The greatest of rich men is he who sympathizes with dervishes and the best of dervishes is he who looks but little towards rich men. Who trusts in Allah, he will be his sufficient support.' After this the qazi turned the face of reproof from me to the dervish and said: `O thou who hast alleged that the wealthy are engaged in wickedness and intoxicated with pleasure, some certainly are of the kind thou hast described; of defective aspirations, and ungrateful for benefits received. Sometimes they accumulate and put by, eat and give not; if for instance the rain were to fail or a deluge were to distress the world, they, trusting in their own power, would not care for the misery of dervishes, would not fear God and would say:

If another perishes for want of food I have some; what cares a duck for the deluge?

The women riding on camels in their howdahs Take no notice of him who sinks in the sana.

The base when they have saved their own blankets Say: What boots it if all mankind perishes?

`There are people of the kind thou hast heard of, and other persons who keep the table of beneficence spread out, the hand of liberality open, seeking a good name and pardon from God. They are the possessors of this world and of the next, like the slaves of His Majesty Padshah of the world who is aided by devine grace, conqueror, possessor of authority among nations, defender of the frontiers of Islam, heir of the realm of Solomon, the most righteous of the kings of the period, Muzaffar-ud-dunia wa uddin Atabek Abu Bekr Ben Sa'd Ben Zanki, may Allah prolong his days and aid his banners.

`A father never shows the kindness to his son Which the hand of thy liberality has bestowed on mankind. God desired to vouchsafe a blessing to the world And in his mercy made thee padshah of the world.'

When the qazi had thus far protracted his remarks and had caused the horse of his eloquence to roam beyond the limits of our expectation, we submitted to his judicial decision, condoned to each other what had passed between us, took the path of reconciliation, placed our heads on each other's feet by way of apology, kissed each other's head and face, terminating the discussion with the following two distichs:

Complain not of the turning of the spheres, O dervish, Because thou wilt be luckless if thou diest in this frame of mind. O wealthy man, since thy heart and hand are successful Eat and be liberal for thou hast conquered this world and the next.

ON RULES FOR CONDUCT IN LIFE

Maxim 1

Property is for the comfort of life, not for the accumulation of wealth. A sage, having been asked who is lucky and who is not, replied: `He is lucky who has eaten and sowed but he is unlucky who has died and not enjoyed.'

Pray not for the nobody who has done nothing, Who spent his life in accumulating property but has not enjoyed it.

Moses, upon whom be peace, thus advised Quran: `Do thou good as Allah has done unto thee.' But he would not listen and thou hast heard of his end: Who has not accumulated good with dirhems and dinars Has staked his end upon his dirhems and dinars. If thou desirest to profit by riches of the world Be liberal to mankind as God has been liberal to thee. The Arab says: Be liberal without imposing obligations and verily the profit will return to thee. Wherever the tree of beneficence has taken root Its tallness and branches pass beyond the sky. If thou art desirous to eat the fruit thereof Do not put a saw to its foot by imposing obligations.

Thank God that thou hast been divinely aided And not excluded from his gifts and bounty. Think not thou conferrest an obligation on the sultan by serving him But be obliged to him for having kept thee in his service.

Maxim 2

Two men took useless trouble and strove without any profit, when one of them accumulated property without enjoying it, and the other learnt without practising what he had learnt.

However much science thou mayest acquire Thou art ignorant when there is no practice in thee. Neither deeply learned nor a scholar will be A quadruped loaded with some books. What information or knowledge does the silly beast posses Whether it is carrying a load of wood or of books?

Maxim 3

Knowledge is for the cherishing of religion, not for amassing wealth. Who sold abstinence, knowledge and piety Filled a granary but burnt it clean away.

Maxim 4

A learned man who is not abstinent resembles a torchbearer who guides others but does not guide himself.

Who has spent a profitless life Bought nothing and threw away his gold.

Maxim 5

The country is adorned by intelligent and the religion by virtuous men. Padshahs stand more in need of the advice of intelligent men than intelligent men of the proximity of padshahs.

If thou wilt listen to advice, padshah, There is none better in all books than this: `Entrust a business to an intelligent man Although it may not be his occupation.'

Maxim 6

Three things cannot subsist without three things: property without trade, science without controversy and a country without punishment.

Speak sometimes in a friendly, conciliatory, manly way Perhaps thou wilt ensnare a heart with the lasso. Sometimes speak in anger; for a hundred jars of sugar Will on occasion not have the effect of one dose of colocynth.

Maxim 7

To have mercy upon the bad is to injure the good; to pardon tyrants is to do violence to dervishes. If thou associatest and art friendly with a wretch He will commit sin with thy wealth and make thee his partner.

Admonition 1

The amity of princes and the sweet voice of children are not to be trusted, because the former is changed by fancy and the latter in the course of one night.

Give not thy heart to a sweetheart of a thousand lovers, And if thou givest it, thou givest that heart for separation.

Admonition 2

Confide not to a friend every secret thou possessest. How knowest thou that he will not some time become thy foe? Inflict not every injury thou canst upon an enemy because it is possible that one day he may become thy friend.

Admonition 3

Reveal not thy secret to any man although he may be trustworthy, because no one can keep thy secret better than thyself.

Silence is preferable than to tell thy mind To anyone; saying what is to remain unsaid. O simpleton, stop the source of the spring. When it becomes full, the brook cannot be stopped.

Maxim 8

A weak foe, who professes submission and shows friendship, has no other object than to become a strong enemy. It has been said that as the friendship of friends is unreliable, what trust can be put in the flattery of enemies?

Admonition 4

Who despises an insignificant enemy resembles him who is careless about fire.

Extinguish it today, while it may be quenched, Because when fire is high, it burns the world. Allow not the bow to be spanned By a foe because an arrow may pierce.

Admonition 5

Speak so between two enemies that thou mayest not be put to shame if they become friends.

Between two men contention is like fire, The ill-starred back-biter being the wood-carrier. When both of them become friends again He will among them be unhappy and ashamed. To kindle fire between two men Is not wise but is to burn oneself therein.

Converse in whispers with thy friends Lest thy sanguinary foe may hear thee. Take care of what thou sayest in front of a wall Because an ear may be behind the wall.

Admonition 6

Whoever makes peace with the enemies of his friends greatly injures his friends. Wash thy hands, O wise man, from a friend Who is sitting together with thy foes.

Admonition 7

When thou art uncertain in transacting an affair, select that portion of it which will entail no danger to thee.

Speak not harshly to a man of gentle speech. Seek not to fight with him who knocks at the door of peace.

Admonition 8

As long as an affair can be arranged with gold, it is not proper to endanger life.

When the hand is foiled in every stratagem It is licit to put the hand to the sword.

Admonition 9

Do not pity the weakness of a foe because when he gains strength he will not spare thee.

Boast not of thy moustaches when thou seest thy foe is weak. There is marrow in every bone, a man in every coat.

Maxim 9

Whoever slays a bad fellow saves mankind from a calamity and him from the wrath of God.

Condonation is laudable but nevertheless Apply no salve to the wound of an oppressor of the people. He who had mercy upon a serpent Knew not that it was an injury to the sons of Adam.

Maxim 10

It is a mistake to accept advice from an enemy but permissible to hear it; and to act contrary to it is perfectly correct.

Be cautious of what a foe tells thee to do Lest thou strike thy knee with the hand of pain. If he points thy way to the right like an arrow Deflect therefrom and take that to the left hand.

Admonition 10

Wrath beyond measure produces estrangement and untimely kindness destroys authority. Be neither so harsh as to disgust the people with thee nor so mild as to embolden them.

Severity and mildness together are best Like a bleeder who is a surgeon and also applies a salve. A wise man uses neither severity to excess Nor mildness; for it lessens his authority. He neither exalts himself too much Nor exposes himself at once to contempt.

A youth said to his father: `O wise man, Give me for instruction one advice like an aged person.' He said: `Be kind but not to such a degree That a sharp-toothed wolf may become audacious.'

Maxim 11

May that prince never govern a kingdom Who is not an obedient slave to God.

Admonition 11

It is incumbent upon a padshah to give way to anger towards his slaves only so far as to retain the confidence of his friends. The fire of anger first burns him who has given cause for it and afterwards the flame may or may not reach the foe.

It is not proper for sons of Adam born of earth To inflate their heads with pride, violence and wind. Thou who displayest so much heat and obstinacy Must be, I think, not of earth but of fire.

I visited a hermit in the country of Bilqan And requested him to purge me of ignorance by instruction. He replied: `Be patient like earth, O lawyer, Or else, bury under the earth all thy learning.'

Maxim 12

An ill-humoured man is captive in the hands of a foe, from the grasp of whose punishment he cannot be delivered wherever he may go.

If from the hand of calamity an ill-natured man escapes into the sky The evil disposition of his own nature retains him in calamity.

Admonition 12

When thou perceivest that discord is in the army of the foe, be thou at ease; but if they are united, be apprehensive of thy own distress.

Go and sit in repose with thy friends When thou seest war among the enemies; But if thou perceivest that they all agree Span thy bow and carry stones upon the rampart.

Maxim 13

When all the artifices of an enemy have failed he shakes the chain of friendship, and thereon performs acts of friendship which no enemy is able to do.

Admonition 13

Strike the head of a serpent with the hand of a foe because one of two advantages will result. If the enemy succeeds thou hast killed the snake and if the latter, thou hast been delivered from a foe.

Advice: If thou art aware of news which will grieve a heart, remain silent that others may convey it.

Nightingale, bring tidings of spring. Leave bad news to the owl.

Caution: Give not information to a padshah of the treachery of anyone, unless thou art sure he will accept it; else thou wilt only be preparing thy own destruction.

Prepare to speak only when Thy words are likely to have effect. Speech is a perfection in the soul of man But do not ruin thyself by speaking.

Maxim 14

Whoever gives advice to a self-willed man stands himself in need of advice.

Admonition 14

Swallow not the deception of a foe. Purchase not conceit from a panegyrist. The one has laid out a snare for provisions and the other has opened the jaws of covetousness.

Maxim 15

A fool is pleased by flattery like the inflated heel of a corpse that has the appearance of fatness.

Take care not to listen to the voice of a flatterer Who expects cheaply to derive profit from thee. If one day thou failest to satisfy his wishes He enumerates two hundred faults of thine.

Maxim 16

Unless an orator's defects are mentioned by someone, his good points will not be praised. Be not proud of the beauty of thy speech, Of the approbation of an ignoramus and of thy own opinion.

Maxim 17

Everyone thinks himself perfect in intellect and his child in beauty.

A Jew was debating with a Musalman Till I shook with laughter at their dispute. The Moslem said in anger: `If this deed of mine Is not correct, may God cause me to die a Jew.' The Jew said: `I swear by the Pentateuch That if my oath is false, I shall die a Moslem like thee.' Should from the surface of the earth wisdom disappear Still no one will acknowledge his own ignorance.

Maxim 18

Ten men eat at a table but two dogs will contend for one piece of carrion. A greedy person will stir be hungry with the whole world, whilst a contented man will be satisfied with one bread. Wise men have said that poverty with content is better than wealth and not abundance.

Narrow intestines may be filled with dry bread But the wealth of the surface of the world will not fill a greedy eye.

When the term of my father's life had come to an end He gave me this one advice and passed away: Lust is fire, abstain therefrom, Make not the fire of hell sharp for thee. In that fire the burning thou wilt not be able to bear, Quench this fire with water today.

Admonition 15

Whoever does no good in the time of ability will see distress in the time of inability.

No one is more unlucky than an oppressor of men Because in the day of calamity no one is his friend.

Maxim 19

Life is in the keeping of a single breath and the world is an existence between two annihilations. Those who sell the religion for the world `are asses', they sell Joseph but what do `they buy'? Did I not command you, O sons of Adam, that ye should not worship Satan?

On the word of a foe thou hast broken faith with a friend. See from whom thou hast cut thyself off and to whom united.

Maxim 20

Satan cannot conquer the righteous and the sultan the poor.

Lend nothing to a prayerless man Although his mouth may gasp from penury; Because he who neglects the commands of God Will also not care for what he may be indebted to thee.

Maxim 21

Whatever takes place quickly is not permanent.

I have heard that eastern loam is made In forty days into a porcelain cup. A hundred are daily made in Baghdad. Hence thou seest also their price is vile.

A little fowl issues from the egg and seeks food Whilst man's progeny has no knowledge, sense or discernment. Nevertheless the former attains nothing when grown up Whilst the latter surpasses all beings in dignity and excellence. Glass is everywhere, and therefore of no account, But a ruby difficult to get, and therefore precious.

Maxim 22

Affairs succeed by patience and a hasty man fails.

I saw with my eyes in the desert That a slow man overtook a fast one. A galloping horse, fleet like the wind, fell back Whilst the camel-man continued slowly his progress.

Maxim 23

Nothing is better for an ignorant man than silence, and if he were to consider it to be suitable, he would not be ignorant.

If thou possessest not the perfection of excellence It is best to keep thy tongue within thy mouth. Disgrace is brought on a man by his tongue. A walnut, having no kernel, will be light.

A fool was trying to teach a donkey, Spending all his time and efforts in the task. A sage observed: `O ignorant man, what sayest thou? Fear blame from the censorious in this vain attempt.

A brute cannot learn speech from thee. Learn thou silence from a brute.'

Who does not reflect what he is to answer Will mostly speak improperly. Come. Either arrange thy words like a wise man Or remain sitting silent like a brute.

Admonition 16

Whenever a man disputes with one who is more learned than himself to make people know of his learning, they will know that he is ignorant.

If one better than thyself begins to speak, Although thou mayest know better, contradict him not.

Maxim 24

Whoever associates with bad people will see no good.

If an angel associates with a demon He will learn from him fear, fraud and hypocrisy. Of the wicked thou canst learn only wickedness. A wolf will not take to sewing jackets.

Admonition 17

Reveal not the secret faults of men because thou wilt put them to shame and wilt forfeit thy own confidence.

Maxim 25

Who acquires science and does not practise it, resembles him who possesses an ox but does not use him to plough or to sow seed.

Maxim 26

From a body without a heart obedience does not arise and a husk without a kernel is no stock in trade.

Not everyone who is brisk in dispute is correct in business.

Many a stature concealed by a sheet If revealed appears to be the mother of one's mother.

Maxim 27

If every night were to be the night of Qadr, the night of Qadr would be without Qadr.

If all stones were rubies of Badakhshan, The price of rubies and of stones would be the same.

Maxim 28

Not everyone who is handsome in form possesses a good character; the qualities are inside not upon the skin.

It is possible in one day to know from a man's qualities What degree of science he has reached. Be however not sure of his mind nor deceived. A wicked spirit is not detected sometimes for years.

Caution 2: Who quarrels with great men sheds his own blood. One who thinks that he is great Is truly said to be squinting. Thou wilt soon see thy forehead broken If thou buttest it in play against a ram.

Maxim 29

To strike one's fist on a lion, and to grasp the sharp edge of a sword with the hand, is not the part of an intelligent man.

Do not fight or try thy strength with a furious man. Hide thy hands in thy arm-pits to avoid his finger-nails.

Caution 3: A weak man trying to show his prowess off against a strong one only aids his foe to encompass his own destruction.

What strength has one brought up in the shade To go against champions in a fight? A man with weak arms in his folly throws His fist upon a man with iron claws.

Maxim 30

Whoever does not listen to advice will have occasion to hear reproof.

If admonition enters not thy ear Be silent when I blame thee.

Elegant saying 1: Men void of accomplishments cannot behold those who possess some, without barking like the curs of the bazar on seeing a hunting dog, but dare not come forward; that is to say, when a base fellow is unable to vie with an accomplished man he sets about slandering him according to his own wickedness. The envious mean fellow will certainly slander, Whose tongue of speech is dumb when face to face.

Maxim 31

If there were no craving of the stomach, no bird would enter the snare of the fowler; nay, he would not even set the snare.

Maxim 32

Sages eat slow, devotees half satisfy their appetite, recluses only eat to preserve life, youths until the dishes are removed, old men till they begin to perspire, but qalandars till no room remains in the bowels for drawing breath and no food on the table for anybody.

A slave to constipation spends two sleepless nights, One night from repletion and another from distress.

Maxim 33

To consult women brings on ruin and to be liberal to rebellious men crime. To have mercy on sharp-toothed tigers Is to be tyrannical towards sheep.

Admonition 18

Who has power over his foe and does not slay him is his own enemy.

With a stone in the hand and a snake on a stone It is folly to consider and to delay.

Others, however, enounce a contrary opinion and say that it is preferable to respite captives because the option of killing or not killing remains; but if they be slain without delay, it is possible that some advantage may be lost, the like of which cannot be again obtained.

It is quite easy to deprive a man of life. When he is slain he cannot be resuscitaied again. It is a condition of wisdom in the archer to be patient Because when the arrow leaves the bow it returns no more.

Maxim 34

When a sage comes in contact with fools, he must not expect to be honoured, and if an ignorant man overcomes a sage in an oratorical contest, it is no wonder, because even a stone breaks a jewel. What wonder is there that the song Of a nightingale ceases when imprisoned with a crow Or that a virtuous man under the tyranny of vagabonds Feels affliction in his heart and is irate. Although a base stone may break a golden vase, The price of the stone is not enhanced nor of the gold lost.

Maxim 35

Be not astonished when a wise man ceases to speak in company of vile persons, since the melody of a harp cannot overcome the noise of a drum and the perfume of ambergris must succumb to the stench of rotten garlic.

A blatant ignoramus proudly lifted his neck Because he had overcome a scholar by his impudence. Knowest thou not that the Hejazi musical tune Succumbs to the roar of the drum of war?

Maxim 36

Even after falling into mud a jewel retains its costliness, and dust, although it may rise into the sky, is as contemptible as before. Capacity without education is deplorable and education without capacity is thrown away. Ashes are of high origin because the nature of fire is superior, but as they have no value of their own, they are similar to earth and the price of sugar arises not from. the cane but from its own quality.

The land of Canaan having no natural excellence, The birth of a prophet therein could not enhance its worth. Display thy virtue if thou hast any, not thy origin. The rose is the offspring of thorns and Abraham of Azer.

Maxim 37

Musk is known by its perfume and not by what the druggist says. A scholar is silent like the perfumer's casket but displays accomplishments, whilst an ignoramus is loud-voiced and intrinsically empty like a war-drum.

A learned man among blockheads (So says the parable of our friends) Is like a sweetheart among the blind Or a Quran among unbelievers.

Maxim 38

A friend whom people have been cherishing during a lifetime they must not suddenly insult. It takes a stone many a year to become a ruby. Beware not to break it in a moment with a stone.

Maxim 39

Intellect may become captive to lust like a weak man in the hands of an artful woman. Bid farewell to pleasure in a house Where the shouting of a woman is loud.

Maxim 40

A design without strength to execute it is fraud and deception and application of strength without a design is ignorance and lunacy. Discernment is necessary. Arrangement and intellect, then a realm; For realm and wealth with an ignorant man are weapons against himself.

Maxim 41

A liberal man who eats and bestows is better than a devote who fasts and hoards.

Maxim 42

Who has renounced appetites for the sake of approbation by men has fallen from licit into illicit appetites.

A devotee who sits in a corner not for God's sake Is helpless. What can he see in a dark mirror?

Little by little becomes much and drop by drop will be a torrent; that is to say, he who has no power gathers small stones that he may at the proper opportunity annihilate the pride of his foe.

Drop upon drop collected will make a river. Rivers upon rivers collected will make a sea. Little and little together will become much. The granary is but grain upon grain.

Maxim 43

A scholar is not meekly to overlook the folly of a common person because thus both parties are injured; the dignity of the former being lessened, and the ignorance of the latter confirmed.

Speak gracefully and kindly to a low fellow, His pride and obstinacy will augment.

Maxim 44

Transgression by whomsoever committed is blamable but more so in learned men, because learning is a weapon for combating Satan and, when the possessor of a weapon is made prisoner, his shame will be greater.

It is better to be an ignorant poor fellow Then a learned man who is not abstemious; Because the former loses the way by his blindness While the latter falls into a well with both eyes open.

Maxim 45

Whose bread is not eaten by others while he is alive, he will not be remembered when he is dead. A widow knows the delight of grapes and not the lord of fruits. Joseph the just, salutation to him, never ate to satiety in the Egyptian dearth for fear he might forget the hungry people.

How can he who lives in comfort and abundance Know what the state of the famished is? He is aware of the condition of the poor Who has himself fallen into a state of distress. O thou who art riding a fleet horse, consider That the poor thorn-carrying ass is in water and mud. Ask not for fire from thy poor neighbour's house Because what passes out of his window is the smoke of his heart.

Admonition 19

Ask not a dervish in poor circumstances, and in the distress of a year of famine, how he feels, unless thou art ready to apply a salve to his wound or to provide him with a maintenance.

When thou seest an ass, fallen in mud with his load, Have mercy in thy heart and step not on his head. But when thou hast gone and asked him how he fell, Gird thy loins and take hold of his tail like a man.

Maxim 46

Two things are contrary to reason: to enjoy more than is decreed and to die before the time appointed.

Fate will not change by a thousand laments and sighs, By thanks or complaints, issuing from the mouth. The angel appointed over the treasures of wind Cares not if the lamp of a widow dies.

Admonition 20

O thou asker of food, sit for thou wilt eat; and 0 thou asked by death, run not for thou wilt not save thy life. Whether thou strivest for a maintenance or not God the most high and glorious will send it to thee; And if thou rushest into the jaw of a lion or tiger They will not devour thee unless on the day decreed.

Maxim 47

What is not placed cannot be reached by the hand and whatever is placed will be reached wherever it is.

Hast thou heard that Alexander went into the darkness And after all his efforts could not taste the water of immortality?

Maxim 48

A rich profligate is a lump of earth gilded and a pious dervish is a sweetheart besmeared with earth. The latter is the patched garment of Moses and the former is the bejewelled beard of Pharaoh. Nevertheless good men retain a cheerful countenance in adversity whilst the rich droop their heads even in prosperity.

Who possesses wealth and dignity but therewith Succours not those whose minds are distressed, Inform him that no kind of wealth and dignity He will enjoy in the mansion of the next world.

Maxim 49

An envious man is avaricious with the wealth of God and hates the guiltless as foes. I saw a crackbrained little man, Reviling a possessor of dignity, Who replied: `O fellow, if thou art unlucky, What guilt is there in lucky men?'

Forbear to wish evil to an envious man Because the ill-starred fellow is an evil to himself. What needest thou to show enmity to him Who has such a foe on the nape of his neck?

Maxim 50

A disciple without intention is a lover without money; a traveller without knowledge is a bird without wings; a scholar without practice is a tree without fruit, and a devotee without science is a house without a door. The Quran was revealed for the acquisition of a good character, not for chanting written chapters. A pious unlettered man is like one who travels on foot, whilst a negligent scholar is like a sleeping rider. A sinner who lifts his hands in supplication is better than a devotee who keeps them proudly on his head. A good humoured and pleasant military officer Is superior to a theologian who injures men.

One being asked what a learned man without practice resembled, replied: `A bee without honey.'

Say to the rude and unkind bee, `At least forbear to sting, if thou givest no honey.'

Maxim 51

A man without virility is a woman and an avaricious devote is a highway robber.

O thou, who hast put on a white robe for a show, To be approved of men, whilst the book of thy acts is black. The hand is to be restrained from the world, No matter whether the sleeve be short or long.

Maxim 52

Regret will not leave the hearts of two persons and their feet of contention will not emerge from the mire: a merchant with a wrecked ship and a youth sitting with qalandars.

Dervishes will consider it licit to shed thy blood If they can have no access to thy property. Either associate not with a friend who dons the blue garb, Or bid farewell to all thy property. Either make no friends with elephant-keepers Or build a house suitable for elephants.

Maxim 53

Although a sultan's garment of honour is dear yet one's own old robe is more dear; and though the food of a great man may be delicious, the broken crumbs of one's own sack are more delicious. Vinegar by one's own labour and vegetables Are better than bread received as alms, and veal.

Maxim 54

It is contrary to what is proper, and against the opinion of to partake of medicine by guess and to go after a caravan without seeing the road. The Imam Murshid Muhammad Ghazali, upon whom be the mercy of Allah, having been asked in what manner he had attained such a degree of knowledge, replied: `By not being ashamed to ask about things I did not know.'

The hope of recovery is according to reason, That he should feel thy pulse who knows thy nature. Ask what thou knowest not; for the trouble of asking Will indicate to thee the way to the dignity of knowledge.

Admonition 21

Whatever thou perceivest will become known to thee in due course of time. Make no haste in asking for it, else the awe of thy dignity will be lessened.

When Loqman saw that in the hands of David All iron became by miracle soft like wax, He asked not: `What art thou doing?' Because He knew he would learn it without asking.

Maxim 55

One of the requirements for society is to attend to the affairs of thy household and also at the house of God.

Tell thy tale according to thy hearer's temper, If thou knowest him to be biased to thee. Every wise man who sits with Mejnun Speaks of nothing but the story of Laila's love.

Maxim 56

Anyone associating with bad people, although their nature may not infect his own, is supposed to follow their ways to such a degree that if he goes to a tavern to say his prayers, he will be supposed to do so for drinking wine.

Thou hast branded thyself with the mark of ignorance, When thou hast selected an ignoramus for thy companion. I asked some scholars for a piece of advice. They said: `Connect thyself not with an ignorant man, For if thou be learned, thou wilt be an ass in course of time And if unlearned thou wilt become a greater fool.'

Maxim 57

The meekness of the camel is known to be such that if a child takes hold of its bridle and goes a hundred farsakhs, it will not refuse to follow, but if a dangerous portion occurs which may occasion death and the child ignorantly desires to approach it, the camel tears the bridle from his hand, refusing any longer to obey because compliance in times of calamity is blamable. It is also said that by complaisance an enemy will not become a friend but that his greed will only be augmented. To him who is kind to thee, be dust at his feet But if he opposes thee fill his two eyes with dust. Speak not kindly or gently to an ill-humoured fellow Because a soft file cannot clean off inveterate rust.

Maxim 58

Who interrupts the conversation of others that they may know his excellence, they will become acquainted only with the degree of his folly. An intelligent man will not give a reply Unless he be asked a question. Because though his words may be based on truth, His claim to veracity may be deemed impossible.

Maxim 59

I had a wound under my robe and a sheikh asked me daily how, but not where it is, and I learned that he refrained because it is not admissible to mention every member; and wise men have also said that whoever does not ponder his question will be grieved by the answer. Until thou knowest thy words to be perfectly suitable Thou must not open thy mouth in speech. If thou speakest truth and remainest in captivity, It is better than that thy mendacity deliver thee therefrom.

Maxim 60

Mendacity resembles a violent blow, the scar of which remains, though the wound may be healed. Seest thou not how the brothers of Joseph became noted for falsehood, and no trust in their veracity remained, as Allah the most high has said: Nay but ye yourselves have contrived the thing for your own sake.

One habitually speaking the truth Is pardoned when he once makes a slip But if he becomes noted for lying, People do not believe him even when speaking truth.

Maxim 61

The noblest of beings is evidently man, and the meanest a dog, but intelligent persons agree that a grateful dog is better than an ungrateful man.

A dog never forgets a morsel received Though thou throwest a stone at him a hundred times. But if thou cherishest a base fellow a lifetime, He will for a trifle suddenly fight with thee.

Maxim 62

Who panders to his passions will not cultivate accomplishments and who possesses none is not suitable for a high position.

Have no mercy on a voracious ox Who sleeps a great deal and eats much. If thou wantest to have fatness like an ox, Yield thy body to the tyranny of people like an ass.

Maxim 63

It is written in the Evangel: `O son of Adam, if I give thee riches, thou wilt turn away from me with mundane cares, and if I make thee poor thou wilt sit down with a sad heart; then where wilt thou enjoy the sweetness of adoring me, and when wilt thou hasten to serve me?'

Sometimes thou art made haughty, and careless by wealth, Sometimes art in distress from exhaustion and penury. If thy state be such in joy and in distress, I know not when thou wilt turn to God from thyself.

Maxim 64

The will of the Inscrutable brings down one from the royal throne, and protects the other in the belly of a fish.

Happy is the time of the man Who spends it in adoring thee.

Maxim 65

When God draws the sword of wrath, prophets and saints draw in their heads, but if he casts a look of grace, he converts wicked into virtuous men.

If at the resurrection he addresses us in anger What chance of pardon will even prophets have? Say: `Remove the veil from the face of mercy Because sinners entertain hopes of pardon.'

Maxim 66

Whoever does not betake himself to the path of rectitude in consequence of the castigations of this world will fall under eternal punishment in the next. Allah the most high has said: And we will cause them to taste the nearer punishment of this world besides the more grievous punishment of the next.

Admonition is the address of superiors and then fetters. If they give advice and thou listenest not, they put thee in fetters.

Maxim 67

Fortunate men are admonished by the adventures and similes of those who have preceded them, before those who follow them can use the event as a proverb, like thieves who shorten their hands, lest their hands be cut off.

The bird does not go to the grain displayed When it beholds another fowl in the trap. Take advice by the misfortunes of others That others may not take advice from thee.

Maxim 68

How can he hear whose organ of audition has been created dull, and how can he avoid progressing upon whom the noose of happiness has been flung?

To the friends of God a dark night Shines like the brilliant day. This felicity is not by strength of arm Unless God the giver bestows it.

To whom shall I complain of thee? There is no other judge And there is no other hand superior to thine. Whom thou guidest -- no one can lead astray. Whom thou castest off no one can guide.

Maxim 69

The earth receives showers from heaven and gives to it only dust. Every vessel exudes what it contains.

If my humour appears to thee unbecoming Lose not thy own good humour.

Maxim 70

A mendicant with a good end is better than a padshah with a bad end.

The grief thou sufferest before the joy Is better than the grief endured after joy.

Maxim 71

The Most High sees a fault and conceals it, and a neighbour sees it not, but shouts.

Let us take refuge with Allah. If people knew our faults No one could have rest from interference by others.

Maxim 72

Gold is obtained from a mine by digging it, but from a miser by digging the soul.

Vile men spend not, but preserve. They say hope of spending is better than spending.

One day thou seest the wish of the foe fulfilled The gold remaining and the vile man dead.

Maxim 73

Who has no mercy upon inferiors will suffer from the tyranny of superiors.

Not every arm which contains strength Breaks the hand of the weak for showing bravery. Injure not the heart of the helpless For thou wilt succumb to the force of a strong man.

Maxim 74

When a wise man encounters obstacles, he leaps away and casts anchor at the proper opportunity, for thus he will be in the former instance safe on shore, and in the latter he will enjoy himself.

Maxim 75

The gambler requires three sixes and only three aces turn up.

The pasture is a thousand times more pleasant than the racecourse But the steed has not the bridle at its option.

Story 1

A dervish prayed thus: `O Lord, have mercy upon the wicked, because thou hast already had mercy upon good men by creating them to be good.'

Maxim 76

The first sovereign who laid stress on costume and wore rings on his left hand was Jamshid; and being asked why he had adorned his left whereas excellence resides in the right hand, he replied: `The right hand is fully ornamented by its own rectitude.'

Feridun ordered Chinese embroiderers To write around the borders of his tent: `Keep the wicked well, O intelligent man, Because the good are in themselves great and fortunate.'

Story 2

A great man having been asked why he wore his seal-ring on his left hand, whereas the right possesses so much excellence, replied: 'Knowest thou not that the meritorious are always neglected?'

He who has created joy and distress Apportions either excellence or luck.

Maxim 77

He may freely warn who neither fears to lose his life nor hopes for gold.

Pour either gold at the feet of a monotheist Or place an Indian sabre to his head. He entertains no hope nor fear from anyone And this is a sufficient basis of monotheism.

Maxim 78

The padshah is to remove oppressors; the police, murderers; and the qazi to hear complaints about thieves; but two enemies willing to agree to what is right will not apply to him.

When thou seest that it must be given what is right Pay it rather with grace than fighting and distressed. If a man pays not his tax of his own accord The officer's man will take it by force.

Maxim 79

The teeth of all men are blunted by sourness, but those of the qazi by sweetness.

The qazi whom thou bribest with five cucumbers Will prove that ten melon-fields are due to thee.

Maxim 80

What can an old prostitute do but vow to become chaste, and an policeman not to commit oppression upon men?

A youth who sits in a corner is a hero in the path of God Because an old man is unable to rise from his corner.

A youth must be strong minded to abstain from lust, Because even the sexual tool of an old man, of sluggish desire, rises not.

Maxim 81

A sage was asked: `Of so many notable, high and fertile trees which God the most high has created, not one is called free, except the cypress, which bears no fruit. What is the reason of this?'

He replied: `Every tree has its appropriate season of fruit, so that it is sometimes flourishing therewith, and looks sometimes withered by its absence; with the cypress, however, neither is the case, it being fresh at all times, and this is the quality of those who are free.'

Place not thy heart on what passes away; for the Tigris Will flow after the Khalifs have passed away in Baghdad. If thou art able, be liberal like the date tree, And if thy hand cannot afford it, be liberal like the cypress.

Maxim 82

Two men died, bearing away their grief One had possessed wealth and not enjoyed it, the other knowledge and not practised it.

No one sees an excellent but avaricious man Without publishing his defect But if a liberal man has a hundred faults His generosity covers his imperfections.

BIBLIOGRAPHY

Atil, Esin: *Exhibition of 2500 Years of Persian Art,* Washington D.C., 1971.

Bayat, Mojdeh: *Tales from the Land of the Sufis,* Boston, Mass., Shambhala Publications, 1994.

Bly, Robert: *When Grapes Turn to Wine,* Cambridge, Mass., Yellow Moon Press, 1986

Browne, Edward Granville*: A Persian Anthology: Being Translations From the Persian,* London, E. Benn, 1927.

Chandra, Moti: *The Technique of Mughal Painting*, Lucknow, 1949.

Cave, George.*Sufi Poetry*. Rawalpindin, Pakistan, R.C.D. Cultural Association, 1986.

Chittick, William: *The Sufi Path of Love: the Spiritual Teaching of Rumi.* N.Y., State University of New York Press, 1983.

Cowan, James: *Where Two Oceans Meet: A Selection of Odes from the Divan of Shems of Tabriz,* Rockport, Mass., Element, 1992.

Curzon, George N.: *Persia and the Persian Question*, London, 1892.

DeLamotte, Roy C.: *Jalaluddin Rumi, Songbird of Sufism,* Lanham, Md., University Press of America, 1980.

Dole, Nathan Haskell: *Flowers from Persian Poets,* New York, Thomas Y. Crowell, 1901.

Ergin, Nevit Oguz: *Crazy as We Are: Selected Rubais from Divan-i Kebir,* Prescott, Ariz., Hohn Press, 1992.

Ernst, Carl: *Teaching Sufism,* Boston, Shambhala Press, 1999.

Feild, Reshad: *The Last Barrier*: *A Sufi Journey*, Rockport, Element, 1993

Guest, Grace Dunham: *Shiraz Painting in the Sixteenth Century*, Washington D.C., 1948.

Guvenc, R. Oruc: *Lovers of God, Mevlana*, Vaduz, Liechtenstein, Aconcagua, 1986.

Hakim, Khalifa Abdul: *The Metaphysics of Rumi, a Critical and Historical Sketch*, Lahore, Pakistan, Institute of Islamic Culture, 1959.

Holter, Kurt: *Persische Miniaturen*, Vienna, 1921.

Losty, J. P.: *The Art of the Book in India*, London, 1982.

Lowry, Glenn, and Nemazee, Susan: *A Jeweler's Eye: Islamic Arts of the Book from the Vever Collection*, Washington D.C., 1988.

Robinson, B. W.: *A Descriptive Catalogue of the Persian Paintings in the Bodleian Library*, Oxford, 1958.

Robinson, B. W.: *Islamic Painting and the Arts of the Book*, London: 1976.

Rohani, Nasrin: *A Bibliography of Persian Miniature Painting*, Boston, 1982.

Schimmel, Annemarie: *Calligraphy and Islamic Culture*, New York, 1984.

Schmitz Barbara: *Islamic Manuscripts in the New York Public Library*, New York, 1992.

Schmitz Barbara: *Islamic and Indian Manuscripts and Paintings in the Pierpont Morgan Library*, New York, 1997.

Titley, Norah M.: *Persian Miniature Painting and its Influence on the Art of Turkey and India*, Austin, 1984.

Welch, Stuart Cary: *Artists for the Shah: Late Sixteenth-Century Painting at the Imperial Court of Iran*, New Haven, 1976.

Welch, S. C., and Dickinson, Martin B.: *The Houghton Shahnameh*, Cambridge, 1981.

INDEX

□□□